In Search of Corky

In Search of Corky

Paul J. Greenhalgh, Jr.

Copyright © 2008 by Paul J. Greenhalgh, Jr.

ISBN: Hardcover   978-1-4363-5876-7
        Softcover   978-1-4363-5875-0

All rights reserved. No part of this book may be reproduced or transmitted in any form or by any means, electronic or mechanical, including photocopying, recording, or by any information storage and retrieval system, without permission in writing from the copyright owner.

COVER PICTURES

Front   Jim Murray and Corky Devlin kneel over the graves of Mathew Fox and Thomas Merton. Gethsemani, Ky.
Back   The author and Jim Murray kneel over headstone of Corky. Gethsemani, Ky.

ACKNOWLEDGEMENT OF ASSISTANCE BY:
American Academy of the Sacred Arts
1629 Porter St., Philadelphia, Pa. 19145

This book was printed in the United States of America.

To order additional copies of this book, contact:
Xlibris Corporation
1-888-795-4274
www.Xlibris.com
Orders@Xlibris.com

49121

Contents

Chapter		Page
	Preface	9
I	A Chance Meeting	11
II	The Harpoon is Sunk	16
III	Running with the Hooked	26
IV	More Punishment	32
V	Stardom In College	38
VI	I Played with the Things of a Child	42
VII	The Flip Side of the Fight	46
VIII	The Backcourt for the Pistons	51
IX	Gethsemani	56
X	Bob Hardy's Rescue Mission	61
XI	Unlikely Encouragement	69
XII	My Best Friend, Corky	74
XIII	Discovering the Caves	83
XIV	Relatively Strange	96
XV	League Headquarters	106
XVI	Remember the Warriors	112
XVII	The Draft that Split	118
XVIII	Mining Gucci Pearls	123
XIX	My Paradigm	129
XX	Taking it out of the Cheese	146
XXI	Working Relationships that Didn't	157
XXII	For Him the Bell Told	167
XXIII	This, the Autumn of His Life	176
XXIV	Healey's Bridge to Corky	181
XXV	Thankfully, Only *Like* a Thief in the Night	193
XXVI	Corky Dearest	201
XXVII	The Biggest Kid in the Yards	213

XXVIII	George Washington Speaks	219
XXIX	Alone and on the Go	228
XXX	The Nature of Addiction	231
XXXI	Just One More Good Day	239
XXXII	Stretching in Kentucky	248
XXXIII	Crossing the Finish Line	256
XXXIV	Blind, But Now I See	265
XXXV	Corky's Legacy	270

Dedicated to:

Professor Henry Doehler, Helen Greenhalgh,

Peg Hardy and Bill McKay

Preface

A mystic sees beyond the senses. He personifies the question, "Are we spiritual beings having a physical experience or are we physical beings having a mystical experience?" His answer, uniquely, is both. In pursuing Corky, I have learned to accept his limitations while absorbing his spirituality in a way similar to experiencing bifocals underwater.

To understand him, abstain from applying moral judgments or boundaries. I myself pounced on conclusions like, "This is Corky," only to encounter a contradiction resulting in a loss of meaning. "My life's motivation is profound. Find me, and you will find yourself. I want my story written." Corky will not let me rest until his entire story is told.

Believe in the Communion of Saints and lifting the veil for communication with souls who have passed beyond. Only then, can his agony and transformation provide answers. In life, he wallowed in apparent failure. Can desiring to please God lead to sainthood? How he prods me! "My life has meaning. Write my story."

Corky challenged me to love a scoundrel. God has always graced the world with saints who reflect their times. Do we need reminders of how evil grips our times? Murder, greed, and degradation are commonplace. Centuries ago, on the day of our redemption, the Son hid from His Light. Shadowed by failure and addiction, Corky, too, has dared to reach for that same Light.

Come with me on a privileged journey. I want to help you know him through enlightened eyes. Meet him in his glory. He speaks to us now without limits. Listen and believe simply that Corky does indeed speak. His stories live through the words of those who knew him. My questions are preceded by a Q:. Answers are preceded by an A:. I have also placed my questions in italics.

I

A CHANCE MEETING

In June, 1993, the stones crackled under my tires as I drove up the dirt road to Bob Hardy's farmhouse. The prayer meeting had started, so I eased through the crooked screen door and entered the parlor. In the next room twenty men prayed together. There he reposed on a worn black couch. He lay so still that he looked stuffed. I gazed at a long body in black clothes, his hands folded on his chest suggesting he was praying. Snow-white hair framed a long pasty face highlighted by hints of pink. His heritage was unmistakably Irish. Even motionless, he demanded attention. I wondered how this comatose chiseled man would look wide awake. How could anyone be secure enough, sleeping in a parlor oblivious to stares from those who walked by?

Later that night, I learned that Corky was a homeless man. He was fighting a disease that caused him to drop out of society and lose all sense of time or responsibility. Episodes mimicked sinking in an ocean. Submerged, he lost communication with reality. During entombment, he forfeited his earthly possessions, then floundered under heavy medication for about six weeks. Before his current spell, he had been living in Washington. His landlord locked him out of his apartment for nonpayment of rent. What remained of Corky's possessions were under lock and key. His friends deserted him. He couldn't hold a job. He couldn't predict when the next attack might occur. Corky lay there homeless, penniless, and without a future.

A Chance Meeting

"Who is that?" I whispered to Bob as I joined the men in the living room.

"That's Corky. He lives on that couch. You will like him." It became much more than like.

I returned the following week to Bob Hardy's farm. This time, Corky joined us. He was alert and participated. He sat next to Bob and described his struggles to find and please God. Corky thought deeply. He also had a charming delivery. He resembled an older, gaunt Irishman from my past. Such men strained under a burden of pathos—they experienced more suffering than their share. High ideals assured continual misunderstanding, then came failure. Pain from ridicule festered always beneath the surface. Sad men struggled, isolated by their unique view of life. Celtic whimsy concealed their hidden world of spirits. Corky accepted never-ending struggle, striving for unimagined goals, driven by hidden values. How lonely! People he loved, he hurt the most. He yearned for happiness. He reaped failure and pain. Because Corky's comments were insightful, I considered him spiritual. He watched, aware of his listeners. He evaluated us while gaining our acceptance. In hindsight, Corky was a con.

Corky's apparent sincerity merited my trust. He must be a good man. He told colorful stories. My responses encouraged him. He guided me into his inner world where dreams drew him onward. Home lay somewhere just ahead. I trusted Corky as I was drawn into his journey.

Q: You played basketball in the National Basketball Association in the '50s?

A: Basketball was the biggest part of my life. I graduated from George Washington University in 1955. I wouldn't trade those days, but they led me into some pretty disastrous times.

Q: The glory and limelight must have been pretty exciting. Did you have trouble handling the fame?

A: Corky didn't hold back. The exposure to the big time gave me some pretty wild ideas. You meet all kinds of people, and you are in and out of their lives quickly. It's hard to really care about people you meet on the fast track. I care about people. That's why I struggle in life.

Q: When you turned pro, I was just entering college. How were you drafted?

A: I was drafted seventh overall, just behind Tom Gola, by the Philadelphia Warriors. Gola became the territorial pick and for a short time we were teammates. The owner, Eddie Gottlieb, traded me to the

Fort Wayne Pistons. I played in Indiana and later with the Lakers. In Los Angeles, I got into real trouble.

Q: I saw you last week. You slept on the couch. Nothing woke you. Were you really tired?

A: I was coming out of one of my down periods. This one lasted about a month. Bob took me in. I'm living here. I can't do anything when I'm down. Now I don't know where I'm headed. I really feel good here, like part of Bob Hardy's family. The Hardy's are good people. Somehow, I have to get my life going.

Corky had been around. He behaved differently from the rest of us. The little boy inside me loved the glamour of basketball. I had met a player who had been famous. I would see him at future meetings. His era (the '50s) was an innocent age in basketball. Television was a novelty. Players weren't paid much. I liked talking openly with one of the stars of that era.

I drifted around the room talking to other men. I left without thinking much more about Corky.

Later that week, Bob Hardy called me. Corky and I had hit it off. Corky needed friends to help him out of his depression. "Corky is homeless. He came to us with nothing but a duffel bag. I've allowed him to become part of my family. My girls love him. He tells wild stories. He has met famous people. A major problem is his gambling. I'm trying to give him a home. I think he is harmless."

Q: I wanted to help. *Why is he sleeping on the couch? When I walked in last week, I thought he might be dead. Nobody seemed to notice him. It's hard for me to understand sleeping in front of complete strangers.*

A: Bob's knowledge was limited. "Corky experiences chemical spells. I think they call it bipolar. About once a year, he drops out. He disappears. He leaves everything unattended; his home, his clothes, his work. He goes incognito for weeks. When he comes out of it, he starts all over again. The people he has run out on become angry. That's why he has no one to talk to."

Q: How long do the spells last?

A: At least a month, sometimes a lot more.

I promised Bob that I would try to talk to Corky whenever possible. Reclamation presented a new challenge for me.

Q: Can't he just take medicine? If we try hard enough, we should be able to overcome anything.

These words would come back to haunt me. They still do.

Each week that summer, Corky attended our meetings. We gravitated towards each other. Our friendship became comfortable. He seemed open when I asked him more details about his life. He told me about playing in college. Corky graduated from George Washington University in Washington D.C. in 1955. He is still the all-time leading scorer among three-year players. He excelled as a rawboned rebounder. Corky was proud of his aggressive play. His mouth tensed and his face scowled when he remembered "The Fight".

During my senior year, we played a very good West Virginia University team in their gym. Both teams were striving for first place. Our deciding clash took place in real redneck territory. We sensed hostility from the good old boys. I wondered whether the animals would stay in the stands. We endured a steady ration of boos.

A lot of things went wrong with our play. Early in the second half, we trailed by double digits. West Virginia's star was a real showboat named Hot Rod Hundley. At best, Hot Rod was insensitive to our position. He thrived on demonstrating his dribbling skills and spinning the ball on his index finger. When our guys lunged at the ball, he pulled it back with a big smile. The crowd roared its approval with the southern version of *Olé*. I remember his standing on the foul line, about to spin the ball before a foul shot. I leaned into his face: "If you spin again, I'll punch you in the mouth." Well, he did, and I did. The place went crazy. Everyone grabbed one another. Both benches erupted onto the floor. Fans joined the melee before I was wrestled to the floor. I remember thinking Hot Rod had gotten the message. He wouldn't embarrass us again. He was shouting, but I couldn't hear him.

After order had been restored, I accepted a permanent seat on the bench. The crowd roared threats. I was now a certified villain. Everyone saw the punch as a good-versus-evil confrontation. The fans couldn't imagine any reason why I popped him. Hot Rod sprawled on the West Virginia bench. The scorer's table sat between us. I noticed an occasional brushing of a towel full of ice over his nose and cheek. I triumphed. He wasn't shooting fouls anymore. Behind our bench gathered a line of stone-faced policemen. None of them said anything. They represented our only way out of the gym alive.

The clock wound down to the last minute of play. Suddenly, a force inside lifted me up. I found myself walking towards the West Virginia bench. Play had stopped because of a jump ball. The startled crowd inhaled in unison. I was watching this scene, but I was also part of it. I strode past frozen faces at the scorer's table. I continued past the entire West Virginia bench. Hot Rod sat at the end. He noticed me only when I reached the end of my walk. What was he thinking? I couldn't tell. At our moment of confrontation, when I stood squarely in front of him, I reached out my hand. Only his hand responded. He kept staring at me when he put his hand in mine. I don't know which of us was more surprised. He sat there, as noise started to swell. It wasn't a cheer. It lacked direction. It was just noise. The crowd's anger was gone, and I had experienced Divine Intervention. I still don't understand why I did it. Many things have happened about which I can say, "I don't know why I did it."

* * *

George Washington eventually won The Southern Conference championship. Corky was chosen All-American and played with the College All-Stars who toured with the Harlem Globetrotters. His time had come for a career in professional basketball.

II

THE HARPOON IS SUNK

As summer waned, Corky called. I was headed for a day on the beach (50 miles away.) He asked if he could tag along. I was flattered. It didn't occur to me that he had nothing else to do.

As we entered the beach, Corky elaborated on his professional basketball experiences. They started after the National Basketball Association draft. Eddie Gottlieb didn't want to pay big money to two first-round draft picks. He shipped Corky to the Fort Wayne Pistons. The Pistons' owner made Gottlieb look like a spendthrift. Corky started in the backcourt with Gene Shue.

"It was tough," Corky explained. "I guarded the other team's leading scorer. I got in his face. I also rebounded and only scored when needed. I was not our "go-to guy," so I didn't rack up huge statistics. I was happy mixing it up. Other teams noticed me, especially my elbows. I liked to talk. I used my mouth to throw my man off his game. My comments announced my intention to physically abuse. Today we label it "trash talk." The man I guarded envisioned brawls and unexpected pain. I was a bully who thrived on sowing seeds of conflict and doubt. My head game enhanced my elbows. The following summer the Pistons mailed me a contract offering a fifteen-hundred-dollar raise. The request for my services had been increased by a paltry $1,500. As I said, I utilized graphic mind pictures to get my point across. I wrapped the unsigned contract with barbed wire and sent it back to the owner, Fred Zollner. I scribbled instructions—*USE AS A SUPPOSITORY*.

The battle lines had been drawn. I settled for $2,000 more. The principle mattered. Mr. Zollner knew who I was. A year later, I was traded to the Los Angeles Lakers.

California proved to be the worst place Corky could have landed. He assimilated into the fast lane. "I behaved like a prep school kid at a party university. There were so many distractions. I couldn't decide which way to turn."

Corky stressed that he tried to be good. He experienced the initial battles with bi-polar disease. This unpredictable illness rendered goal-setting and planning impossible. After each attack, he tried to pull his life back together. He started over. Eventually, he let everyone down. Corky's deep pain was that no one could trust him. He couldn't trust himself. Corky believed in God's mercy. While seeking help, Corky applied for admission to virtually every Trappist monastery in the United States. Monastic life would assure that he couldn't hurt himself. He yearned for some safe home hidden from afflictions and embarrassments. Corky, under his debilitations, possessed a strong drive to be good. He wanted to help people. Most of all, he aspired to please God. Inability to reconcile his strong desire for goodness with his afflictions resulted in a continual cycle. He almost succeeded but his efforts would be followed by failure. His favorite author, Winston Churchill, advocated that we never give up. Despite many failures and limited successes, Corky never gave up.

We walked in the shallows of the warm, almost tide-less waters. Corky introduced memories of a famous physicist who was suffering from a terminal disease. Corky nursed this man before his death. They lived together in Strathmere, NJ. Corky served as his friend's constant nurse and companion. During that year, Corky's understanding of life had been put to the test. His world-renowned patient faced death with Corky's help. Corky reached equal status with this great man. Together, they explored their mortality. As life slipped away, Corky's assistance became increasingly necessary. Corky evolved into a single voice of both men. His decisions kept them both alive. After accepting responsibility, Corky wrestled with the "whys" of life. He recognized that none of his dreams would come true. The energy of youth was long spent. Now in his 60s, the charm of his personality was withering with age. His health was declining. The physicist decayed before his eyes. Corky grappled with tough questions while escorting a dying man into the spirit world. Corky nurtured his own capacity and desire for goodness. Corky's virtue seldom triumphed.

Would anyone revere Corky's existence? None of his struggles merited lasting meaning. Only his prayers stirred hope of salvation. He vowed to continue walking, searching

Q: I lightened the conversation, *Did you do anything outstanding in pro basketball?*

A: He smiled. "I set a record for the most missed shots in one game. I took the most shots in a game without making any. I was never shy. That day I took 17 shots. After that game, I concentrated on defense. My teammates never said a word. They acted totally oblivious to my historic accomplishment. My record stands unmatched to this day." He smiled. How appropriate.

Q: *Your real name is Walter Devlin. How did you get the name Corky?*

A: When I was a baby, my father left us. My mother married a man named Joe Corcoran, whom I grew to love. Joe was a rough man. We lived in Newark, NJ. He worked on the docks and could fight with the best. I admired his strong principles. As a kid, I was tall and lean. We lived near a city basketball court. I played mostly with black kids. In those days, black players were segregated from white players. Neither the blacks nor the whites knew much about one another. On the courts, all of the players were black. My nickname was "White Shadow." I shot the jump shot. After only a few pickup games, I was accepted as a player. Many a day, I was the only white player within blocks. When you're caught up in the flow of a basketball game, you don't think about race. I was happy just being included. Later, my game assumed the characteristics of those with whom I played. The guys I played with had been gifted with physical athleticism. Our playing style was free form. Self-expression sometimes overshadowed discipline. I never knew when a pass was coming. But I knew to be ready. Compared to rigidly coached white teams, we played creatively. When our moves came from deep within our spirits, we surprised ourselves. Of course, whatever the move, we acted as if we were in total control. Holding our play together was a deep respect for the game and its rules. Hotheads and cheaters were quickly stigmatized. They drifted away. It was mano e mano with respect. Our environment molded my self-image. The way I walked (loose and rhythmic) stamped me as being from the Courts of Newark. I played and talked like an inner-city kid. This creative style served me well. I was ready and able to mix it up with anyone. Mine was a "challenge everyone for everything" type game. I didn't hesitate to pop anyone whom I didn't like. Later in college, I sensed this style was different.

No one played like me. Everyone else played basketball deliberately under control. I slowly realized the aloneness.

Corky assured me that he did not want to be alone. During the second month of his life, the pain had begun. His father disappeared. His mother raised him in an eight-family tenement house. She married Joe Corcoran, and he became the only father Corky remembered. Joe was wise and a man of principle. His word was his honor. Joe acted tough. He once knocked Corky down a flight of stairs because he had been mouthy to his mother. But the boy idolized his father. The name "Corky" linked Walter Devlin to his father. He felt proud of that nickname.

Newark's Central was the local high school. Corky's city basketball skills allowed him to blend well with friends he respected. Competitive success and his natural talent assured respect from his teammates. Stardom was always his goal. Our clean-cut white kid was quick. He found security because he belonged. Unfortunately, he loved basketball to the exclusion of almost everything, particularly academics. It made little sense to study when he found basketball so enjoyable. His teenage years seemed to last forever. Basketball was everything; not playing unimaginable. Consequently, he graduated in his class—sixth from the bottom. The basketball players congregated among the bottom feeders. They each relied on their own immortality.

In 1949, colleges were not clamoring for athletes, especially ones with low grades and an attitude. Corky tested well. Even though he ignored most of his teachers, he was college material. Joe Corcoran urged his son to attend Potomac State College in Keyser, West Virginia. Admission standards were low and the collegiate atmosphere relaxed. Corky's courses were interesting. His grades improved. He began to understand that a little scholastic effort could pay off in respect. His encounter with southern basketball brought him stardom. His quickness and improvisational offensive skills served him well. Whenever the team needed a basket, Corky was the man. He thrived on the challenge. Corky developed his mantra, "Give me the ball." His teammates tolerated our mouthy kid from Newark. His play was different, but he accomplished wonders. West Virginia served as a launching pad for Corky's career.

After two years as high scorer at Potomac State, Corky signed an agreement to enter George Washington University in our Nation's Capitol. Through his commitment, he entered the big time—Southern Conference Basketball. He still had three more years of varsity eligibility, and he relished playing for Coach Bill Reinhart at Uline Arena.

The Harpoon is Sunk

Later in the spring of 1952, basketball presented an even bigger pay-off. The system recognized Corky's talent. Corky's aggressive style and point production drew attention in far away Kentucky. Adolph Rupp was the most revered basketball coach in America. Great stars like Alex Groza and Ralph Beard led Kentucky to NCAA and NIT championships. The Wildcats were the most prestigious team in the country. Another Kentucky team was so talented that it turned professional as a unit. They formed the original Indianapolis team. Adolph Rupp beckoned, so Corky visited Lexington, KY. NCAA rules of that day permitted recruiting players any time and anywhere. Corky was flattered by the invitation. Kentucky's basketball facilities were state-of-the-art. Alumni lurked everywhere. Playing for Kentucky was a significant rung to basketball stardom. Coach Rupp officially offered Corky a new car and a package worth $20,000. Corky was ecstatic. His trip was a triumph.

Back at Potomac State, Corky called his stepfather. Joe Corcoran listened carefully. The potential glory and promising lucrative career in the pros were excitedly reported. Corky described his intention to raise the entire family's level of living. Adolph Rupp promised to refine Corky's already considerable skills. This combination was obviously his ticket to stardom.

"Where do you plan to spend your summers and holidays?" Joe asked.

"What do you mean?"

"No son of mine gives his word to George Washington and then goes back on his promise."

Corky became forever connected to George Washington. He led the team in scoring and set records that still stand for three-year players. His darting improvisational shooting blended successfully with the steady scoring and rebounding skills of John and Joe Holup. The team rose to the top ten in the nation. The Southern Conference boasted Maryland, Georgetown, and West Virginia among its national powerhouses. Corky scored on a star-studded team. He finished as one of the Colonials' greatest players. As wins mounted, so did national attention. The team's success created intense school spirit. Corky was voted All-Southern Conference for three straight years. Not surprisingly, Corky represented George Washington on the College All-Star team. Today, All-Star teams are merely lists of honored athletes. In the '50s, the All-Stars toured the country and played thirty games against the Harlem Globetrotters. The

Trotters abandoned their clowning for this very serious match-up. Each night, the beloved Trotters fought the respected college players. Battles were close and hotly contested. The combatants traveled from city to city attracting large enthusiastic crowds. Game box scores and the current win/lose totals were reported all over the world.

Corky described the game in Philadelphia's Convention Hall. That game was decided in the last few minutes. Trotter stars, Nat "Sweetwater" Clifton and Marquis Haynes, focused on serious basketball for some of the few times in their careers. Marquis Haynes was the master dribbler. No one could grab the ball from him when his team was leading near the end of a game. His moves could be called illegal by current pro basketball standards. But his quickness was extraordinary. Defending guards groped awkwardly in his wake. He darted across the court, only to stop as if sliding across home plate. He kept the ball dribbling as he performed acrobatic rolls then re-emerged upright. The All-Stars had to have the lead going into the final minutes. The Trotters squeezed out another victory.

Corky smiled as he described the travel, playing the Trotters, and the national exposure. He approved of Marquis. The College All-Stars considered Marquis as a monstrous showboat who didn't belong in their game. Conversely, Corky admired his rhythmic improvisation and inner freedom. Corky nurtured hope for future change. Basketball hovered on the brink of accepting creative expression. Love of creativity made Corky a visionary. Improvisation might bring with it personal acceptance. He embraced this future.

Waves lazily lapped at our feet as I absorbed Corky's stories. We strode, rhythmically disturbing the foam. Behind us, footprints expanded while I grew more absorbed. I sensed that Corky's stories must be true. Slanted maybe, but true. This man's worth revealed his past as he justified its value. He had entered life with so much talent. He tried hard to do the right thing. Seemingly uncontrollable obstacles caused failure. He arose after each fall, determined not to fail again. Great experiences repeatedly generated absorbing stories.

Corky probed, "You know about my gambling problems."

Bob had told me about Corky's addiction. Gambling never made much sense to me. I have a responsibility for everything that I gain in this world. When my life is judged, I expect the question, "What did you do with what you were given?" Then gamblers will get theirs. I don't enjoy losing.

When I win, I'm winning someone else's misery. Also, I accept increased responsibility by my added winnings. Imagine pleading on your Day of Judgment, "Well, I gambled a lot." Gambling is not a good use of talents. I see no real value to its risks.

Q: Corky, explain your slant on gambling.

A: I played in the big time. Remember Leonard Tose—he owned the Philadelphia Eagles football team. Well, I became a close friend of his. He had a group. Jim Murray, general manager of the Eagles, was also in our group. I was the driver. They liked to gamble. I contributed a wealth of experience. Those were great times. When Mr. Tose sued the casinos for getting him drunk then grabbing his money, I joined his team. The trial made all the headlines. Halfway through the fight, our team split. I went with Jim Murray. Both men lost. But, gambling has been my life. I drifted to Gamblers Anonymous. I was interviewed on national radio. I was talking on the Larry King Show when a buddy from my past called. I had stayed at his home in Nebraska during my wanderings out west. He asked what had happened to me. On the show, he invited me to visit. I did. Gambling led to a nomadic existence. I followed the action. I bet on practically anything. The betting drive was overpowering. Some people are consumed by their sex drive. All they think about is their next sexual encounter. Well, I had an all-consuming mind-set about gambling. I opened the newspaper to the horseracing page. No other page interested me. I knew which horses were running at any moment. I was observing some other person when I saw myself pry money from friends to gamble. I grabbed what I wanted. A small voice wanted to scream, "Don't do it; he's a liar." That inner voice *never* surfaced. I wrote a $2,000 check to my own mother knowing it would bounce. I maintained multiple bank accounts. I transferred cash between accounts, manipulating the float to stay ahead. While I was on that merry-go-round, I forgot about a holiday and bounced a big check. Subsequently, I was convicted and spent two years in jail. I was in jail multiple times. I knew what I was doing, and I hated myself. I despised the way I was. My gambling passion became so powerful that I could no longer fight it. Worse, I watched myself perform the scams I loathed.

Q: Why is gambling so overpowering? Can't you control yourself?

A: All I remember is the rush. I changed into that person I always craved to be. There were no boundaries. Excitement fed on itself. I heard the crowds cheering. Fast music quickened my heart. When I won, I felt like the most powerful person alive. I was important, just as I should have been. No other experience has ever approached that rush.

Let me describe a recent high profile case in Canada. A guy named Brian Moloney embezzled $6 million from his bank. An ordinary employee, he developed a scheme to steal money from his institution. He carried the money to Atlantic City where he lost it all. After he was caught, he was put on trial. I volunteered to join his defense team. I sensed how Moloney felt, so I offered my services to his lawyer. Gary Ross wrote a book about the case. It is titled, "No Limit." I'm part of Brian's story. I'll lend you my copy.

Q: This small paperback was among Corky's few possessions. I never returned it to him. Sadly, I failed to ask Corky whether he learned to control his gambling. *Describe your efforts to help other gamblers.*

A: I served as spokesman for the National Council of Gamblers Anonymous. I counseled such athletes as Pete Rose and Art Schlichter from Ohio State. I maintain contact with Art. We have found no real cure for our disease. We just stay in touch to encourage each other. When the thrill of gambling gets in your head, you really need help.

At one time I was commissioned by the Catholic Church in Philadelphia to help priests overcome gambling problems. One night, I was sitting in Cardinal Krol's office. The Pope called from Rome. The Cardinal spoke Polish to the Pope. They chattered away. After they hung up, I asked what they were discussing. He said, "We were discussing what we had for dinner."

I encountered many famous people outside of basketball. I had dinner with the President of Mexico. That experience developed from my friendship with Jim Murray. We had created a food kitchen to feed hungry peasants. That kitchen progressed into a food bank that still feeds thousands of people every day. I helped him start the Ronald McDonald Houses for the families of children with long-term illnesses. The first house, created in Philadelphia, provided a home for families visiting their sick children. Now McDonald Houses are open all over our country.

Q: *What did you contribute?*

A: I was the driver. When you assess who brought what to the table, I was low in the chain of command. Due to my addiction and bipolar lifestyle, I never assumed a position of authority. I contributed on the periphery. I have always read people well. God gave me insights and instincts to size up people. With little material wealth or pedigree, I listened well and I cultivated a way of influencing others. In my role, I introduced ideas. Then, I nurtured them until another person assumed it as his own idea. I read personalities, then instinctively know how to motivate people. It took a while, but many of my ideas prevailed. The men surrounding Jim Murray usually forgot that I was only the driver at decision time. I was motivated for good. I contributed good ideas. They shepherded them through implementation. Jim Murray is a wonderful, exciting person. We shared many enchanted days at the casinos whenever we hung out.

It had become late afternoon. We reversed direction as we continued together in the surf. Talk continued while we retraced our steps. The beach was crowded with bathers, but in my mind, we were alone. Corky, the angular storyteller, lured me into his world of contradictions. He appeared open to any question. As we walked, the joints of his arms and legs seem elastic. His loose-jointed gait perfectly matched my own measured steps. There was a joyful lilt to his voice. I repressed my own insecurity with his attention. I sensed that he was describing his life through chosen anecdotes. He revealed just enough to solicit my follow-up question. Was he becoming my friend only because I wanted him to be? He offered vulnerability on his own terms. I found myself wanting to become his friend. His pain fascinated me. Inexorably, I was investing myself in his quest. His struggle for good over evil pulled me relentlessly into his life. His battle enlisted me deeply at the level of my soul. This man of contradictions had enticed a companion for his struggle. Far from apprehension, I only felt excitement. I chose to become part of Corky's life. His battle stirred my passion. Years later, I understood that Corky had touched the part of me that has always struggled, unsuccessfully, to be good. He echoed my time of pure innocence and goodness, which my journey had long since left behind. His story reinforced the truth that my interior child experienced corruption through life's hardships. "Why do I do the things I loathe? I am unable to control my actions even though I want desperately to do the right thing. Humanness permeates all that I think and do. I fall often. Getting up seems my only merit. In my hopes and dreams, I never intended to become like this." My struggle resonated with Corky's. We were destined to walk a common journey into eternity.

The afternoon darkened. We strode through the cooling sand and headed for my car. I was certain that I had been profoundly touched. Neither of us knew the direction of our lives. He must have sensed my inner response. One question needed to be asked. Corky understood what I was about to say.

Q; With all the people and your life experiences, why have you been so open with me? You are not guarding or withholding anything. Why me?

A: Corky was serious. "If there is any gift that I am sure of, it is that I can read people. Through success and failure, I have counted on this one constant. As we talked, I sensed your sincerity. I knew then that I was safe. You gravitate to the truth, so I am able to trust you. You have an open heart."

I didn't respond. Truth can be relative. On that day, this was Corky's truth.

III

RUNNING WITH THE HOOKED

    The weekly prayer meetings rolled by. Just after Labor Day, Corky announced new plans. Once again he would try to enter a monastery. He was driving the next day to Kentucky. If accepted, he would enter Gethsemani, the Trappist Monastery that housed the famous mystic Thomas Merton for most of his life. Corky explained that he had applied to numerous monasteries throughout his life. He had never been accepted. His attendance at the prayer meetings with his spiritual insights convinced me that he would be accepted. Corky whispered that the monastery would be a safe place for him. Here, the world couldn't hurt him. Nor would he hurt others. His choice seemed wise. The group prayed with him before sending him on his journey. I expected never again to see Corky. He would remain one of the most likable yet confusing people I had ever met.

    Bob Hardy's wife, Peg, joined us at our next prayer meeting. Peg had been injured in an automobile accident. She spent six years confined to a wheelchair. Because she was homebound, she and Corky spent a lot of time together. They would sit on Hardy's back porch each morning talking about life's mysteries.

"My girls really love Corky," Peg shared. "He tells great stories. They are convinced that all are true. Mostly, he listens to them. They are convinced that he genuinely cares. They look forward to dinners when he reveals his life. In a way, Corky is still a child. He relates to children and describes interesting experiences to them. Did you know that he has seen almost every show of Bishop Fulton Sheen? He reads the Bishop's books so he can quote him on any topic. Inside of that charismatic demeanor lives a very spiritual man. Even with all of his problems, Corky is very good. His behavior was bad, but somehow he is good." Wouldn't that describe most of us?

Two weeks later I rushed into the prayer meeting. Corky was sitting next to Bob. He wore a white shirt and a black blazer. He grinned, relaxed and comfortable. I gave him a look that asked "What?" as I sat down. In a whispering voice, he answered, "They didn't accept me." When he had filled out the monk's questionnaire, he checked off too many in the "bad" columns. Anyway, Corky was home to stay. The surprise started me thinking.

I develop computer systems in the medical field. I own my company, so I have never accepted outside investors. Because resources are limited, I have been unable to expand company sales. I enjoy writing programs and creating systems. My Achilles heel has always been sales. I find it impossible to develop systems, keep clients happy, and spend adequate time marketing products. Over 25 years, I have hired and trained a half dozen salesmen. None proved successful. My systems are complex. Salesmen in the medical field really have to understand their product. Could my answer be Corky's persuasive personality? Obviously, Corky could sell snowballs to Eskimos. Maybe he could use basketballs to sell to medical administrators. Besides, Corky wasn't doing anything nor going anywhere. My underlying motive was reclamation. I could offer him a chance (perhaps his last) at monetary success. One advantage was open communication. There seemed nothing about his life that he wouldn't tell me. Were his past problems not his fault?

Toward the end of the meeting, Corky handed me a card. "I picked this up for you at Gethsemani. I found it very meaningful, and I wanted you to have it." One of the men heard Corky and asked me to share it aloud.

The card read as follows:

> MY LORD GOD, *I have no idea where I am going. I do not see the road ahead of me. I cannot know for certain where it will end. Nor do I really know myself, and the fact that I think that I am following your will does not mean that I am actually doing so. But I believe that the desire to please you does in fact please you. And I hope I have that desire in all that I am doing. I hope that I will never do anything apart from that desire. And I know that if I do this, you will lead me by the right road though I may know nothing about it. Therefore I will trust you always though I may seem to be lost and in the shadow of death. I will not fear, for you are ever with me, and you will never leave me to face my perils alone.*
>
> THOMAS MERTON
> —*Thoughts in Solitude*
> © Abbey of Gethsemani

Two sentences leapt off the page. "Nor do I really know myself, and the fact that I think that I am following your will does not mean that I am actually doing so. But I believe that the desire to please you does in fact please you." If ever a thought captured Corky's life, this was it. Corky knew that his life couldn't always please his Maker. At his core, Corky desired to please God. This desire provided his only hope. In his humanity he reached, overwhelmed by chemical imbalance, addiction, and frustration. He still nurtured a conscience. His trump card was that he truly loathed this existence. As Marley said to Scrooge, "I cannot eat. I cannot sleep. I cannot rest. I wander from place to place acting out my destiny." How often he falls doesn't matter most. What counts is how many times he gets up. Corky continues determined to arise until hope manifests itself by God's approval.

I understood that Merton's card was Corky's plea for understanding. Corky never again mentioned the prayer or its message. Two things kept churning in my head. First, I pondered whether this charismatic man could be the answer to my search for a salesman. Growing stronger was a desire to break the bonds that imprisoned the man I had grown to care about. I decided to join in his crusade.

My proposal was this: I would offer Corky a late career. At that time, I was attempting to acquire a new client. The decisive meeting was scheduled for the following week. Rogosin Institute (affiliated with Cornell University) was a highly respected dialysis facility on the East Side of New York City. For months they had evaluated my system. Their final decision hinged on a site visit to another of my clients. Larry Maglione, Chief Executive Officer of Rogosin, wanted to see my system in actual operation. It was a very wise request. Unless he could observe the computer system functioning in a live environment, he could not be sure that it would work for him.

I made arrangements for Larry and his entourage to visit another client—South Shore Dialysis in Hempstead, Long Island. Corky joined me for the day. If he liked the environment, he could make good commissions selling my product. Corky's heart seemed in the right place. He certainly had the ability to sell. I wondered how he would thrive in this highly professional medical specialty. I encouraged him, "Remain perfectly mute if you want to." Silence was hard to imagine. Corky always talked from our first meeting. Corky accepted the opportunity immediately.

On a Wednesday morning we drove up the New Jersey Turnpike, crossed the Verrazano Bridge and inched along the Southern State Parkway to Franklin Street in Hempstead, Long Island. As I drove, I described my Dialysis Electronic Billing system and emphasized its advantages. I planned to ask the South Shore Billing Manager, Theresa Thompson, to demonstrate her system. I would only add technical details if the need arose. Corky would not be expected to contribute. He could observe the process. Corky commented that I must have tremendous faith in Theresa to let her do all the talking. I do have faith in Theresa. "Client to client" is the best way to convince a new prospect. Our system is good, so we have nothing to hide. Corky's observation was encouraging. He charged into the challenge. I felt relaxed optimism walking into South Shore Dialysis with Corky. We stood the same height (6-foot-5). I sensed that he could handle difficult-people problems. Larry Maglione arrived with two assistants. Lisa Maggio, South Shore's administrator, joined us and spoke eloquently about the benefits of the system. I sensed mutual respect between Lisa and Larry. I also sensed that Larry had already decided on our system. Theresa was outstanding, demonstrating the ease and power of my system; her enthusiasm, compelling. After 10 minutes Larry announced, "Well I'm convinced. Let's do it." Corky's involvement had been limited to having his name mentioned. As Larry retreated to process his decision with his assistant's, I entertained Lisa and Theresa.

Corky's a basketball player. He played in the NBA in the '50s.

"You're kidding," Theresa was intrigued. "My boyfriend and I love the Knicks. Who did you play for?"

Corky eased onto center stage. His smooth and confident manner took over. "I played for the Pistons and Lakers. In those days we were in different cities."

The questions started coming. Corky seemed delighted. I'm not sure how the word spread, but a crowd gathered. Larry and his Rogosin people planned at one end of the hallway. Corky and a gathering crowd discussed basketball at the other end, near the cafeteria.

"What do you think of Patrick Ewing?"

"Do the Knicks have a chance this year?"

"What position did you play?"

"Is the game that much faster these days?"

"Describe your favorite game."

Before Larry returned to our end, to finalize the deal, Corky was signing autographs. People came from other buildings wanting to meet the celebrity. As we left for our cars, Larry confided that he was a season ticket holder for the Knicks. A stroke of luck. Larry hoped he would see more of us. I felt triumphant. We had a new client.

"What do you think?" I asked as we drove down the Jersey Turnpike.

"If we get our hands on front row seats for Knicks games, I can sell every Dialysis Unit in New York." How could I doubt what Corky could do? Philadelphia had a team in the same league.

"This will be a success; I can sense it." Corky added, "You know I don't usually dress like this. I own some good clothes. They would help me sell to professionals. The last time I went bipolar, I left all my clothes in Washington, under lock and key. I owe three months back rent. If I could get those suits, I would be confident to sell at this level."

"How much would it take to get you back on your feet?" I asked.

"Twenty-five hundred."

Three hours later, we entered my condo in Mt. Laurel, NJ. I sat down and wrote a check for $2,500. To me, it felt right. This was the answer. Corky and I must be good for each other. He knew that this was his last chance to capitalize on his talents. He left. I called, "Take your time over the weekend. Call me on Monday so we can schedule sales calls. This will be great for both of us." Corky smiled and left with a bounce in his step. I didn't question how enthusiastic about our project he really was.

That was Wednesday. Bob Hardy called on Friday, "Have you seen Corky?"

"He was with me on Wednesday. He left for Washington to retrieve clothes. I think we are in business together."

Bob sounded concerned, "He has disappeared. My children are very upset. He left some old clothes and just disappeared. I hope he's not dead or wandering somewhere. I'm going to call the police. They'll put out an APB on him. I'll keep you posted." Bob sounded serious. I hoped Corky wasn't in trouble.

I called Bob on Sunday night. He responded, "They found him. Did you lend him any money?"

"Yes, but why?"

"There are six of us. Corky lined us all up for the same day. He went south on a gambling spree. We probably won't see him again. He got me, too. I completely misread him. My family is devastated. We trusted him. Now we see him as cruel."

I didn't want to believe that Corky could be so *cunning* and so insincere. I thought back. He had revealed to me exactly who he was. Why should I be surprised? Because I had viewed this man's soul, I attempted to justify his evil actions. I was sure he would eventually return to make restitution. My hope was more for his sake than for mine.

IV

MORE PUNISHMENT

In February, 1996, I lay on the massage table as Joe Gorman prepared to administer his Treager massage.

Joe questioned, "Tell me more about Corky Devlin. Have you heard anything about where he is?"

"Joe, I can't believe he just took off and his conscience doesn't bother him. Bob Hardy tells me that he squandered the money. Then he retreated to Gethsemani and reapplied for admission."

"His conscience led him there," Joe murmured.

"Bob thinks he might have been accepted. He claimed a heart condition and they bought his story. Interesting combination—Corky the con with a monastery full of monks. Who will win over whom? Wouldn't it be awful if he founded Trappist Anonymous?"

Corky had been on Joe's mind. Joe had somehow connected with Corky. He only envisioned Corky through my descriptions, but he felt connected. Did Joe find some of Corky's traits attractive? If so, which ones?

Joe Gorman is a very intuitive person. He, like me, is convinced that we are spiritual people living a physical experience. The spiritual world is real. Joe served as head counselor for a mental health consortium in Burlington County, NJ. He was known as the counselor's counselor. He mentored counselors he supervised. Joe specialized in children, particularly teenage boys. I took one of my sons to him for help. We became friends after we shared life experiences. I valued him as the consummate shrink.

He viewed me as an idealist. Our friendship probably began as a rescue mission for him. We talked about the unseen freely. Treager massage was Joe's second profession. His treatments gave me flexibility and relieved tension. For three months, Joe worked on me weekly. He asked me to keep him informed of any news about Corky.

One night in June, Corky called me. He was living in Kentucky at the monastery. He said he was sorry for taking off. He did not mention the money or plans to pay me back. Instead, he talked about his heart problem.

"The doctors removed half of my heart. I am weak and can't do much of anything. They told me that I have six months to live. I am the greeter at the main entrance. I meet people and answer the phone. I belong here and I'm [at last] happy.

Peace at last. He promised to stay in touch with me and wished me well. Still puzzled, I stored the story for Joe.

The following week, Joe seemed excited when he arrived with his massage board.

"Wait till you hear this story. My sister Kathleen is a Mother Superior for an order of nuns across the river in Philadelphia. She attended a conference in Cleveland, Ohio, where she sat in seminars all day. She never does anything like this, but she decided to play hooky. She drove to Bardstown, Kentucky to visit the Trappist Monastery where Thomas Merton had lived. She met this charming white-haired man who greeted her at the door.

"He spent the day with her. He was so spiritual and we became close friends," Kathleen told me.

Joe interrupted, "He is tall and thin about 6-foot-5 and his name is Corky."

My sister's eyes widened, "How did you know?"

A stronger link was forming between Joe and Corky. The seed planted in my mind was growing. I didn't believe what Corky told me on the phone. I couldn't believe he was dying. I did sense that his life had some strange connection. My own journey seemed joined to his life. How could there be good in an utter failure? His habitual lying and addiction-driven scamming were mysterious. The world judged him a hurtful failure. Money and power make right. Those who have little are ignored and branded worthless. Only God accurately judges men who strive all their lives to be good. Does Corky belong to the ash heap? There must be some reason why we met. Deep within me, a conviction was forming that Corky's life had meaning. Many of us, I think, share his struggle. His apparent lack of accomplishment cancel consideration by the world. His failure warns us. Corky points an accusing finger from our own dark side.

I decided to return his call. "Corky, it's Paul. Two months have passed since we talked. How is your health?"

"I'm better some days than others. I just don't have much strength. Did you hear that my record in the NBA has been broken by Tim Hardaway of the Golden State Warriors? He missed 18 straight shots. How ironic that a Warrior would wipe me out of the record book."

"You have my condolences," I murmured. "I have a reason for calling. I've decided to write a book about your life. You have had some wonderful experiences. I think your story needs to be told."

There was a long pause. "Your story needs to be told," confused him. He asked how I would do it.

"I own a video camera and a tripod. I will fly to Gethsemani next weekend and interview you for a few hours each day." By the time the call ended, Corky had grown enthusiastic about our project.

The night before my flight, I encountered Bob Hardy at a **Cursillio** meeting. We talked before the meeting started. I told him of my plan with Corky.

"You better not take your wallet along. He'll pick you clean. I wouldn't trust that man in anything. You'll come back in a barrel."

Bob's words stunned me. I saw the wisdom in what he was saying. Was I ready to deal with Corky's cunning? This wasn't the appropriate time to travel to Kentucky. I called Corky and begged off of the trip. We would reschedule sometime in the future. I wasn't sure when that would be. Corky sounded disappointed. I wondered whether he expected to fleece me. It was August. I forgot the project.

Eleven months later, I uncovered the unused airplane ticket to Louisville in a drawer. The ticket's one-year guarantee was about to expire. I called US Airways to book a flight for the following weekend. Then I called the monastery.

A Brother answered politely. I asked for Corky Devlin. He responded, "Corky passed away last April. He is buried here at Gethsemani."

My first impulse was to say, "Are you sure?" Thankfully, I didn't. As I hung the phone up, I thought, "Well, this takes me off the hook. Now, I don't have to write the book."

Distinctly, Corky spoke to me. "You already know enough about me to write our book. My life has meaning. I want it written. I will help you."

Souls in the spirit world sometimes communicate through thought transfer. In this way, whole ideas are received intact without any voice being heard. Corky's response was distinctly linear. His voice was clear. I had no doubt about what I heard. Nor could I doubt its source.

Joe Gorman hurried into my condo for the Traeger the following week. Before I could tell him about Corky's message, he blurted out that he awoke in the middle of last night. A poem flowed into his head about Corky. It just entered into his mind nonstop as he wrote it down. Joe pleaded, "I know he was there. He wants his story written." His poem follows:

"For Corky"
An instrument less minstrel
Skipped a beat and lost the rhythm
Replaced by dances on the high-wire
Searching for balance without a pole.

The light locked in chambered heart
Scared by dynamite found by the side of road
Temporarily diffused by temporal visions
Later found empty—transparent.

Hallowed wholes bored by life's course
Left questions of detours taken on un-lit nights
And maps sketched by another's unsteady hand.
Downside-up-experiences temporarily
Failing course adjustment.

Left turns cul-de-sacs
Right turns stop signs met him.
Trade-ins, radar detectors, suits of Klein
The heart of the matter—missed.

Unfailing smiles support by will
Turned to the sky—and matched
An unseen eye he began to fly
Directions form inside altered faulty maps.

Directionless signals followed and steered.
Verbal erasers shared with journeymen
Whose mountains he shared.
Kneeling in sunlight—moonlight—and his light.

Letting go of the strings—He found wings
Supported and guided by contemplative friends
That witnesses the miracle of the everyday
In seeds—in green—and pyramided hands.

A shift in tides amidst waterless mountains
The rudder—his soul steering
New stakes—eighteen months of grace
Amongst ringing bells and smiles of worth.

Yesterday's—tomorrow's left in the harbor of memory
Released from earth-bound seduction
I'd spotted the depth of it all
In errands and measured security.

He left holding his hand
Opening doors
A dream realized
No longer penalized for fortunes outside his grasp.

Now bound to his soul
The instrument less minstrel
Plays songs and whispers to us
From his home.

—Joe Gorman August 15

    Joe had deeply experienced Corky. The two men, never in each other's presence, had been drawn together spiritually. I informed Joe that Corky was dead. We agreed that his book should be written.

    Corky's death launched this search. One aspect of his story puzzled me. Months earlier he promised when I undertook this investigatory project, "In finding me, you will find yourself." Corky's life became somehow universal. He and I experienced a similar struggle. Enlightenment visits through our individual search. On the other hand, Corky's story might never be read. This shield of anonymity permits me to write uncompromised truth disregarding a potential reader. All effort must lead me to truth. I assure any potential reader, this account of Corky's life will be the truth.

V

STARDOM IN COLLEGE

George Washington University has a proud basketball history. Ed McKee, GW Athletics Department, spent a day with me in September of 1997. He described the current Colonials squad. Corky had attended many of their home games. Ed located articles written about Corky with his teammates during Corky's second and third seasons. The stories appeared in *The Hatchet* (George Washington newspaper). They were all written by Bob Alden.

> *High Scoring Devlin Becomes GW Star.* (December 15, 1953)
> Walter (Corky) Devlin was a pretty good player for George Washington University's basketball team last winter. He even surpassed the former all time GW scoring record for one season by scoring 334 points last year, although a guy by the name of Joe Holup set a new mark of 427.
> Corky also established a new mark for shots taken, although records in this field aren't too complete. Devlin took 336 attempts for the basket, and hit on 139, for a very respectable 41.4%. (In fact, only Joe Holup and Elliot Karver achieved better averages, despite the general rumor that Corky took quite a few shots.)
> Devlin may have been a good player last year, but this year he has laid the groundwork for a really great season. In two games (although two games are not a reliable basis to determine

greatness) Corky has averaged an amazing 61.9% accuracy on his field goal attempts. He has also averaged 90% accuracy on his free throw attempts. Both figures would have won him the individual high marks among major college players last year.

In scoring 33 points against West Virginia in GW's opener, Corky tied the single game mark for points set by Joe Holup in the 113-87 rout of Duke here last year. Corky also set a new mark for most field goals in one game (15), bettering the former record of 13 set by himself and Joe Holup.

Corky established a new scoring mark for two consecutive games by adding 28 points in the Richmond game to his 33 against West Virginia. No player in GW annals has ever approached the start that Devlin is off to this season.

. . . And with Joe Holup and Devlin returning next year, and with the contemplated development of George Klein, another transfer student from Potomac State, the Buff should be about as strong next year.

Corky is a pretty independent sort of person. He is the only basketball regular, with the exception of the wedded John Holup, who lives away from Welling Hall, the domicile of most GW athletes.

Devlin lives at a fraternity house on G Street (known as Sigma Chi). Corky does most of his own cooking. He and one of his fraternity brothers share a whole refrigerator, which they padlock to assure that they will be the ones to eat the food stored within.

Young Walter is also known around these parts as a pretty fair dancer. And his 'Arthur Murray' steps seem to be quite a help to him on the basketball floor, for he is developing into one of the shiftiest players in the area.

Devlin Dangerous (December 14, 1954)

Devlin, who averaged 51.2% of his tries in '53-'54, is a dangerous shooter. He is well-equipped with a good repertoire of shots—especially his one-handed jump from near the key. Corky last year blossomed into another All-American prospect in helping lead the Colonials to their 23-3 mark and national ranking. Last year he led all Colonial scoring with 551 points for the season (Holup was right behind with 547), setting a new record and is possessed with one of the best "eyes" in collegiate play.

* * *

The Holup brothers grabbed rebounds, enabling Corky's abundant shooting. John, two years older than Joe, was drafted by the Warriors in his senior year. From 1955 through 1980, John Holup taught, coached, and was principal of high schools in Washington-area high schools. He served as principal of Cardozo High School, one of the original black schools in Washington D.C.

John played with Corky in 1953 and 1954. At 6-foot-5, John played center and forward. He married during his senior year. Before that he had lived in the same suite of dorm rooms with Corky. Because they became close friends, Corky lived only a few feet away.

Q: Do you remember Corky?
A: In college, Corky was flashy. He was always overt and perfected his own way of talking to people. He always had an iron in the fire (I doubt that he really did.) Corky knew someone and always had something going. On the other hand, he was a loner. He could be with you but never close.

On the court, he wanted to be our go-to guy. During one game against Maryland at Cole Fieldhouse, we were losing. Corky kept on shooting. The Cole Fieldhouse's baskets were like tuning forks. The shot either swished or clanged. Corky believed in himself. "It's only a matter of time, so I'll keep shooting." Both teams were nationally ranked, and we knew he would get hot. We were wrong. We lost the game by a few points. Our home rims were like sewers (opposite of Maryland), soft and enough give to hold the ball.

Q: Describe Corky's college life.
A: He was always on the go. He never studied more than he had to. Corky was also a fraternity brother of mine in Sigma Chi. Later as a senior, he ran for class officer. Corky flirted, but I don't think he did much dating. Corky had not experienced a strong family life. He never received much mail. No one visited him. He and I did some things together. I probably became one of his closest friends.

In those days, the University hired some of its athletes to be night watchmen. We were both employed as watchmen. On one occasion, Corky bought a copy of a final exam for five dollars. His grades were fine, but he didn't want to study. Because we were about the same size, I loaned Corky one of my suits. As time went by, I realized that I would have to ask for it back. When he finally returned the suit, he referred to the transaction as a loan to me.

Q: Did you see Corky in later years?

A: Corky experienced tough times in the '80s. One day he visited me in hopes of getting some money. He looked terrible. He had recently been released from jail. He was dressed in a knitted cap, a navy jacket and jeans. Some of his teeth were missing. He seemed very tired. He was always a talker and he told me about his gambling problem. When he returned in 1993, he looked much better. By then, he was well-dressed. He spoke clearly. Corky made a '180' turn and was on his way back.

Q: When did Corky change?

A: Corky was not the same person after he finished playing pro basketball. At the time, I attributed his behavior to drinking. Sadly, I watched him go downhill.

* * *

Could Corky's basketball skills pay off? Could he perform as a starting guard for the champion Pistons in the National Basketball Association? Players like Wilt Chamberlain, playing for Kansas, and Elgin Baylor, in Seattle, were about to dissolve the league's color barrier. 1955 was an exciting year for Corky. World-renowned Swedish psychiatrist Erik Erikson advocated that the final (eighth) step to human maturity centered on a person's belief that he was living in the right place at the right time in the story of his life. As he stepped out of the lights of college basketball, Corky appeared to have his foot on this eighth step. He welcomed being part of basketball's growth and change. Could he successfully grow along with the league? Unfortunately, never again did he step close to maturity.

VI

I PLAYED WITH THE THINGS OF A CHILD

In the late '40s, Corky was among a group of teenagers who hung out in The Clinton Hill section of Newark. Quint Villanueva described Corky as a talented basketball player when he attended Madison Junior High. "He was full of fun, a member of our gang. He loved playing basketball in the schoolyard, before class, during lunch, and after school let out."

Corky was liked by his peers, teachers, and adults in the neighborhood. Occasionally he arrived at Quint's house, with a couple of guys or girls. Quint's folks liked him very much.

Corky had a dental bridge holding his missing front tooth. He manipulated it with his tongue so that it partially slipped out of his mouth. He performed his tricks in front of the girls, teasing them. They screamed in feigned fright (they really enjoyed it). They turned and ran away. Corky had this big grin on his face. The tooth was still hanging from his lower lip. He was very funny.

* * *

While I was having breakfast in Woodbury, NJ, Jim Ryan casually commented, "You are writing a book about Corky Devlin. My family knew him well in the '50s. My brother, Paul, played basketball with him. My sister, Kay, dated him. He often stayed overnight at our house."

In 1954, Paul Ryan was a carefree high school senior enjoying an entire summer at the New Jersey shore. He also attended West Virginia University where he scrimmaged for hours against Hot Rod Hundley. Twice he was invited, but declined, to join the varsity team. Paul's quickness served him well. Paul discussed playing with Corky. He remembered a young untainted Corky Devlin. His stories portrayed Corky before he changed in pro basketball.

Q: Tell me about your time with Corky.

A: My parents owned one of the three houses on the bay at Island Beach, NJ. The township built a sand and gravel court in front of our house. Corky and I spent endless hours every day on that irregular surface. The ball bounced in odd directions when it hit the stones. Our dribbling skills really improved as a result. We played barefoot. By the end of summer you could light a match under our feet and we wouldn't feel it.

Q: You are about 5-10. Were your games evenly matched?

A: I am two years younger. I always had quickness.

Q: Did you play one-on-one?

A: Mostly. Sometimes other guys joined us.

Q: Was there a particular day with Corky that stands out?

A: He had just signed his first contract with the Pistons. He called me. "Stay there. I'll pick you up in my new car. We'll drive to Atlantic City."

Up to the house comes a huge white four-door Oldsmobile convertible with red seats. It was a boat. We drove to Atlantic City and parked near Steel Pier. On the boardwalk, we spotted a three-shots-for-a-quarter basketball cage. Those rims were smaller than regulation. The odds were stacked for the house. Corky refused to play. He didn't want to look bad. I tried my luck. As I fired at the basket, I recognized that the man next to me was Pat Boone (no white bucks). He also was shooting fouls. The three of us held a great conversation. Pat kept glancing around. He didn't want to be recognized. Finally, a voice came from somewhere on the boardwalk, "There's Pat Boone."

Whoosh. Everyone on the boardwalk, including the Planters Peanut man, was in our space. Corky and I managed to slip out of the crowd.

Q: Sounds like Corky was a bit of a showoff.

A: He was. But, he was a wonderful person.

Q: Was he good enough that the girls loved him?

A: Corky dated my sister Kathleen Ryan. She really liked him. When Corky left for California, Kay was very upset.

Q: She was pining away for Corky?
A: Yes. She really liked him.
Q: What year was that?
A: The year he graduated from college (1955).
Q: What did she like about him?
A: His disposition was really good. He always seemed to be happy. He cared about other people. Corky was careful to include everyone in the conversation.
Q: I'm surprised. Some considered him a real stinker.
A: I know. Some things that happened later caused people to feel bad about him. I'm not one of them. He was a fun-loving person. When we lived at the shore, he was "The" basketball player. Everyone looked up to him. He was gracious to everybody. I never saw him in a bad mood.
Q: You know he became a compulsive gambler?
A: I didn't see that at all. But I can see how he could get caught up with gambling. When he was with the Fort Wayne Pistons, he talked about team flights. The place to be was the back part of the airplanes. The "in" players flew there.
Q: Corky was a good person?
A: Yes. My sister, Kathleen, died two years ago. She always had her antennas out for other people. She was well-educated and could have played "the superior" role. Instead, she concentrated on sizing up people. Kathleen really liked Corky. She was hurt when he went to someone else.
Q: Who did he go with?
A: Arleen Adams. Corky brought Arleen over to our house. My point is that Kathleen sized Corky up as a really nice guy. When some players get into the limelight they get caught up with themselves.
Q: Describe Corky of your era.
A: Corky was the type of person that everybody followed. He treated everybody well. He never said anything bad. He never got angry. Corky was my biggest fan. When we played together, I used to be able to get by him.
Q: He didn't get mad at that?
A: No. He got more determined, not mad.
Q: He shot a jump shot. You were a driver?
A: I had a pretty good set shot that I released quickly. I out-rebounded him at times through better timing. Guys 6-foot-5 didn't like me to drive

around them. I could get Corky's feet tangled. I put one foot over his foot and I was past him. We played for hours everyday on our sandy court.

Q: Could Corky guard Bob Cousy well?

A: He did talk about Cousy a lot. Corky talked about shutting Cousy down. Maybe Corky was a little jealous. He said he outscored Bob Cousy in a game.

Q: When was the last time you saw Corky?

A: In 1958. We were living in Trenton. Corky hit my brother for $35. He promised to repay in two days. He still hasn't.

VII

THE FLIP SIDE OF THE FIGHT

SOUTHERN CONFERENCE LAURELS DOOMED BY W. VIRGINIA, 58-48 (March 8, 1955)
...The championship tilt was tied at 46-46 when the regulation game ended. The next five minutes saw "Hot Rod" Hundley and his friends score 12 points to the Colonials' pair. Thus, the Buff closed out the year with 24-6.

...The Buff-Mountaineer tilt will be long remembered by the fans that witnessed the game. After a sluggish first half, the West Virginia team, henceforth known as Hot Rod Hundley and his Friends, led, 28-23. The Colonials, always a great third period team, rallied sharply and rattled off ten quick points. The Colonials nursed a small lead until there were less than three minutes to go. The Hot Rod and his Hillbillies tied the score at 46-46, when Corky Devlin attempted a jump shot. It missed, and the game went into overtime.

The next five minutes were a nightmare for the Buff. They were outscored by the Rod and his Friends, 12-2. Hundley blitzed the Buff for four quick points, and the handwriting was more than on the wall for the Colonials.

The torture was soon over. The Friends won, 58-48, and face LaSalle in Madison Square Garden tonight in the NCAA play offs.

> ... Devlin tallied 24 points and played one of his greatest games ... He was a real tiger in the game.

Good sense prompted me to verify Corky's fight with Hot Rod Hundley of West Virginia. Corky repeated his story of punching Hundley on many occasions.

I went to Hundley himself to verify Corky's story. In March, 1998, I called the office of the Philadelphia 76ers. The Sixers had relocated from Syracuse, replacing the Philadelphia Warriors (they migrated to San Francisco in the '70s). The Sixers' executive secretary put me in contact with Kim Turner, Director of Public Relations for the Utah Jazz. Rod Hundley, a few years removed from announcing the National game of the week, broadcast Utah Jazz games. Kim wanted to help. First, he cleared my request with Rod. Then he gave me Rod's home number. Our time difference compounded the broadcaster's busy schedule. Finally, I caught Rod. I repeated Corky's account of their fight. Rod sounded annoyed, "That never happened, I was never in a fight."

I welcomed his side of the story. I suggested an interview before the Jazz—Sixers game in Philadelphia. Rod agreed to 20 minutes if I would meet him at courtside an hour before the game. I sensed that he was going to contradict Corky. Rod's account might enhance my understanding of Corky.

On game night a cold north wind chilled South Philadelphia. The pre-game crowd was large and enthusiastic.

I bought two tickets in the nose-bleed level. Rod was happy to meet me at press row. He promised to remember as much about Corky as possible. My 32-year-old son, Paul, wanted to experience the game. Was Corky smiling? It was St. Patrick's Day.

Courtside at the NBA game was fascinating. Celebrities were everywhere. The players from both teams warmed up. They seemed so calm (focused). Some Sixers players messed and joked with Jazz players. They seemed to genuinely like each other. All over, players paired to practice one on one moves. Just about every shot nestled in the basket.

Paul pointed out Iverson, Lynch, and Snow. They seemed serene. No excitement. Players lay on the floor in acrobatic positions as trainers stretched their leg muscles. Basketball players are lean and limber. I counted six Sixers who were about the same height, seven feet tall. My height made me feel self-conscious in crowds. These guys stood proudly straight and tall, comfortable on court, enjoying the land of giants.

The Flip Side of the Fight

I had never seen Rod Hundley. My son Paul thought he remembered Rod when he announced the National Basketball Association Game of the Week. I was mesmerized by the players. Paul nudged me. We leaned against a railing. In front of us were two rows of red folding chairs. At courtside sat the visitors' scoring table. Rod strode easily down the aisle. I called his name. He responded by motioning for us to climb over the railing. Rod's hair was gray, but he had maintained his slim build. At 6-foot-5 he appeared to be in good shape. He smiled graciously. His demeanor was confident, but not at all intimidating. He asked us to wait while he announced a promo for the game back to Utah. He spoke from the table directly in front of us. With his back to us, he became animated. Sometimes he shouted into the microphone. We couldn't hear what he was saying because the crowd murmured around us. Then he totally focused on us.

We sat alone with him on press row. We had 45 minutes before game time. The ushers kept close watch on who entered press row. An usherette approached and offered to bring us drinks. Paul ordered a beer, I ordered a soda. She smiled warmly. I told her we didn't belong. During this important moment, Paul left for the men's room. I suggested that he prepare for his return by contacting an usher. Our nosebleed tickets were in my pocket. Rod was ready. In his sincere, slightly southern accent, he spoke to me about Corky. They had become friends.

Q: Tell me what really happened during and after the game in 1955.

A: He never hit me. No punches were ever exchanged. During my entire career, I was never in a fight. We were playing the Southern Conference finals in Richmond, Virginia. The game was a showdown. Both teams were really psyched. The final score was 58-48 and we won in overtime. I scored 10 points in the overtime. Corky was crushed. He had tears in his eyes. They were tears of disappointment. Both of our seasons ended. I remember that he refused to shake hands. Later, he got himself together. We did shake hands.

We both went on to play professional basketball. I remember him as a marginal player. He never excelled after college. Basketball was very important to Corky. He was scrappy and tough, but he never quite fit into the pro scheme. In college, he was a high scorer and a star. He never became a star with the Pistons or the Lakers. He was just average. After a few years, he couldn't hang on any longer.

Q: Did you see him in recent years?

A: As time passed, we became friends. We talked a lot about how life had changed in the League. We both mellowed. I saw him last in Baltimore.

We had become good friends by then. I felt a little sorry for him. He was a wanderer, and life seemed to pass him by.

Q: Can you remember anything about his play in the pros?

A: He sometimes drank before the games. That wasn't so unusual in those days. He liked martinis. The pressure Corky felt came from deep within. I knew that he was bipolar, a compulsive gambler, and had a drinking problem. After he retired, we saw each other from time to time as he criss-crossed the country. I considered him my friend.

Rod Hundley was gracious to me. He seemed to be in no hurry. He genuinely liked Corky. He recalled the exact date of the Richmond game so many years ago. Rod's account of the fight contradicted Corky's. I wondered if Corky made up the story to save face? Probably, Corky believed that his version was true. His lie probably envisioned what he wished he had done. How many more of Corky's stories had been altered to reflect what he wished he had done? This man challenged me to write his story. Is he not to be trusted? The murky path continues.

* * *

The following box score describes that conference final game in Richmond. Corky performed well. The game was lost on the foul line. Rod Hundley's smiles on the foul line really frustrated Corky. It was an unhappy ending to his career.

Saturday, March 5, 1955 Richmond Arena, VA

George Washington Colonials	FG	FGA	FT	FTA	REB	PTS
Basil Ciriello	0	7	0	0	3	0
Joe Petcavich	0	5	8	9	9	8
Joe Holup	4	14	0	2	8	8
Walt Devlin	11	25	2	2	9	24
George Klein	2	5	0	1	6	4
Jay Manning	0	1	1	2	2	1
Bob Sweeney	0	1	0	0	1	0
Stan Walowac	0	1	0	0	0	0
Ed Catino	1	6	1	2	2	3
	18	65	12	18	40	48

West Virginia Mountaineers	FG	FGA	FT	FTA	REB	PTS
Pete White	1	8	5	6	15	7
Willie Bergines	1	3	1	6	8	3
Clayce Kishbaugh	4	10	6	6	3	14
Frank Spadafore	1	3	0	0	4	2
Rod Hundley	10	26	10	16	12	30
Paul Witting	0	2	2	3	1	2
	17	52	24	37	43	58

	First	Second	OT	Final
George Washington	23	23	2	48
West Virginia	28	18	12	58

VIII

THE BACKCOURT FOR THE PISTONS

CORKY DEVLIN STARS AGAIN IN FORT WAYNE
(October 23, 1955)
   It looks like Walter "Corky" Devlin has made the jump from college ball to professional ball without any trouble.
   A small note from Fort Wayne last week noted that Corky was high scorer for the College All-Stars basketball team with 16 points as the All-Stars lost to the National Basketball Association champion, the Fort Wayne Pistons, 97-93.
   Corky was drafted by the Philadelphia Warriors after ending a great cage career at George Washington last year. At the time of his drafting, Corky preferred to play semi-pro ball. He was supposedly signing with the Peoria Caterpillars team, when Corky was selected to go on a "goodwill" trip to Turkey, sponsored by the U.S. State Department.

* * *

   Chuck Noble graduated from University of Louisville in 1954. At 6-foot-4 and 195 pounds, The Philadelphia Warriors drafted him. He played one year for the Goodyear Wingfoots of the National Industrial League. Corky and Chuck became rookies together with the Pistons in

1955. Chuck played the next seven years for the Fort Wayne Pistons (now the Detroit Pistons). I spoke with Chuck by telephone.

Q: Why did you sit out a year before joining the NBA?

A: Ed Gottlieb wouldn't pay, so I played a year in Akron where I was raised.

Q: Corky told me he earned $15,000 his first year. Does that sound right?

A: I don't know. I doubt if he ever made that much. (laughter)

Q: You're saying that you never made that much?

A: Yes.

Q: That's awful; players now make more than that playing a quarter.

A: Well, yes. Our top player was George (the Bird) Yardley and he never made more than $27,000 in any year. He was also the league's scoring champion. We also had Mel Hutchins and Larry Foust (from Philadelphia.). Our center was Foust with Yardley and Hutchins at forward. Andy Phillip, who played for everyone, played guard for us. The three of us alternated at guard depending on the team we were playing. We tried to match up. The Pistons had won the Western Division, then lost in the finals to the Syracuse Nationals in 1954. In my first year, we again won the Western Division but lost to the Philadelphia Warriors. We had a strong team. We moved the ball well.

Q: Were black players in the league?

A: The first black player with the Pistons was Jesse Arnelle. He was an All-American football player at Penn State. He came in my first year, so all three of us were rookies together.

Q: With three strong rookies, whom did the Pistons have to cut to make room?

A: Max Zaslofsky (from St. John's) and Dick Rosenthal. I cannot remember the other player.

Q: You seemed incredulous when I told you Corky died in a monastery. Why?

A: (After a laugh) Well you know he led a pretty fast life. After our playing days, I saw him only when he came through town. He married a gal named Arleen Adams, and our wives became close friends. They stayed in Fort Wayne during the summers. We saw a lot of them during those years. He had a little girl at that time. After basketball, he went to work for Jostens, Inc. They manufactured graduation rings for high schools.

Q: He played two years with the Pistons and one year with the Lakers. I have his stats. I'll try to get yours from the league.

A: (Chuckle) Mine are nothing exciting.

Q: Wilt Chamberlain entered the league in 1959.

A: Is that the year? I know Bill Russell started in the fall of 1956. The Olympics were held that year. Bill played in the Olympics before he went to Boston. It's kind of funny; we beat Boston every time we played before they got Russell. We never beat them again. He was a great all-around ball player. He didn't score as much as Chamberlain, but the Celts had other guys who scored. They were all team ballplayers. The Celtics were the greatest team I ever saw. I don't care how good these guys are today, they would have a tough time beating those Celtics.

Q: You are my first source of stories about Corky.

A: All I can tell you is that he and Arleen were very much in love when they started. Then, Corky couldn't acclimate himself. He really didn't do a very good job of supporting his wife while they were married. He squandered tremendous talent. He was very good with people. He made friends easily. I just don't know why he didn't make it in marriage. He did well with Jostens so they moved to California. Then I lost touch. Arleen accompanied him to California. All of a sudden, she met someone else. They got a divorce. Corky told me he attempted suicide when she confessed that she was running with another guy.

Q: He was Corky's best friend.

A: I didn't know that. He was a performer. I can't remember his name, but they were both musicians. Arleen began singing with him. Corky told me that he wanted to hang this guy's suit up in the closet with him in it. That's how he explained it to me. Sounds like Corky, doesn't it?

Q: It does. Did you know that Corky was treated for mental depression?

A: No. He went through a lot. I think he was put in jail in California after acting as a strikebreaker for one of the unions. I didn't see him for a long time. I was living in Des Moines, Iowa at the time. He came through town. I had been appointed president of a company and he called me. He arrived on the edge of town while hitchhiking back to New Jersey. I got him and he stayed at my house for a week or so. I gave him money to catch a bus back to New Jersey. He reappeared back in town periodically. One time, I came home and he was sitting in my kitchen drinking a beer, talking to my wife. He hitchhiked back and forth across the country. Unfortunately, I don't think he worked at the time. He told me he had developed a real gambling problem. A few years later, I'm sitting in the boardroom at my office and someone comes in and says, "Turn on the TV.

There is a buddy of yours on the Phil Donahue Show!" Corky was talking about Gambler's Anonymous. The next time I heard from him was 10 years later. He wanted to know who he could get to publish his gambler's book (analyzing the odds). "What did you do, go the other way?" I gave him some guy's name in New York.

Q: Describe Corky's personality.

A: He was a good friend of mine, a good buddy, and fun to be around. He experienced tough times like a lot of athletes after playing ball. They had been pampered their entire life. Their career ends so they have to get a job. They can't acclimate. Corky was not lazy, but his attention span was not very good. He wanted to be on top but he didn't want to work to get there. He lacked patience.

Q: Do you remember playing with him?

A: Corky and I would coast through the game. Then the coach would say, "Ok, you rookies get out there and win the game."

Q: You were also a good shot?

A: Yes, I shot the one-hand set shot and the jump shot. In those days, the two-hand set shot was a weapon. Gene Shue, Billy Kenville, and Larry Costello all shot two-handers. Also, Dolph Schayes was a two-hander. We had a very good ball club. We played Bob Houbregs as backup center. Larry Foust was our starter. Foust, Yardley and Houbregs are all in the Hall of Fame. Andy Phillip was probably our fourth Hall of Famer.

Q: You were, almost?

A: (Laugh) I don't think so.

Q: You must have had a lot of assists.

A: I played pretty well. We had a team concept then. Everyone plays one-on-one now. There was more thinking. We were not allowed to play zone. During my first year, the 24-second clock started.

Q: Do you remember when Corky was traded to the Lakers?

A: Yes, he and Larry Foust were traded for Walter Dukes.

Q: Walter was a 7-footer from Seton Hall. Was he good when he got to your team?

A: He was a heck of a ball player, a great defensive player. I had played against him for three years in college, so I was happy to have him on our team.

Q: Corky claimed to be receptive to the influx of black players. The league was changing colors and he championed those changes. Does that make sense to you?

A: I don't know how much he championed it. I don't think any of us were prejudiced. If a guy could play ball, he could play ball. I didn't care if he was orange. I can't think of any ball players who were prejudiced. If a guy comes in with talent, you know it right away.

Q: Do you remember Convention Hall in Philadelphia?

A: Yes, I remember that their fans were pretty tough. Paul Arizin was probably the greatest player I ever saw. He was also a great person. I didn't get to know him very well because he was quiet. He became perpetual motion during the game. He had asthma and you thought he was going to die half the time. He and Yardley used to guard each other. They both had asthma. It sounded like a steam shop. Yardley was also a good guy.

Q: In summary, would you consider Corky a friend?

A; Yes, whenever he was in town, I was glad to see him and I tried to help him out.

IX

GETHSEMANI

It had not rained for 90 days in southwestern Kentucky. The rolling hills were parched brown as I drove into the Abbey of Gethsemani. A light rain began to fall. I hoped the water might make the monks glad to see me. To my right, on top of a 100-foot knoll stood a giant cross. The evening sun was setting behind the cross. It reflected on the Trappist monastery. To my left, stood a large rambling set of white buildings. I was about to meet a thriving community of Trappist monks.

I entered the monastery building through a large heavy door (gate). Corky once served as gatekeeper. How many times had he opened this door? Just inside I saw a desk, part of a large reception area. I sat and breathed deeply. No one else was in the room. The monks must be having dinner. I closed my eyes. I realized how nervous I had become. Would Bro. Alban (the only name I had) be cooperative? I had driven so far. Mine was a solitary mission. Three or four men filed into the room during the next hour. All carried suitcases. Obviously, they were prepared for a directed retreat. One man gestured that I could go first when the monks arrived. I wondered what they were thinking as they anticipated the silence and solace of a few days at Gethsemani. When one man asked, I stated that I was here for a different purpose. I was seeking information about Corky, but I wasn't sure how my visit would be received. The retreat business had always fascinated me. I had experienced a few spiritual journeys. Retreat masters always seemed so wise. They possessed all the answers. I felt like a soft paper towel blotting up their wisdom. Gethsemani retreats appeared to be casual yet business-like. How could I approach these monks about Corky? This place is so large. I am not holy. Help me, Corky.

A young monk with a closely shaved head took his seat at the desk. The eyes of the other visitors followed me to the desk. "I'm here to see Bro. Alban. I have an appointment." He picked up the phone. I sat down.

All of the visitors had left for their accommodations by the time Bro. Alban appeared in the doorway. He beckoned. We found ourselves at home in an unused conference room. He sat at the front desk while I sat in the front row. He seemed puzzled by what I hoped to accomplish. Joe Gorman and I had visited him over a year earlier. I reminded him that he had offered to help in any way that he could.

Q: Could you repeat the stories you told us about Thomas Merton?(Bro. Alban had lived at Gethsemani for over 40 years. In his younger days, he had been assigned to deliver daily supplies to the monks living the hermit life.)

A: One day as I was delivering oil, bread, mail and the New York Times to Thomas Merton's hut, I blurted out, "You know, you are not really a hermit."

Merton answered quizzically, "Why do you say that?"

Bro. Alban stood his ground. "You are in touch with the outside world through the newspaper and your correspondence. That's not a hermit's life."

There was silence in the hut for over a minute. Then Merton poked his head out and muttered, "I guess you're right. I'm not really a hermit."

This realization was typical of the great theologian Thomas Merton. If you spent an hour with him, you would really like him. He was unassuming and very human. He disliked pomposity. Another well-known Trappist monk cherished opportunities to debate with Merton. Their conversations were enchanted moments. The monks gathered to listen carefully to the two theologians arguing their views on deep moral issues. One night in the middle of a particularly intellectual debate, Merton uttered, "We know that God is all-knowing, we know that God is all-loving, and we know that God is omnipotent. We also know now one other truth, God is definitely not a moral theologian." That ended the debate.

Q: Bro. Alban, repeat the story about the ax.

A: (Bro. Alban smiled). "In those days, we were never permitted to walk alone in the woods. We engaged in communal activities. Merton always followed his own drummer. Many times we observed him under a tree or wandering in the woods. He was usually in prayer. No one dared to interrupt his worship. Well, we were anticipating a visit by the highest-ranking Abbot (from Europe) in our order. Naturally, everyone wanted to be on his best behavior. The question arose, what could we do about Merton wandering in the woods? Our Abbot solved the problem by putting an ax in Merton's belt so he looked like a forest ranger. We never volunteered his real identity. He was responsible for initiating a lot of changes and freedoms around here. Most of them were good."

Q: You were Corky's best friend. Can you elaborate on how you became close?

A: First of all, Corky knew the difference between right and wrong. He had a finely developed conscience and consistently tried to do right. At times, he agonized. Corky had been an athlete and I have always enjoyed basketball. We spent endless hours talking about the NBA's current teams and players. Corky always rooted for the underdog. Every game represented a quest. He knew everyone. One of his favorite sayings was, "I can drop enough names on you to give you a hernia." It was true. He always had a story about someone famous. He stressed the good, then defended the famous people he knew. Once, when working with the McDonald House, he escorted an ill child to see the guy with the glove, Michael Jackson. The visit had been the child's wish. Michael Jackson, in the middle of his show, came backstage to spend 10 minutes with the little boy. Then, he returned and finished his show.

In another incident, Corky brought an ill child to a sports auction. The bidding for a shirt approached a thousand dollars. The child kept bidding. The auctioneer asked him if he really had enough money. "The boy has the money," came a deep voice from the back of the room. The voice belonged to Michael Jordan. The child got the shirt. Jordan wanted no credit. There is good in all of us. Don't forget that. Corky was able to befriend, then defend, famous people who by reputation were not nice people.

Corky was also compassionate. His favorite movie was *To Kill a Mockingbird*. He watched it over and over. I enjoyed many discussions about its message. Corky's favorite author was Bishop Fulton Sheen. He read many of the Bishop's books. One day Corky was painting a house. The owner of the house returned with (you guessed it) Fulton Sheen. They started talking in the kitchen, and the conversation went on for hours. He never mentioned who talked more, but I started to feel a hernia.

Corky joined the National Council for Gambler's Anonymous. He also worked with Cardinal Krol in Philadelphia helping priests with gambling problems.

Another aspect of Corky's character was that he was a hard worker. Whenever the monks started a project, Corky was there wanting to do his part. Although he was sick, he always tried to keep up. At one point, he helped wrap cheese. Selling cheese evolved into the main revenue of the monastery. Cheese paid our bills. Corky decided that we needed his marketing skills. He approached retreatants about buying cheese when they were leaving the monastery. Whatever they ordered, their cheese was available for their departure. Sales started to grow. He fanaticized a company called the H and D corporation (our last initials). I assure you, it would have been a moneymaker.

Q: Gambling was always Corky's downfall. Was gambling like alcoholism?
A: He said; "When I gamble, it's like play money, it doesn't matter if I win or lose. The thrill is there either way." Gambling differs from drinking in that there is no hangover. The damage is more emotional than physical. Once he won forty thousand dollars in Las Vegas. He decided to save it so he put it in a locker at the airport. Just his luck, his flight was cancelled. He took the money back to the tables where he lost it all. He hitchhiked back to New Jersey.

Q: Did Corky describe his trip to the University of Kentucky?
A: Adolph Rupp's people observed Corky during one of his hottest games. They were scouting him in West Virginia. That night, Corky couldn't miss. The rim grew so big he could score from anywhere. Not only did Corky score over 50 points, but all other parts of his game were on too. He handed out a bunch of assists. During subsequent visits to Kentucky, he found a new suit hanging in his closet. Hundred dollar bills were in every pocket. No wonder he became sold on Kentucky. But his father wasn't. That's what counted.

Corky always tried to beat the system. He considered himself the underdog and thrilled at taking risks. On a trip to Canada he hoped to change his luck. Corky escorted a 26-year-old friend named Mark. Mark had marital problems and needed a change of scenery. Corky decided to smuggle Mark out of the United States. He drove up to the border with Mark hiding in the trunk of his car. The guard asked why Corky was visiting Canada. Corky produced a racing sheet from one of the Canadian Tracks. He grumbled about bad information he had received. Corky acted so charming and so convincing that the guard never checked the trunk. Once they were beyond the border, they drove to the track. They celebrated beating the system. Mark had served as a watchman at our monastery.

On April 29, 1995, Corky did not show up for his shift as gatekeeper. One hour later, Bro. Alban became concerned. Mark went to Corky's room. He found Corky face down on the floor. His pills were sprayed all over the floor. He had failed to take them. His pinkish white complexion had turned to black. Corky had suffocated.

X

BOB HARDY'S RESCUE MISSION

Bob Hardy is one of the most interesting and inspiring men I have ever known. Corky said about him: "Bob is the only person I ever met who truly and completely lives the Bible message. Everything that Bob does revolves around his understanding of Scripture." This dedication has resulted in a life characterized by triumphs and sufferings. He has, at times, been highly exalted by his peers; some later despised him.

During the '60s, Bob raised his family on 30th Street in Camden, NJ. His skill in carpentry led to his own business—repairs and building home additions. At that time, he approached the FBI and became an informant on anti-war activists. One night he tipped the FBI about a planned break-in by the Camden 28. They targeted draft records. Catholic clergy led this conscience driven religious organization. The perpetrators were arrested during the break-in and brought to trial. During the trial, Bob realized the ensnarement. He realigned his allegiance to the side of the defendants. His defection angered the FBI who retaliated by causing his business to suffer. It finally dissolved.

In 1975, I visited Bob's house for my first Monday night prayer meeting. We became instant friends. I agree with Corky. Bob is an inspiring but complex man. He believes in the Word of God as it leads the dictates of his conscience. He assumed leadership of a Christian movement known as the South Jersey Cursillio. People in trouble (physically, morally, or financially) turned to Bob. In almost every case, Bob helped. Just hanging around the prayer group gave me a tremendous source of comfort. He served as a shepherd whose flock thrived even though it was always changing. Many hurting men joined for awhile, got what they needed, and moved on.

At that time, I couldn't guess that I would be one of the few men destined to remain in Bob's life. Three years later, I learned that my wife was leaving me alone to raise three young children. Bob was the first person I called. At times, only his faith kept me going. I shared my deepest fears and relied on his strength. We became like brothers. Only a few people in each of our lives attained the commitment to remain friends for life. Turning my back on Bob is unthinkable.

In the late '80s, Bob moved his family from the city. He bought a farm in Pedrickstown, NJ. His first family had included five children. One son, Billy, died in an accident at the age of nine. Bob's wife, Peg, was a very strong supportive mother. Together, they adopted three more girls, Patricia, Theresa, and Sarah. The older children moved out as they married. The three little girls kept the farm busy and noisy.

In 1987, Peg experienced a debilitating car accident. She was paralyzed from the waist down and confined to a wheelchair. Nevertheless, she mothered the girls, and the Hardy's were happy on their farm. Bob worked hard to keep enough money coming in. Peg ran the daily activities, so life seemed reasonably secure. But slowly the money ran out.

One day Corky arrived looking for help. He lived with the Hardy's for a few months. He spent hours sitting on the porch chatting with Peg. She liked Corky. Her acceptance helped Corky re-consider his dreams. He drove to Kentucky, seeking entrance into Gethsmani Monastery. The monastery did not accept him.

In November, 1995, Peg died suddenly. With difficulty, Bob took care of his girls while working enough to keep the farm. Then, the bank foreclosed, and Bob moved the girls to a rehab home in Swedesboro, NJ. He refurbished the twin home where he now lives.

With my tape recorder, I visited Bob to relive the past. His misfortunes had overpowered him. I asked him to tell me all that he could remember about Corky.

Q: When did you meet Corky?
A: Corky called me. He had gotten my name from Fr. Joe Messina. At that time, he was living out at Bob Healey's place in Hainesport, NJ. He said that he represented Bob Healey, the owner of the Viking Yacht Company. Bob Healey wanted to help us avoid losing our farm. This was

in 1992. Peg had been injured for four years. We made arrangements, and Corky came down.

He showed up with great bravado. "Here I am, the answer to God's prayers." As if God prays! Joe Messina had told him what a great family we were, etc. Bob Healey, who was a wonderful person, had decided to help us. While we talked he mentioned that his face once appeared on the front cover of Life magazine. The NBA was just starting. Corky was voted "MAN OF THE YEAR." His story was printed in the magazine. Maybe there wasn't an article inside. But, knowing my friend Corky, he appeared on the cover.

He continually regaled us with stories. He described his Far East Basketball tour representing our country. He spent that year in oil-rich countries, fraternizing with sheiks and barons. He taught basketball clinics. This preceded the time he spent in jail. Incarceration took place sometime in the '60s. He played NBA ball for a while after his eight-month tour with a group of athletes for the State Department. I don't know whether he was paid or just had his expenses covered. He married during that time. As I remember, he got married in the '60s. Jail came in the early '70s. By then he had a child.

Anyway, Fr. Joe Messina called me before he and Corky arrived at our farm. He described Bob Healey's proposal. Bob would lend us the money to pay off all debts. After we settled our lawsuit (regarding Peg's accident) he expected us to pay everything back. That was the deal. Corky would make it happen. Healey put him in charge. I spent the next three months pondering the deal. In Hainesport, a weekly men's prayer group was meeting. It included Corky, Fr. Joe Messina, Bob Healey, myself, and about seven or eight millionaires. Corky visited me regularly. He had been appointed the go-between. Corky eased in and out of our lives during that period of time. Everyone liked him. Suddenly, he disappeared for over a year.

One day in the summer of 1993, he resurfaced on our doorstep. He hadn't slept for three days. He had been living in Baltimore with people I didn't know. It was Monday night so we held our usual prayer meeting in my living room. Corky just lay down on our couch and fell asleep. He needed a deep sleep. You met and talked to him during his second prayer meeting. Anyway, Peg accepted him and the children liked him. I established guidelines for his life in our house. He agreed to be up and gone every morning by eight o'clock. He must either get a job or do something.

I didn't want him just hanging around. I introduced him to Dr. Frank Iula. Frank prescribed Prozac or something like that.

Corky and I had some really good times. We engaged in great conversations. His heart certainly was right. He continually spun fantastic stories.

Before he came to live with us that first time, he called to admit that he was desperate. I told him to come on down (to the farm). It was a weekday. He pleaded, "They are going to shut off my phone. I ran up over a $1,000 worth of bills. I really need $1,000 bad." I had just about $1,500 in the bank so I gave him $1,000. He promised to repay it. It was a bad move. I couldn't afford that $1,000.

At about that time he made a men's spiritual retreat, a Cursillio. He attended the weekend through the urging of Jim Murray, former general manager of the Philadelphia Eagles. Murray did not attend that Cursillio but he visited my farm a few times with Corky. They came once on the Fourth of July. Fr. Dan Rocco also came with them.

After the Cursillio, Corky disappeared a second time. During that disappearance, I tried to trace him. When an adult disappears, he cannot be considered a missing person. We all can disappear. Without signs of foul play, the police won't help. He stayed away for a while. Then he returned. I ordered him to sleep on our couch. That's when you met him. At that point he was talking about going out west to visit his daughter (if he could find her).

Q: Did you know I gave him $2,500?

A: He was the consummate con artist. Corky was lovable and dangerous. After I realized he was dangerous, I kept him at bay. But I still liked him. I hoped we could do something for him. At that time, he was involved in a bitter fight with Bob Healey. Healey apparently had killed one of his dogs. Healey promised Corky a lot of things. Scriptures are very clear that we shouldn't get involved with people above our rank. They will use you, then chew you up and spit you out.

Peg liked Corky. She valued him as someone to talk to. He proved trustworthy in tasks like picking up our children from school. He drove Trish (Bob's daughter) and me to Deborah Hospital when she needed her heart checked. He knew exactly where the hospital was. He knew where everything was. He referred to himself as the original homing pigeon. One night, he described a dinner with Cardinal Krol in Philadelphia. He met the Cardinal through Jim Murray. The Cardinal became angry.

Corky challenged the Cardinal, "I thought the church was in the forgiving business." Corky would say that. The Cardinal took a step back and adjusted his thinking.

Corky knew a lot of people. He worked for a while for a construction firm in Bellmawr, NJ. He successfully filed paperwork with environmental agencies to launch their project. The company built warehouses. Corky was a doer. But, he had a glaring weakness. He could make money. I don't think his weakness was drugs. It was gambling. I wish people who knew of his weakness had warned me when he entered my life. If I had known about his gambling, I would never have introduced him to you. We were both set up. For him, we were an easy shot.

Q: Did he hit six people on the day he disappeared?

A: He was all over the place. One person I introduced him to, he hit for $800. He must have left town with $5,000 or $6,000. Between the money and his Prozac, he stayed high for six weeks.

While he was working for the construction company, I went with him to Leesburg Prison to visit the brother of the owner. It turned into an adventure. I did what Corky, the owner, and his sister asked me to do. I visited their brother in prison. I brought some light into his life. Later, I learned that the family owned a non-profit corporation which provided equipment to handicapped people. That is how Peg got her kiln and potter's wheel. Corky was key. He knew how to sell. In return for a day's ride to the prison, we received $2,100 worth of equipment, a nice return.

Q: Was Corky connected with a Mexican adoption agency?

A: Oh yes, Living Bridges. A person named Bob runs one of them. Corky was still friendly with Bob Healey when the Bishop of Trenton got him involved. The state of New Jersey was attempting to exchange dollars with Mexico because Mexico couldn't repay its debt. New Jersey wanted to trade dollars for pesos on paper if someone could put up the money. Healey promised the Bishop that he would put up $500,000. Corky planted the story in the newspaper. Healey was furious. Healey liked talking about it, but he wasn't enthusiastic about doing it. His anger was justified. Obviously, I don't care for the guy, so I'm being careful what I say. I trust people. If they promise to do something and then can't do it, that's one thing. If they promise to do something and don't do it, that's another thing.

So Corky ends up in Mexico. The Living Bridges Ministry, our State Department, and El Presidente attended a state dinner. They built a school or a couple of orphanages in the borattos—the poorest section of Mexico

City. Corky became a major player. The project happened as a result of Corky's article. The Bishop called Bob Healey asking about the project. The timeframe was 1993. That same Bishop is still in Trenton. Living Bridges is currently based across the Delaware River in Villanova, PA. They could give you details about Corky's involvement. Corky had admiration for people who worked. That's why he liked me so much.

Corky once said, "You're the only guy I know who thinks in homiletic terms. You analyze everything as if you are preparing a homily. You give your energy to prayer groups, Cursillio, Peg, the children, the farm, and helping this great buffoon (Corky)."

Q: *Corky once confided, "Bob is the only person who totally believes and lives Scripture."*

A: Thank you.

Q: *Interesting. He recognized your commitment, then took your money.*

A: I feel no bitterness against the man. If he were alive, I would greet him. The last time he disappeared, he left for Gethsemani. I found his suitcase and his phonebook with all his numbers. I called every number trying to find him. A half dozen were ladies. One lady in Baltimore told me Corky worked for her company for eight months. He actually lived with her family. He functioned as an answering service. He greeted customers at the door. Her name was Maureen Thompson. I called her to identify myself. Corky had been missing for three months. At first she was furious. I offered to call back. Then she started talking, "That guy has been gone for six months. He took our car." She rambled on and on. I really got an earful. After a while, she apologized.

He was also active with the Ronald McDonald House golf tournament. McDonald House was founded in Philadelphia. I don't know the details. Jim Murray visited our farm. He has about 10 children, a very Irish Catholic family.

Q: *Peg would have been a good source because of their talks on the porch. What would Peg have told me?*

A: She was a woman and mother. She talked to Corky about his daughter, the showgirl. He had a couple of grandchildren. Corky talked to Peg about spiritual things. Peg liked him. I never revealed to her that he hustled us. She didn't need to know. Mistakenly, I sheltered Peg too much. It was because I loved her.

Corky was a big help. If she needed oregano from the store, he had the car going. He deeply respected Peg. He loved Peg as a sister. Peg

...at quality about her. Real men like you loved her. A half dozen men loved her. It didn't interfere with our marriage. I had a half dozen women who loved me. Neither one of us were challenged by attention. It is natural to love someone. It doesn't have to be sexual. Peg considered Corky and me to be very much alike. We shared an ability to get our way. We could charm (manipulate) to get what we wanted. I once told Corky, "It's a good thing that we are both Christians, or we would both be in jail." We were capable of charming old women out of their money before leaving town. My father was like that. He also had a gambling problem. Gambling destroyed him. That's why I don't gamble. I once liked gambling. Our Lord literally healed me of my desire. I recognized the beginnings of an addiction.

Anyway, we both could walk into any situation and fear nothing. We knew that we could talk our way out of everything. The trouble was that we had to lie sometimes. Maybe not lie, just not tell all the truth. We lived in denial. We actually believed what we were saying. I know Corky didn't see his con when he took our money. He believed that he would eventually repay us.

The last time I talked to him, he had been away six months. He called me from Gethsemani. He asked if I had his suitcase and notebook. I mailed them to him.

He pleaded, "I'd really like to come back."

I said, "I'm not sure I would let you come back. You did great harm to my family. I haven't told anyone. What good would it do?"

Corky questioned, "Well, we could still be friends."

I said, "I don't know about that either. Call me again in six months. Let me adjust to thinking about your return."

I didn't know he was dead until four months after he died. You were the one who told me. I remember your question, "Are you sure he is dead?"

Q: I couldn't believe it. I only thought that question. I never verbalized.

A: He seemed bigger than life. For those who have forgiven much, much will be forgiven. I have been forgiven so much that I am embarrassed to refuse him forgiveness.

Q: Did he mention a young woman in Atlantic City?

A: No, that must have been someone else.

Q: She fell in love with Corky. She brought him home to meet her family. It turned out that her father had played basketball against Corky. Corky did the noble thing and refused to marry her.

A: He quoted 'The Tale of Two Cities.' "It's a far better thing I have done today, than I have ever done before." During the French revolution, a man switched places with another and lost his head while uttering that quote. Corky reveled in that noble fantasy. It was also his kind of humor.

Q: Corky met his daughter for reconciliation. Did he mention that to you?

A: While he was staying here, he left for Las Vegas or Reno to meet with her. He found her through her social security number. She was in her 40's and had two children. She offered him a joint and he was crushed.

Q: Did Corky work at all relationships and want them to work?

A: Oh yes. Corky was sincere. He wanted friendships to work. Whatever his problems emotionally, he relied on Prozac to keep him level.

Q: I met Corky when he was comatose.

A: He arrived at three that afternoon. We talked for a while; he had not slept for three days. I didn't know whether to believe him, but I was happy that he was back. The prodigal son had returned. After dinner, I told him about our prayer meeting. I urged him to lie on the couch to get some rest. As people arrived, he didn't budge. He didn't wake up until the next morning. I don't know whether he remembered how he got to our farm. He borrowed a little car from the lady in Baltimore. Corky wasn't a groupie, he was a group. He attracted wealthy and famous people. He considered people of wealth his way out.

XI

UNLIKELY ENCOURAGEMENT

 In May of 2000, Philadelphia welcomed spring, its annual embrace of new life. My search for Corky had slowed to a crawl. My book might be advancing towards a quiet death. I had contacted six people in search of Jim Murray. The result was a long list of Jim Murray's telephone numbers. Numbers had been disconnected. Others had changed. Increasingly, I worried about finally finding him. Would Jim be receptive? Jim was a vital source of information about Corky. I had uncovered only Corky's gambling and weaknesses. Everyone liked Corky, but were there any redeeming qualities? His earthly journey seemed greased. He slipped and slid through life. Had he ever walked erect in pursuit of his lofty goals? I was sharing Corky's frustration, walking a similar greased path. The questions were ever-present. "Why write about a scoundrel? Why continue to write?" These questions loomed louder as I wrestled with whether I could continue.

 Bring on new beginnings. My new activity was ballroom dancing. Outside of Philadelphia, I discovered a swing-dancing group. Dances were held every Sunday afternoon at the Cynwyd Club, instructed by Tish Sweeney. Her veteran staff had taught even the most awkward students for many years. During my first appearance, I learned that male dancers are becoming an endangered species. Dancing has never been macho. Forget the new; the activity assures a woman's undivided attention.

 My first action was a waltz. My partner stopped, stepped back, and scolded, "You don't know how to do this?" Crushed. Since childhood, I had lived blissfully unaware that my dancing wasn't adequate. I married a 5-foot-1 woman. Gini and I agreed not to dance. After marriage ended, I entered a state of bluff and denial. I bluffed dancing and denied tactical problems. When dance partners showed signs of displeasure, I labeled them bitchy.

Men lead in ballroom dancing. If the leader isn't adept, the couple flounders. That first afternoon, the Cynwyd Club's dance floor was overpowering. I spotted a table at which to hide. Every woman and most of the men had simultaneously branded me a fraud. Mortified, I flopped, clinging to my chair. I avoided eye contact with all females.

In front of me, the really good dancers enjoyed a Tango. I felt safe. No woman dancer would expect me to dance a Tango. An exceptionally beautiful dancer caught my eye. Her perfect figure was accentuated in a short white dress. Her long dark hair moved rhythmically as she glided easily through the Tango's intricacies. She was perfection. My breathing became shallow as I observed this beautiful confident woman dancing effortlessly. Really good dancers don't seem to smile. Stoicism makes them more aloof. Could I ever be aloof? I set a goal. I vowed to return every week for six months. My hope was that with practice, I could become confident enough to ask the Tango lady to dance. It was silly, but my vow kept me coming back.

Ten weeks later, I was greeted by the perfect Tango dancer. She was collecting money at the door. Carpe Diem. Could I risk discovery as a Non-dancer? She probably spotted my scarlet "N" but she was gracious enough to talk to me for a half hour. I learned that she is a literature professor at a Philadelphia University. I maneuvered our conversation into writing. She empathized with my difficulty in contacting Jim Murray. She volunteered that she had torn up 200 pages of her doctoral thesis because it wasn't her best. Then she tried to help me. She suggested, "Why don't you dialogue with Corky?" It was an intuitive suggestion. I agreed to give dialogue a try. What could I lose? The Tango dancer's name was Donna.

I knew the perfect spot to hold a dialogue. I lived in a condo on the beach. It was summer. I carried my beach chair to the shallows of the ocean. It was late morning. The sun in Brigantine, NJ danced on the water. While I wrote, waves lapped over my toes. The sound of the surf calmed my doubts. I breathed deeply and approached the man who had promised to help.

* * *

Corky,

It is Labor Day. Seven years ago we shared a memorable day on the beach. You surprised me when you confided that you trusted me with your story. Now, I am alone. For an entire summer I have been unable to write about you. Although I have tried to contact Jim Murray many times, nothing has materialized. It is difficult to keep positive about your life. Hints of your spirituality sometimes surface. Your life appears desperate, an endless series of hardships. When you told me you wanted your story written, you also promised to help. If you are able to help me, intercede with God. My summer has been filled with loneliness. I have tried to believe that my work and my finances are going to improve. The pain continues as the summer wanes. I love sitting with my feet in the ocean. The sound of the waves eases the pain in my heart. The brightness of the autumn sun stirs hope. I know the Spirit comes and goes as He pleases. At the same time, He is always with us. Corky, hear this intercession. Help me to continue your life story. At the suggestion of Donna, I ask you for direction. Does your spirit live? I am open. I will listen deep within my being for your response:

* * *

Paul,

Yes, I hear you. Yes, I want my life story told. Your writer's block has resulted from your inability to contact Jim. You will speak with Jim this week. He will cooperate when he meets you. As you and I walked the beach, I saw your openness. You and I share the burden of being misunderstood. I was different. My inner life was more real than my physical life, my journey sometimes seemed unbearable. You share the journey. With every step, you move further from safety in the world around you. Although you listen to people, you find less sense in their motivation. Many of your friends have disappeared. They could not see what you see. They dared not go where you are most comfortable; within your heart. My constant pain was that of not being understood. Bro. Alban was one of the very few who could really hear me. I knew I was safe with him. I could be myself. He knew me. He knew how I tried to follow God. The desire to please God pulled me through life. My addictions and the sense of being alien to the world's values drove me to become a liar. Lies served as my way of coping. They expressed wishes that I wanted to be true. When I took your money, I hoped to return it to you multiplied. You financed my last jump into the arms of fate. I wanted so much to catch up. I grabbed one last shot at winning to become a winner. I have been granted one final chance to repay those I hurt. You must give earnings from my story to the monastery to repay my debt. The monks will know what to do with the money. They are truly men of prayer. You are also a man of prayer. I am permitted to communicate with you so that my story can be told. My life has meaning. You must tell my story. There is much about me that you do not know. Jim will prove a good start. Keep your enthusiasm. I will help you finish this project. Call Jim again. He will continue my story. He will recognize what I saw in you. Write what you hear. I will guide you.

* * *

Could I trust what I heard? Were the words just self-talk? It was worth testing. The following Friday I called Jim Murray's number again. To my surprise, Jim answered. He had received some of my messages. Before I could ask, he volunteered, "I'll do anything I can for the Corkster."

Q: You will meet with me and tell me all you can about Corky?
A: I will. You know Corky lied to everyone. It will be difficult to sort out the truth. He was manipulative. Under it all, he was good.

We made plans to meet. Corky's message had anticipated Jim's lament about stretching the truth. I was destined to identify truth within his stories. Jim Murray proved to be a very busy man. After two cancellations, we finally selected a firm date, November 2, 2000—The Feast of all Souls.

I first laid eyes on Jim sitting in the back pew of the Cathedral of Sts. Peter and Paul on the Parkway in Philadelphia. I had been worried that I might not recognize him. He was the only person in that back row. He greeted me cordially so I settled down. As Mass progressed, I found myself glancing over, sizing up his mood. He appeared very relaxed.

After Mass, he chose his favorite deli restaurant. As we pushed inside, everyone knew and liked him. Jim's easy manner, his genuine interest in all people, disarmed me. I looked forward to hearing his story.

XII

MY BEST FRIEND, CORKY

Lunch finished, we drove to the Pink Chapel at 22nd and Green Street. The church was an old stone building with ornate facing surrounded by cement. Dedicated nuns dressed in pink habits lived inside the building. Each nun knelt for 30 minutes praying before the Blessed Sacrament. We had picked a beautiful sun-filled day. We sat alone on a wall in front of the Church. Jim began discussing Corky while the good nuns prayed perpetually behind us.

Q: How did you meet Corky?

A: My name is Jim Murray. At the time I met Walter "Corky" Devlin, I was employed as the general manager of the Philadelphia Eagles football team. My boss was Leonard Tose, the Eagles owner. He had asked me to drive (60 miles) to Atlantic City to meet with Steve Wynn. Steve was owner, president, and CEO of the Golden Nugget Casino. My assignment was to sell Steve a $2 million Eagles season ticket plan. Our presentation was a cold call. Before my buddy, Sam, and I got very far, Steve put up his hand, "Listen, I really don't want your boss coming in here to gamble. He's a compulsive gambler."

What a put down! Strangely, an hour later we found ourselves alone with Billy Weinberg, manager at Bally's. He confided that he would really love to meet our boss.

"I would love him to come here," Billy said. "I'm probably the only casino operator who ever gave money to the Institute for Pathological Gambling in Washington DC. That Center is run by Dr. Robert Custer."

Billy's comment highlighted a three-hour meeting. It proved to be an important exchange of information.

Our trip ended well. We didn't get $2 million, but we did get Bally's half a million-dollar investment in Eagles' season tickets. Leonard Tose wasn't happy, of course. He wanted $2 million. I was upset; I asked my buddy Sam if he remembered that doctor's name.

He responded, "What doctor?"

"Remember when we first met with Billy. He said his father and his wife's father went to their graves as compulsive gamblers. How hard could it be? Dr. Custer, Washington DC, Institute for Pathological Gambling, or whatever that nifty name was."

I dialed and Information gave me the number. A guy named Gar answered. I told him I needed help for somebody else. He probably figured I was talking about myself. I didn't want him to know that I was General Manager of an NFL team. I was Jim. He was Gar. We began calling back and forth on a daily basis. He gave me news flashes on the whereabouts of Dr. Custer. I was calling places like the Fairmont Hotel in San Francisco. The Institute for Pathological Gambling was a storefront with a phone. Dr. Custer had become the national guru on compulsive gambling. He doubled as head shrink (Psychiatrist) for the Veterans Administration Hospital in Washington. For many months, we played telephone tag. I never left my phone number. I kept calling hotels. Gar and I became good phone buddies. Once, we prayed together for his wife who had developed a brain tumor.

Finally, (Christmas week) I pleaded with Gar, "You know I really need help. My friend really has problems." He knew a person who might be able to help. He sent Corky Devlin. My first meeting with Corky was at the Bellevue Stratford hotel in Philadelphia. It was Christmas Eve, 1982.

Q: Corky represented the Institute?

A: Yes. That's how I met Corky. He eventually explained that he had read about Dr. Custer. Corky was planning to kill himself. He located the Veterans Hospital in Washington. Although he was not a veteran, he barged into the doctor's office.

"If you don't help me, I'm going to jump off the 14th Street Bridge."

Corky could be very persuasive. He evolved into a disciple of Dr. Custer. He easily absorbed clinical terminology. He was already familiar with the emotional and spiritual dimensions of compulsive gambling.

Q: Quite a beginning.

A: Yeah. Corky and I became friends before I introduced him to Susan Fletcher. She was Leonard Tose's daughter. She was taking over her father's team. With her consent, I arranged a meeting for Leonard with Dr. Custer. I knew this bold step could possibly cost me my job. I was right. Dr. Custer described that meeting to me long after I got fired.

"When I met Leonard Tose, he had a scotch in one hand and a cigarette in the other. We sat at a bar on Presidential Boulevard."

Leonard questioned "What are you here for?"

Dr. Custer replied, "I'm here to help you with your compulsive gambling."

Leonard looked him in the eye and said, "Hell. I gave up drinking and smoking, what makes you think I can't beat gambling?"

Dr. Custer whispered to me, "He needs a busload of guys like me, Jimmy. He is the biggest narcissist I ever met."

A few days later, Corky hit me with a word that really disturbed me. Remember, I am an Irish Catholic, full of guilt and freckles.

Corky said, "You're Leonard's enabler."

He really got to me. He meant that every time Leonard got in a jam, I cleaned up after him. I enabled him to avoid responsibility. Leonard Tose would never admit that. He never imagined that I contributed to his gambling. When I examined my conscience (part of our faith), there was a lot of truth in what Corky said.

We had numerous discussions before Corky met Susan Fletcher. She wanted to get Leonard help because, "He's messing with my money and inheritance." The Leonard Tose story: compulsive gambling caused his demise. He lost his football team because he incurred incredible loses in Atlantic City. He was forced to sell the team to Norman Bramen. There is a lot more to the story, but one gift I cherish (I consider it a gift), resulted from that call to Dr. Custer. God's timing was precise. I met Walter "Corky" Devlin. An accomplished storyteller, he embellished tales with great veracity. Some were Paul Bunyan tales. He lived on many different levels, but he could speak. Corky was a handsome man. He claimed to be the first 6'5" guard in the NBA. He was one of the first to room with a black player. This occurred before southern hotels were integrated.

Corky and I literally traveled millions of miles together. Our ride was incredible. His compulsive gambling broke his heart. Gambling compelled him to steal his mother's life savings. He took the money, and he bet on a horse in Atlantic City. It came in second. He remembered the horse's colors, the other horse's names, and the time of the race. Crushed, he stood sobbing in the racetrack parking lot. All the cars had left. He drove back to Alexandria, Virginia and appeared before a judge.

He pleaded, "I gotta be sick. There is something wrong with me. Please commit me."

Corky signed his own papers before entering a mental institution, a real black hole. As fate would have it, the administrators lost his paper work.

He spent months pleading with the Doctors, "Hey I'm not crazy; I signed myself in here."

They pumped him full of something he called Thorazine. He had been diagnosed as anti-social. One of my favorite memories occurred after another inmate advised him,

"Look Corky, you're never going to get out of here unless you go upstairs and socialize." The institution held a tea at about four o'clock in the afternoon.

Corky recounted, "I was the last one on the elevator because I had never been to a tea. We arrived upstairs. The elevator doors opened. There in front of us, twelve different kinds of dances were going on. I recognized one as the Virginia Reel. Guys were pouring milk on their heads and crushing cookies. A 400 pound nymphomaniac screamed and started ripping her clothes off. She charged toward me like a raging bull yelling, 'He's mine.' I couldn't get the elevator doors closed fast enough. I don't care if I stay here forever. I'm never going back for tea."

Q: It was a coed tea?

A: Yes. He finally met a female doctor who became enamored with him. She made a few moves before taking him home on a weekend pass. After a year, he talked his way out. Years later, during one of our many The Ronald McDonald House trips, we stopped and rode around the grounds of that Institution. It *was* scary, right out of a Stephen King movie.

Corky attempted to end his life several times. He fell into compulsive gambling after he caught his wife with another man. Arleen had been a featured singer on the Arthur Godfrey Show. Her infidelity so shocked him that it changed his life. He became homeless before anybody knew what the word meant. Gambling grew into an addiction. He never stole to eat nor would he steal for shelter. Yet he would do anything, (lie, or make up stories) to get a bankroll. He approached the National Basketball Association headquarters to lie about his situation for money to gamble. He fractured every relationship. He described how he evaluated everyone to determine how much he could get. He pushed each envelope. Oddly, after meeting Dr. Custer, he wanted to help other gamblers. When Corky identified compulsive gamblers, he became their advocate. He would call them up, drive to where they were, and try to create an effective defense. He worked with a lawyer named Ronny Kidd. On one occasion, he helped a guy in Canada who faced a 16-year to life sentence. This former banker had stolen $10 million from Caesars.

Q: Brian Moloney?

A: Yeah. If you read Brian's book, Corky received recognition. The world contains a lot of Brian Moloney's.

He amazed me. Art Schlichter was an All-American quarterback at Ohio State. He was a very talented football player. Because of his skill, he was drafted in the first round. Today he is in jail for some scam related to gambling. Art grew suicidal. It was Christmas week. Corky jumped into his van and drove to Schlichter's father's farm in Ohio. He empathized with and understood compulsive gambling. Corky literally held Art's hand during that crisis. Our world shows little empathy to gamblers. It's not like drinking or drugs where there are visible manifestations. Gamblers deal with the false god of our society, money. Their addiction is overpowering and unforgiving. People can't understand gambling. Corky considered gambling the most compelling addiction. Every state but Utah and Hawaii permits and encourages some kind of gambling. Gambling has become epidemic in America. Corky distrusted Gamblers Anonymous. In his view, their meetings became bragging contests:

"I lost two houses and two wives."

"Well, I lost three houses and three wives."

Although he rarely attended GA, he knew all their meeting places. He encouraged his friends to participate in the meetings. At one meeting, Corky and I met Chet Forte, the great television producer and former basketball player at Columbia. He fought gambling all his life. Most important, while we attempted to help gamblers, Corky and I became inseparable.

Q: You switched to "we" from "he." Did you take on the same causes as Corky?

A: Let me explain. I had my own ministry, the Ronald McDonald Houses. I traveled all over the world but primarily in the United States. Corky loved to drive. I was experiencing problems with my equilibrium. I couldn't drive. He loved to drive.

Our most memorable experiences occurred after Chuck Sullivan, owner of the New England Patriots, bankrolled a nationwide Freedom Tour for Michael Jackson. We bought a van. It was painted the Ohio State colors, red and gray. We nicknamed our van "Artie Schlichter." We were going to call it "Woody Hayes." Our name changed when we encountered the Ohio State quarterback. We drove "Artie" to Kansas City on a 4th of July to inaugurate the Michael Jackson Tour. We drove all over America's heartland with Michael and his entourage.

Q: Did you get to know Michael Jackson well?

A: No, nobody knew Michael well, including Michael. Corky and I had a wonderful experience. We were so diverse. The tour lost so much money that it cost Chuck Sullivan his team. He had borrowed $40 million to finance us. Everybody made money except the guy who put up the money. Corky and I grew close. He was interesting in so many ways.

After signing a pro contract, Corky thought he was making big money. He bought a red Olds and six Armani suits. The Warriors had traded him. He drove to Indiana for the Pistons training camp. Corky was on top of the world when he spotted the team hotel.

He sauntered in, slammed his fist on the desk and bellowed, "I'm Walter (Corky) Devlin, and I'm here to bring you the NBA championship."

The guy behind the desk smiled. "That's fine, where's your luggage?"

Corky paused, "I gave it to the valet."

The desk clerk gasped, "We don't have a valet."

Corky never saw his new car or his suits again. This episode foreshadowed Corky's destiny. Similar events punctuated Corky's destructive march into obscurity.

Q: He never saw his suits again?

A No. Their new owner had posed as a valet. He now resides in Guatemala or South Korea. Life's irony. Corky bet on many wrong horses. His temper had a pretty short fuse. Without warning, he went off. In contrast, he was a voracious reader. If asked to choose my most unforgettable character, it would be Walter (Corky) Devlin.

Q: Wasn't Fulton Sheen his favorite author?

A: He never shared that with me. Corky was a great one for telling you what he thought you wanted to hear.

Q: Really?

A: I'm not trying to turn the page, saying he didn't love Fulton Sheen. Corky absorbed everything. He played back every idea. He was quite verbal. Eloquence branded him a natural salesman. He claimed to have played with Elgin Baylor of the Los Angeles Lakers. He survived a plane crash transporting the Lakers team. He told that crash story many times. The plane landed in a cornfield in Nebraska.

After retirement, he landed a great first job. Jostens Jewelers employed him. His was the perfect life. He thrived in Southern California. He drove a boat and a fancy car. He also loved a beautiful wife and a baby daughter.

We were on the road on October 18, the day I will never forget. Corky had lied to me most of the time. He was reminiscing about his daughter. Suddenly he switched to talking the truth. She had worked for Walt Disney; he fabricated that he had visited with her often. First, Corky dined with her in San Francisco. Then, she was working in Hawaii. We were driving through the hills of West Virginia.

Corky blurted, "Murray, I have been lying to you. I haven't seen my daughter since she was five. She wrapped her arms around my leg crying because I was leaving my wife. We split."

My response was instantaneous. "Pull over, Corky." He stopped the car. I called 212 Plaza 8 1500 (the phone number of the NFL). I asked for Warren Welsh, Director of Security for the Eagles. Warren was a former FBI agent. Previously, Corky assisted the NFL with some gambling problems. Warren knew and liked Corky. We needed to find Corky's daughter. I put Corky on the phone.

"Corky, what does she look like?" I remember how tough that question was. Corky was sure she was a singer like her mother. Warren wrote down all available information; such as birth date, place of birth, mother's name.

My life really changed after that call. I bought a new car, a Lincoln. I named the car "St. Francis." It was Franciscan brown. I decided that our next stop would be Chicago. We had just opened a new Ronald McDonald House in Salt Lake City. I promised Corky that we would not return from our road trip before we found his daughter. My car had a bad lease (25,000 miles a year). Off we went. We landed at a Trappist Monastery in Utah. An old monk greeted us. I asked to use his phone.

I called Warren Welsh. He replied, "Bingo, we know where his daughter is."

"Are you kidding me?"

"No we checked through the postal authorities."

Warren traced her to a P.O. box in Truckee, California. Time to strategize. We did the "Columbo thing." Our plan was to park our car in front of her home. We would recognize her picking up her mail. Now, we had a real fix. Warren sounded like a law enforcement official.

He concealed his joy. "I talked to the head of the FBI in San Francisco. He sent his son to watch her perform. He met her. He concocted a story that he might be interested in having her sing at his wedding. He learned that she lives in a town called Calpine, California. Her home is a four-story free-standing dwelling at the corner of Main and Ferrar."

I will never forget that address. Calpine was so small it wasn't on the map. The next morning, Corky and I left after an ample breakfast. In the diner we met a good-looking waitress. She told us her brother had been an NFL tight end. I forget her brother's name. As usual, Corky became instantly enamored.

Off we went. We drove towards a deeply touching experience. The scenery was magnificent. It was a perfect fall day. The evergreen trees were beautiful. We approached Lake Tahoe. I kept searching for Calpine. Signs were announcing campgrounds. With each mile the road grew more rustic. Suddenly, I spotted a little sign. It read simply, 'Calpine.' As we turned left, we both started laughing. There were only five buildings in the whole town. It would have been impossible to miss Main and Ferrar. In front of us stood her building. Next door was a motel and the entertainment building where she performed. We also observed a post office and a fire station. We parked in front of his daughter's house. A guy was standing outside. Corky panicked. Fear gripped him about going inside.

"I don't look right."

He was wearing a jump suit. Corky always looked good. He looked fine. He was just not ready for this moment. He imagined every kind of greeting. He assumed his ex-wife had been pretty vicious describing Corky and the reason he left. His mind conjured only negative thoughts.

I suggested, "Let's say a Hail Mary."

We prayed together. I prodded him to re-think this meeting. Suddenly, out of the car we jumped. We approached the guy in front of the house. I told him who we were looking for.

He smiled, "Oh yeah, the second floor."

As we climbed the steps, I saw the door open. Inside sat a little guy who closely resembled the comic strip character, Dondi. Corky's daughter (her name was Dawn) had a little boy, a beautiful child. Her husband, a drummer, sat over to the right. From where I stood, I couldn't see Dawn.

For all Corky's verbosity, all his practicing for this moment, he could only stumble through the door.

He announced in a stammering way, "M-my n-name's W-Walter D-Devlin, my friends call me Corky."

The woman suddenly rushed the doorway. She erupted like a Nike missile launched from the couch.

She screamed at the top of her lungs, "You're my daddy!"

Well, we Irish guys started bawling. She's hugging her father whom she hasn't seen since she had grasped his appendage. It had been 25 years. The reunion consummated triumphantly. The tenderness was magnificent. It was spontaneous. It was blessed. More than one Hail Mary had been answered. I still see those two embracing. This was the single moment in my life with Corky that I shall never forget. In freeze frame I see it right now, with visions of sugarplums. Later that same day, we went to see her perform.

She sang with a Janis Joplin-type voice. Very throaty. Very good. The two of them began their honeymoon. They spent four or five days just catching up. Each night we went out to dinner. Corky was eager to know Dawn's husband and their son, his grandson. Their reunion couldn't have been more touching or more joyous.

After five days, I was obligated to return to Salt Lake City to finish opening their Ronald McDonald House. Happily, Corky and I drove back to Utah in St. Francis.

Then an idea struck me. "Why don't you drive back and spend more time with your daughter? I'll fly back to Philadelphia." Corky agreed. It was October 18, the day that Kirk Gibson of the Dodgers hit his famous World Series home run. I jumped on a plane and flew home with some Philly guys. The home run somehow resembled Corky's reunion. We had two home runs. I asked a guy on the plane, Buzz Satau from New Jersey, "What happened in the press box when Kirk Gibson hit it?"

I fancied a bunch of different reactions. His answer was, "Silence. Everyone was stunned."

XIII

DISCOVERING THE CAVES

Corky's reunion was a real stunner. He prepared for everything except something good. Dawn's embrace of him was unexpected. Later their relationship dipped into pathos.

We returned St. Francis to my buddy Franny McGowan's Lincoln Mercury dealership. The car had 10,000 new miles. "29 days. Did you guys take the car to Indianapolis and just ride it around the tracks?"

Everyone liked Corky. He tried to fix people's problems. He had little success fixing his own. His newfound relationship with his daughter proved imperfect. Her problems were very deep. Her addictions were serious. We both tried to stay in touch with her for a few years. Eventually she disappeared. It would have been nice if she had attended his funeral. I don't know whether she knew he was dead.

Q: Finding his daughter, then recognizing her problems, crushed Corky. Would you agree?

A: When you drive through Virginia you discover places called caverns. Each cavern is filled with caves. Corky's brain resembled a labyrinth of caves. I agree with Bro. Alban. Maybe talking with his brothers at the Monastery opened him up. Corky's mind contained cubicles, little caves, where he protected the most painful episodes of his life. During his final years he fell often. He never beat his gambling addiction. Shame prevented him from sharing his weakness with me.

My final memory of Corky was at Mass while he lived at Gethsmani. We had become so comfortable. I even knelt in the Abbot's stall. It was a Sunday. My son, Brian, accompanied me on that trip. Later, Corky drove us to a little town outside Gethsemani. We laughed, repeating the old stories and enjoying a big breakfast.

Corky turned serious. "Jimmy, I suffered this violent heart attack. I was driving myself to Jewish Hospital in Louisville. I thought I had finally straightened my butt out. Now, I'm going to die in this happy place. The doctor predicted that I will just keel over watching television."

Months later, the call came to my home in Villanova.

My son warned, "Abbot Kelly wants you to call. Corky died."

Diane and I left immediately for Gethsemani. Corky's brother arrived with his wife. We four represented his immediate family. I delivered Corky's eulogy. As I gazed over the crowd, I knew that Corky had deeply touched many.

Weeks later, a grieving lady, who had learned from my eulogy that I loved him, visited me in Philadelphia. I repeated some funny stories—especially about the car and the suits. The depth of Corky Devlin enthralled her. Far from superficial, he was troubled. He took big punches during his life. He also threw a few. Many body bags remained. Unquestionably, his was a good heart. He saved people's lives, literally and figuratively. He also caused some pain.

During one fond moment, I hugged him outside Gethsemani. I was never to see him again. We were standing on the grounds where Thomas Merton wrote his books. Corky Devlin added his own pages to history in that wonderful holy place. He loved Gethsemani. He loved the monks. They loved him back. For him, sleeping in that Monastery was better than hitting the lottery. After long painful years, he shouted one last heavenly headline: "WALTER DEVLIN EMBRACES THE CATHOLIC CHURCH WHILE PASSING THROUGH THE VEIL OF TEARS."

Gethsemani is extraordinary. I visited his grave recently. His headstone simply states "CORKY." He entered this world on December 21, 1931. He rose to heaven on April 28, 1995. He stood 6-foot-5 and lived almost a year for every inch of his life. He loved enough to make him 9-foot-7.

Q: Did his gambling start the day he learned his wife was leaving and his stepfather died?

A: True. His wife Arleen ran off with a comedian on the Arthur Godfrey show. I think the man was also Corky's next-door neighbor.

Corky's stories were sometimes contrived. He assured me that his gambling began that day.

He spun the following story while we sat at an old cowboy track in Omaha. The track was Aksarben (Nebraska spelled backwards). With us sat our friend, (alcoholic buddy) Rocky. What a wonderful guy—a real character. He was more verbal than either Corky or I. The Track Association published monthly lists of operating tracks in the U.S. The three of us checked off the tracks we had visited. It was no contest. My total was a distant third. Rocky, sure he had been to every track in the western world, finished second. Corky, our champion, had frequented every racetrack. Each had its own story. The stories made sense. At one track, he held a job picking apples in Washington State. That track ran six days a year during the apple season. He bet at numerous tracks that way. He also admitted to serving multiple prison terms. We didn't question whether they were trackless. I don't know how true his prison stories were. He told so many stories, but each was colorful.

Q: Was gambling latent like a light switch? Did it turn on after he got the horrible news?

A: He glanced over his light switch theory with me. Your story matches what he told me. His betting at Arksarben segued to decades of uncontrolled gambling. He loved Las Vegas most. One memorable night he won $144,000 playing poker. Later that weekend, he hitchhiked home to New Jersey. He hadn't been able to hold on to 10 cents.

Q: Did he describe stashing the money in a locker at the airport? The flight was cancelled. Frustrated, he withdrew the money. He lost it all.

A: No. I never heard the airport story. He told two other versions of that story. In one version, he purchased a room and put the money under his pillow. He paid a bodyguard a hundred bucks to sit outside his room for protection.

One of the casino managers visited and offered, "Corky, what do you want; Wine, women, whatever? You know you are just renting the money."

He couldn't stand all that money under his head. He felt compelled so he went downstairs and lost it all. I believe that he won the $144,000. I'm positive he lost it all.

In a second version, Corky slept with the money before losing it the next day. The story of winning and losing is true. The nuances are unimportant. You could spend your entire life researching Corky's stories. You could never chronicle his tortured experiences. Ponder each moment when truth and fiction dissolved into each other. God now holds him in the palm of His hand. His loving arms surround Corky encouraging our search. His thoughts stay hidden. Corky smiles and watches us struggle in front of this convent at 22nd and Green. It's Corky's humor, rooting for us to separate truth from fiction. Look at that statue across the walk. Jesus stands with his palms raised. It's not as if we scored any touchdowns. The statue is encouraging us to find Corky's truth. We need only let it flow!

Q: I expected you to enlighten me through insights into Corky. You haven't. Should I be patient?

A: Ours will be more than a one-time encounter. I prayed, while I waited for you. At Mass, the priest talked about his sainted Irish mother. He described another saint in Atlantic City gambling at the casinos. The priest portrayed how Corky lived his life. Corky assisted people he did not know. He didn't exclusively help people with gambling problems. Helping others was his corporal work of mercy. He walked alone. Life experiences made him very self-reliant. Some projects stirred passions. In the early '80s, the two of us experienced a weekend retreat. We joined 30 men for an emotional deepening, a *Cursillio*. Corky embraced spiritual moments. Fr. Joe Messina and Fr. Dan Rocco profoundly changed him. Later, we became active in an adoption ministry named Living Bridges. Corky and I traveled to Mexico. We touched many children in South America. On paper, Corky's story is a beget journey. This guy begat someone who begat someone else. You will meet people with wonderful stories. Conversely, you will also encounter embarrassingly negative stories.

Q: Getting to know Corky feels like unraveling an onion.

A: That's a good one. He was faced with tears and cheers. As an athlete, he made the NBA. He claimed to really guard the great Bob Cousy. He could get Cousy ticked off. Corky held a height advantage. Cousy was small with a great shot. He was also the greatest passer of his era.

Corky seldom excluded anyone from the sting of his creativity. His wild stories about how badly life had treated him found receptive ears. Throughout our adventures, we were always laughing. Doesn't God want us to be happy?

Corky lived alone, so home was very important to him. Corky liked to cook. He enjoyed each of his apartments. There he could be himself. He became very attached to his Doberman. The dog grew tall, lean and loyal.

Q: Were you the lead wit or were funny lines equally distributed?

A: I described him as "Tall, slim and close to the rim." I was, "Small, round and close to the ground." Corky was quite funny.

Q: He was proud of his gift of gab. He once saved a woman's life by not marrying her. He met her as a waitress in Atlantic City. She brought him home to meet her father. The father recognized Corky as an old friend. Does that story sound familiar?

A: Yes. There was a litany of waitresses and professional women. He protected his relationships with women. Women occupied a whole cave. He hid out, then locked the door. He talked only about his ex-wife. Purposely, he named no other women. His relationships seemed convoluted. Many of the women had been battered or suffered from serious problems. Corky was the eternal willing helper. In a similar vein, he described prison. His cellmate had previously killed two inmates. Corky befriended this murderer. He also got along with the prison guards. The guards weren't mean. They were apathetic. Corky hated people with no opinions. Apathetic people really bothered him. Corky admired extreme people. He liked the gambler from Canada, Brian Moloney. Corky interacted well with a man who stole 10 million bucks. Apathetic people were yogurt without fruit. Corky valued passion.

Q: Corky sought out people who were industrious?

A: Yet Corky could be very lazy, operating on cruise control. Don't kill yourself. Once he was working for me when he disappeared for two months. I forgave him by handing him eight weekly paychecks. My co-workers bristled. I learned not to mention the Christian stuff. Corky went on binges. His thing, gambling. He returned to assume his role as the lovable rogue.

Q: When in tough spots, you prayed with Corky. Would he pray along? Did he show faith?

A: Absolutely. Corky was a prayerful person. From the beginning, he had a deep belief in God. He suffered the agony of attempting to end his own life. He experienced unbelievable despair. During those times he could only shriek to God for help. Corky over-coached himself. He projected. He protected. He probed. He despaired. Conversely, he enjoyed a good time. His life was a true dichotomy.

Q: The contradiction of Irish wakes? The mourners cry in the living room with the deceased. The revelers sit in the kitchen with the Bushmill.

A: Yes. Whimsy entombed crushing sorrow hidden within his lower caves. Pain resurfaced when he remembered Joe Corcoran. He loved his stepfather. Every time we drove up the Garden State Parkway he mentioned

Joe Corcoran. He also dearly loved his Mom. I witnessed a poignant moment when Corky visited a nursing home in Atlantic City. His Mom suffered from Alzheimer's. She had become a shell of her former self. She had to be strapped down. Corky held her while whispering stories about hurricanes in Atlantic City. I witnessed the Pieta in reverse. The son held his mother. His virility was accented by his wild white mane and chiseled features. He regressed to a little boy. Corky relived that moment over and over. At certain times he zoned out. I noticed in his eyes that he had left me. He returned to that deep experience. When it was over, I reverenced the twinkle in his eye.

Q: *I love the Pieta. He drank deeply from the cup during that painful moment.*

A: Corky loved Henri Nowen, a great spiritual writer. Nowen reached Corky's heart through the metaphor of drinking from the cup.

On one fateful day, I was working at The Garden State Racetrack in NJ. Corky sauntered into my office. My wife, Diane, had just informed me that Corky's mother had died. Not only that, she was already buried. When I told Corky, he snapped. He literally ran out of the room. My approach had been too direct. I should have taken him somewhere else to break the news. He disappeared for quite a while. Pain and anger caused him to weep deeply. In desperation, I asked Mike Mintern, "Help me get him to Gethsemani?"

We arrived on Holy Thursday. That night at service, the monks read seven passages of scripture then blew out a candle after each. By the time they snuffed out that last candle, God was on campus. That profoundly sweet experience lives forever in my heart. Corky's healing began.

Days later, The Abbot, Mike Mintern, Corky and I planned to attend a fundraiser. We drove to the Ronald McDonald House in Louisville. That year's All-American high school basketball team was also visiting the house. The players were the guests of honor. I watched Corky. He would have played on that team during another era. That dinner lifted his spirits, restoring his identity. At that same time he solidified his relationship with the Trappists. He mourned his mother's death. Deep in a cave he dealt with not being able to say good-bye.

Q: *Did you become his closest friend?*

A: I won't be presumptuous. Corky modeled his life after the Heisman Trophy. He kept everyone at arm's length. He didn't stand as acute as the statue. Occasionally we embraced. I probably had more conversations with him than anyone. He was a good poker player. I never knew for sure what thoughts he was holding.

Q: Could he be ripping you off?

A: Yes. He ripped me off. You know, we all rip God off. We start out determined to be perfect people. We thank God for what He has given us. But, we become selfish. Much of the time Corky was selfish. He could be narcissistic. No one understood my relationship with Corky. Disapproving people beat me up. For years, Corky lived in my home. He grew close to my kids. But he was tough. Most of the world keeps score. People hurt when he ripped them off. Each time I buy into any relationship, I get hurt. Corky's complexities stretched our relational equation.

Was I his best friend? At times, I was. He probably revealed more to me than to anyone. Our discussions were often deep and meaningful. Occasionally, he relaxed the Heisman. Only then we embraced as brothers. He was a terrific friend. I never focus on negatives. I value the positives. I couldn't have been happier that he found his way to Merton's place. I hoped that he would eventually call me. I never had control. When he went off radar, everybody called me. I served as conduit for a bill collector, fixing a mistake or comforting someone in love with him. Eventually, he surfaced. I was not contacted when he headed for Gethsemani. When I heard he had been accepted, I rejoiced. I introduced him, but he developed his own relationship with the Trappists. Corky participated in many varied relationships. You could never identify all the people Corky touched. He blended Lewis and Clark, Charlemagne, Charlatan, and Marco Polo.

Q: By Heisman, do you mean that he perfected the stiff arm?

A: Yes. Arm's length.

Corky served as a major player in establishing early Ronald McDonald Houses. I cherish each experience. We received inspiration from the unsung heroes who build and run those houses. Best of all, we met wonderful kids. Theirs were the toughest diagnoses. Children fighting cancer deeply touched Corky. To them, Corky was truly present. I loved introducing his NBA background. Off he went reliving his basketball stories. Two Irish guys turned on our Niagara Falls of words. We inundated people. One faucet ran out only to allow the other to drench everybody. Our humor and imagination complimented each other.

I tried to attend Mass each day. Many times Corky came with me. Sometimes he didn't. Each day, I looked for a church. We discovered new churches together. Many people misunderstood.

Q: Wasn't your forgiveness of Corky miraculous?
A: It's just that I am a sinner. I know how many of my faults God has forgiven. I have visited my own caves and caverns. I count the many times I have failed. I recognize my own addictions. Forgiveness comes easy to me. The closer I draw to my loving God, the more I'm amazed that He forgives and forgets. I sometimes forgive. I never forget. There are many body bags created during my human experience.

You really ask, "Who was Walter James Devlin?"

He was a guy who survived a rough childhood. He was abandoned by his dad who left behind any number of poor role models. His early life was dominated by his ability to play a game. He believed that basketball could lead to a wonderful life. Ultimate defeat was sealed by how he dealt with adversity. He gave logical reasons for turning to gambling. He talked about analgesics and endorphins. He evolved into an expert on scientific psychobabble. He understood and lamented that gambling disguised his real problems. Corky clung to memories and hated his weakness. Gambling, the hideous mask, hid him from reality.

Q: What were his problems?
A: Those things that tortured him. Broken marriage. Loss of his child. Stealing his mother's money. Fractured relationships with his sister and brother. The hearts he broke. He always plunged. He charged ahead with the same passion he displayed at the racetrack.

One season at Santa Anita, Corky hung out at the local bars. He befriended the insiders. During that 50-day meet, he placed only 26 bets. He won 24 times.

He was obsessed with instant gratification. After one win, he bought three new cars. One Corky, three cars, very smart. A few days after those purchases, he drove me to Garden State. Corky had decided to perfect my gambling technique.

He counseled me, "You don't go to the track to win."

"What do you mean?"

"You only go to play; you don't go to win. If you went to win, you wouldn't bet every race."

Corky was 100 percent right. That's gambling. The thrill comes from the action. Only the rush of endorphins counts. If I bet only on sure things, where is the thrill?

Q: He always played to win?

A: Only at times. He never sustained discipline. He gambled with such pathos. During our Michael Jackson Tour, Corky encountered a dilemma. He was forced to lie his butt off to me. We stayed at my buddy's house in Malibu, who owned a box at Hollywood Park. We arrived in his limo on opening day. I enjoy sports history. I like being part of an Inaugural. I hit the first race, lost the rest. I really enjoyed that day. Rather than join us, Corky concocted a story about seeing some guy in the valley. In truth, Corky snuck into the same track. He hid at the track every day we spent in L.A. He invented different lies. One day he hit a $8,000 bet. He couldn't share his joy. He was unable to admit that he had won. We remained close friends. He always drove our car and I never put demands on him. Yet, he felt compelled to lie. I would have enjoyed his company at the track. I avoided inviting him because I didn't want to tempt him. Corky possessed no gambling *off* or *on* button. He eased into addiction when his *off* button short-circuited.

Q: *Corky won $8,000. He couldn't tell you?*

A: His term paper was incomplete. Sharing wins was half the thrill. The banter about winning exceeded the joy of the money.

"Guess what, Mur? I'm a hell of a handicapper."

Our trips to the racetrack were difficult for both of us. Sometimes he handled it well. On other occasions he retreated to his caves.

Q: *Corky must have been very lonely.*

A: He suffered deeply while trying on many masks. Many faces. He really cared about people. For various reasons, he could not risk being truthful in any relationship. For example, he lived in Sea Isle City with Sylvan Thompkins, (The Professor). The professor was ill and dying, yet they engaged in intellectual ping-pong. Corky enjoyed being verbal; he wanted to discuss. He could have made an excellent television talk-show host. He honed skills, discovered while employed as a bartender. That career short-circuited after he stole betting money. Skills ruined by disgrace formed a pattern in the life of this interesting, charming, and tortured man.

Q: *Jim, you cultivate deep relationships. Yet, you were never close to Corky. You grew to love him. Doesn't the one-way dimension of your feelings strike you as strange?*

A: I'm not a scorekeeper. Maybe his love for me exceeded my love for him. I'm unable to judge the depth of love. There is a line in our Church's marriage ceremony. It goes like this, "Only love makes a marriage perfect and perfect love makes it a joy." We all strive for perfect love. I reach for it in my family. We battle an inner voice that wants proof of love. It keeps score. I find your question hard to hear. Was my part of the relationship deep and his wasn't? I don't know. His contribution was at times deeper than mine. I can't peer inside Corky's soul. In addition to free will, God gives us another great gift. He gives us the gift of being able to feel. What we feel helps us struggle with, "Is there really a God?"

You and I are sitting on the steps of this Contemplative Convent. Inside are women who have devoted their entire lives to adoring God. They, more than we, walk the walk. Many of us talk the talk. These women withhold nothing. They totally offer their lives to God. Are any of them perfect? Absolutely not. They aspire to perfect love. They experience joy. But each of them is limited by a human personality. What impresses me most about Contemplatives is their commitment. Commitment is sadly missing in today's world. Far from a cliché, this is true. The sickest ingredient in relationships depicted on television is that writers judge their characters' commitment to one another. Walter Devlin was unforgettable. He was a blur, a point guard, a shooter, and a passer. His appearance was borderline ethereal. The white hair and disjointed movement made him appear ghostly. God loved our dirty-faced Irish friend who stood real tall while constantly rambling about his background. God never counts the times we fall. Corky always got up and continued running.

During all those years, we often drove to Bardstown, Kentucky. We turned left and headed down Route 247. As we entered Gethsemani, our troubles lighten. "Be still and know that I am Lord," filled our hearts. Corky recited that great Psalm, and he was home. He thrived on the stillness. We valued the consolation of quiet time together. At times we talked. At other times, we listened to tapes or listened to the radio. We fell asleep. As we sat alone, I recognized Corky's attributes clearly. They were soul gifts from God.

Q: On the beach in Avalon, he spent the day telling me the story of his life. I felt privileged.

But, I was puzzled, "Why me? Why have you told me so much?"

Corky became very serious. "There is one gift I never doubt. I can read people. When I look into your eyes, I can see your soul."

"Soul" haunts me. I believed he was seeing my soul. You use that same word. Am I probing too deeply?

A: No holds barred here. I won't hold back. I prayed a lot before our meeting. I know how important this book is to you. Corky's memory is important to me. It is no accident that we are initially meeting on All Souls Day. Don't you see the absurdity? We are sitting in front of a convent talking about Corky Devlin. I spent inordinate time with this man. My friends urged me to fly when we opened the McDonald Houses. Corky and I preferred driving across our country. We investigated monasteries along the way. Never before have two guys spent so much time looking for racetracks and Trappist monasteries at the same time. We once invented a name for ourselves, "Trackists." Our word was not an oxymoron. Strangely, we encountered similar people in both places. They shared passionate dedication.

Our gambling fraternity included one other colorful character. He was truly dynamic. I mentioned the Professor who has passed on. Our other Damon Runyun character was Rocky. Racetrack escapades included the Professor, Rocky, Corky and myself. Poor Rocky. If still alive, he could entertain you with Corky's funniest stories. We took a picture of the four of us outside Saratoga Racetrack. I stopped a passerby and asked him to snap our picture. A year later, it arrived in the mail. It is my favorite picture. All four guys were preparing to engage in our passion. If pictures could talk! Rocky was full of colorful insights, a verbal student of life. He described himself as a stone alcoholic and survivor of 27 rehabs. One fateful day, I met Rocky at the track in Atlantic City. We stood next to each other in the men's room.

He turned to me to announce, "You piss me off."

I blinked, "Pardon me?"

He barked, "I see you around here. You're always smiling. Why are you so happy?"

I murmured, "It's not because I'm winning. I'd be interested in finding out who you are."

The next day we met for lunch. We became instant friends. Rocky accumulated his money as the consummate salesman. He had been very successful in the lighting business. He talked and acted like a South Philly guy. He conversed direct and colorful. He was old vaudeville. His stage name had been "Rex Dale." You could write eight books about Rocky. Corky and Rocky were constantly chirping like the mongoose and the cobra. Each was competitive but so similar. Rocky's name for Corky was "little brother."

When Rocky's only brother died, the four of us attended his wake. I walked up to the casket to say my last goodbye. Rocky walked beside me. He reached into his pocket to take out a $20 win ticket from The Atlantic City Track. It touched me. This horse had won. Rocky slipped the ticket into his brother's pocket. He mumbled, "I want him to go out a winner." That night there were probably eight gravediggers fighting over digging up the casket.

After Rocky died, we all gave his eulogy, including Corky. Not to be outdone, Corky did the same thing for Rocky. Somehow he found a horse named "Rocky." It was only a $2 ticket, but he lovingly put it in Rocky's pocket. I never found out whether "Rocky" was a winner.

Q: Wasn't that a great story?

A: All of Rocky's stories were like that. He was an outright liar when it came to gambling. We shared some great trips to the track. Rocky acted as our entertainer.

Q: He was comfortable in your group?

A: Oh, we were meant for each other. Imagine the picture. We weren't Mount Rushmore but we deserve to be the four faces of something. Our lives intertwined. Our comments were rapid fire. I can't remember laughing so deeply. It was magic. The professor had taught at Princeton. We were a strange combination.

Q: The Professor was a world famous physicist. Did Corky nurse him in the last year of his life?

A: No, no. The Professor gave shelter to Corky. Some woman close to the Professor let him use her house in Sea Isle, New Jersey. The Professor had been writing his book forever. His work in progress was all over the house. Corky just hung out with him.

Q: Corky had me picturing "Tuesdays with Maury." Corky nursed. The professor faced death.

A: No, no, no. How can I say it? Corky grubbed off the guy. They lived together for a year. Corky could talk to anyone. If Corky were a tennis player, he could have returned anyone's serve. He spent that year playing word games with the Professor. Believe me, there was no nursing.

Q: The last day I saw Corky we traveled to New York for a sales presentation. By the end of the day, everyone loved Corky. He dressed in business clothes but nothing matched. He had a way of shrugging while swinging his arms to keep loose. Wasn't he a natural salesman?

A: Yeah, and he probably grabbed his crotch. He was great at fondling himself.

Q: The people in New York found him fascinating. They had never heard of him. He convinced them of his greatness anyway. They liked being around him.

A: Once again, he lived without deadlines. He had no clock. Life was simple. All he had to do was eat, sleep and plot his next bankroll. He loved being with me because we never missed meals.

Q: Have you heard of the Meyers Briggs personality test? Corky was an ENFP—someone who goes with the flow.

A: Corky and I created a bumper sticker, "Life is an audible." You and I had no plans to meet today. I procrastinated so long that I couldn't disappoint you. I didn't feel guilty. I just felt bad. In truth, Corky's memory is very important to me. Obviously, it's important to you. It is not accidental that we are sitting here. I'm sure God's timing is precise.

XIV

RELATIVELY STRANGE

Corky's mother, Anna Maehad, remarried a man named Joe Corcoran. Corky's younger stepbrother, Bob, graciously recalled his family memories.

Jim Murray and I drove to Bob's office in Central New Jersey. He was not a tall man, but I spotted facial resemblances. Jim remarked that we were meeting on the day that marked the seven-year anniversary of Corky's funeral.

Bob: I was nine years old when Walter left home for college. I remember how my family sacrificed to get him through high school. He was never a good student. He and I were never real close. There was such a difference in our ages. He went off to college for four years before he spent another year in Turkey. Eventually, he turned pro. He never spent much time at home while I was growing up. Our family tried not to speak about negative things. My father was very hurt by the things Walter did. He could have really accomplished something with his life. My father, a product of the depression, couldn't understand anyone wasting so many opportunities. I never called him Corky. He was Walter to me.

After basketball, he encountered serious problems with the law. For about a year, he lived in a psychiatric hospital. According to his letters, he had feigned insanity. He orchestrated his discharge as soon as possible. Through that devious process, he avoided serious jail time.

Jim Murray: Corky told me that just before admission, he had ripped off his mother for her last $2,000. He had stolen her life savings. He felt remorseful, so he approached a judge and begged to be admitted. He pleaded that he must be crazy.

Bob: Our family had a different version. There was a warrant for his arrest signed by The Jostens Jewelry Company. He had embezzled $50,000. An internal audit caught him. According to Walter, he broke down during the trial. He convinced the court to admit him to Stanton. In his letters, he took credit for working the system to avoid going to jail.

Q: He claimed to have been an inmate for a year. During his stay, he befriended a female doctor who helped him get out.

Bob: That story is probably true.

Q: Did you ever see him play?

Bob: We went to many of his games in New York. I remember watching the 1955 East-West College All-Star game at the Garden. I saw most games during the first year he played for the Pistons. Immediately after that season, he spent four weeks with my family at the Jersey Shore. That vacation was the most time I had seen him in 10 years.

Later that same year, Arleen Adams (his wife) lived with my family for four months. While Walter played basketball in Fort Wayne, Arleen sang each day on the Arthur Godfrey Show in New York.

Q: Have you met his daughter?

Bob: Dawn. I met her once or twice through Arleen. I never saw her after Walter split with Arleen.

Jim Murray: Corky tried to help a lot of people with gambling problems.

Bob: Walter's helping other people is what bothers me most. Call it baggage. He disappointed my entire family. He showed up only when he needed something and disappeared when he didn't. His behavior was unforgivable. He never hurt me directly except that he was always after money. I gave him money to get rid of him.

Later in his life, Walter visited my family. His last hurrah happened a year before he died. He attempted to con me by telling stories about the good things he had done recently. I never believed his change. Any good he did was not out of kindness. Good acts merely fed his ego.

Jim Murray: Corky once accused me of being Leonard Tose's enabler. I also enabled Corky.

Q: Was there ever a brother-to-brother relationship?
Bob: Maybe very early. I was always very proud of his notoriety. No one got very close to Walter. We never just hung around. I now have two sons, ages 29 and 21. They have been close since my youngest was able to walk. They look out for each other. Imagine the emotional problems Walter dealt with before my mother and father married. His biological father's name was Bill Devlin.

I remarried in 1972. Walter called. I invited him to visit for dinner. But I would never let him stay in my house. We all hid our credit cards, jewelry and money when he was here. I assured my new wife that I was not being cruel. I had dealt with Walter's visits. The dinner was pleasant. He was his charming self. I wasn't conned. He invited himself to stay at my ex-wife's house. He stole her new boyfriend's wallet and all of her credit cards. Just after my father died, he destroyed our relationship. I was in the service and I came home for the funeral. A few months later, my mother and sister moved to Atlantic City. Walter, the great protector, decided to live with them. He stole my sister's money and her car before he took off. That was enough for me. How could he steal from his closest relatives whose husband and stepfather had just died?

Jim Murray: Is your dad buried in the cemetery off the New Jersey Turnpike? Corky always pointed to it when we drove through Northern Jersey.

Bob: No.

Q: Did you really live in a cold-water flat in Newark?
Bob: That is true.

Q: Did he survive a plane crash with the Lakers and Elgin Baylor?
Bob: Walter claimed that when he boarded a plane, he suffered an anxiety attack and had to be carried off.

Q: When did your father die?
Bob: February, 1961. He was only 52 years old.

Jim Murray: Corky told me that he had been recruited by Kentucky. Joe Corcoran warned him that he couldn't come home if he broke his word to George Washington.

Bob: That sounds like my father. He worked all his life for RCA.

Q: Your father was Corky's hero. He described a confrontation in high school. Your father thought Corky had disrespected your mother. He punched Corky who fell down a flight of stairs.

Bob: My father punched Walter? My father wouldn't hit anyone on a bet. He didn't have to. He was a Depression-era guy. During 29 years, he never missed a day's work. He died on the job. He had a temper. But he was never physical. All he had to do was look at you. If you talked back to our mother, he sent you away from the table. We were equally his kids. The greatest disappointment in his life was Walter's getting caught stealing from the jewelry company. That stigma caused heartache for our entire family.

Jim Murray: Corky told me that his marriage ended when his wife ran off with another man.

Bob: I think not. Ultimately, Arleen married a comedian named Bill Styles. But her first marriage had not been happy. Walter gave Arleen a hard time about everything. She was a farm girl. Even after she became a successful singer, she was very unsophisticated. I really liked her. I knew her better than I knew Walter. She lived at my house for over a year. Arleen was short and very pretty when she got made up. She was always pleasant to everyone.

Q: Do you remember her daughter?

Bob: Dawn was born after Arleen lived with us.

Q: Corky's sister doesn't want anything to do with him?

Bob: She has had enough. He victimized her most. If you haven't experienced a relative who brings nothing but trouble, you can't feel what we feel. We had an alcoholic comical uncle. He visited every year at Christmas time. One year, Walter happened to be home for the holiday. He was playing basketball. Therefore, he had plenty of money. The local jail employed my uncle as a cook. A real sweet guy, he drank himself to death. My uncle arrived wearing only a tee shirt. Walter (amid bravado) took him up to 16th Avenue to buy him a topcoat.

My uncle vowed: "I'll wear this coat until I die. You'll see this in my coffin." The next day, my uncle arrived with a bottle of wine and without a coat.

Q: Were there any happy memories of Walter?

Bob: I wish there were. I was young and trying to eke out a living. Walter appeared every four or five years. He grabbed as much money as possible before he disappeared. That's why we didn't know where to find him when my mother died.

Q: At the time of her death, was he hiding from you?

Bob: No. We just didn't know where he was. One day he came to my house carrying $70,000 in a brown paper bag. At the time, I was earning about $10,000 a year. He was carrying seven years' salary. He returned the next day with an empty bag.

Q: He wanted to show off the seventy?

Bob: Yes. He entered carrying a bottle of scotch and the rolled-up bag. He smiled when he asked me to loan him $300 traveling money. We sat at the kitchen table drinking the scotch. I told him, "No." He picked up the cap, put it back on the bottle, returned the bottle to the bag and took off.

Q: What kind of relationship did Corky have with your kids?

Bob: My kids liked him. He brought them hats and pictures from the Michael Jackson Tour. His visits were hit and run. He also brought sports stuff from The Meadowlands.

Q: Did you ever think Corky might find redemption?

Bob: When I think of redemption, it includes a change in his ways. Conversion must lead to physical restitution. He expressed sorrow to the people he harmed. I am not aware that he sought forgiveness. He certainly didn't approach my family. To locate all of those he hurt, you need to take out an advertisement in the *New York Times*. He hit everyone he knew. His was the who's who of bad checks. To avoid family embarrassment, I myself covered many of them.

Q: How was the relationship between Corky and your mom?

Bob: Not real good. In many ways she had been strict with him. She wanted him to excel in school. My mother was very nervous and afraid of everything. Our family never seemed to have enough money. Mom was very, very high strung. I do know that she had a loving relationship with my father.

Q: Corky claimed to have played on an all-black basketball team in Newark.

Bob: I would say it was 50-50. He was definitely not the white shadow.

Q: He told me that he graduated last in his class?

Bob: That could be true. He had a hard time getting accepted by any junior college. George Washington helped him gain admittance to Potomac State.

Our family kept a scrapbook of Walter's exploits. At the time that I entered the service, everything disappeared.

Q: Do you remember Corky's having a best friend?
Bob: He was friends with Sal Eldridge from Newark. Walter acted aloof. He was never well-liked in our neighborhood. I don't remember why.
Q: Did he gamble?
Bob: At a young age, he played cards in the schoolyard. Kids played a lot of card games in our neighborhood.
Q: Did Corky go to jail multiple times?
Bob: He put us through five years of blanks at a time. I just don't know.
Q: You didn't know where Corky was at the time your mother died? Would he have been invited?
Bob: Sure. Walter avoided me in later years. He seemed embarrassed that I had become his last resort.
Q: After his heart attack at Gethsemani, did he try to mend some fences?
Bob: He journeyed to our house and stayed about a week. He seemed more peaceful. I always felt compassion toward him because his life had turned out so sadly. Things came very easy to him. My father had a strong work ethic. He instilled it in us as children. In my younger years, I switched jobs from managing a warehouse to selling office equipment. My father told me I was crazy for quitting any job.
Q: Men in his era worked only one job.
Bob: This is ironic. The only reward Walter ever promised was, "Do well in school and I'll get you a new car." I graduated from high school on the honor role. I'm still waiting for that '57 Chevy.

My father didn't have the money, but he took me to get a car. We found a used '53 Ford. The purchase required a $2,000 bank loan. My father was a tough guy. As we prepared to enter the bank, he sat shaking. He was terrified of being turned down for a loan. My good father was totally intimidated by the suits.

Q: He left you a great legacy. How old are you?
Bob: Sixty-two. I have two boys, a daughter and two grandchildren.
Q: Corky would probably declare you the success and he the failure.
Bob: I would think so. Walter was never happy. What happened to him made me very sad. He was driven to stay one step ahead of everyone.
Q: Before he started gambling in 1961, what were his interests?
Bob: He liked jazz. He always enjoyed sports. In college, he found success as a basketball player. After college, he didn't experience great success. That he could no longer be a star gnawed at his ego. Just before he turned pro, he came to New York for the East-West All-Star game.

He started the game, drilling eight straight baskets and scoring 16 points. He was a streaky shooter. But he had problems with his coach. He knew better than every coach.

Jim Murray: Seven years ago today, you were driving home from Corky's funeral in Kentucky. What were your thoughts?

Bob: I was very sad. The service proved very emotional. I cherish my family. Walter never had that. I have reached the stage where I don't need more. My wife and I plan to shop for a new house tomorrow. I don't need it. I probably have 10 good years left. My wife spends more time at home. I want her to enjoy these good times. I inherited not being a material person from my father.

I feel deep compassion for Walter. I observed several unattached women at his funeral. He attracted vulnerable women. He dressed well and looked the part.

The best time the two of us spent together was three weeks during one summer at the shore. We hung out with guys Walter's age. Walter didn't put pressure on himself. He was not yet married.

Q: Any other good times?

Bob: Again, down at the shore. Years later he tended bar at the Rugby Inn in Northfield, NJ. He seemed to have friends there.

Q: Do you know whether he married twice?

Bob: I'm not sure whether he actually married the second woman. When I started my previous job, I spotted Walter's picture among people wanted by the police. He and his girlfriend crossed the country cashing bad checks.

I assured my superior, "This man is my brother. You don't have to worry about me. I haven't seen him in five years."

Walter and his traveling companion had a daughter. That baby was given up for adoption. My sister unsuccessfully tried to adopt the baby. I cannot remember the child's name.

Q: What was Corky's life like before he went to college?

Bob: We lived in Newark. Later, we moved to the Atlantic City area (Northfield, N.J.) with my sister and my mother. My mother was originally employed as my father's housekeeper. After their marriage, they lived in Jersey City before moving to Newark. I was born in Newark. Corky attended Newark's Central High School. He did not mingle much in our neighborhood. After basketball, he worked for Josten's Jewelry on the West Coast. Then he embezzled the money.

Q: The Arthur Godfrey Show broadcast from New York?

Bob: Yes. Walter and Arleen lived with us at that time. Arleen stayed alone during the six-month basketball season. Walter resented Arleen because she made more money than he did. In those days she sang on both the radio and the television show. The two shows were broadcast simultaneously. She earned $700 for each song, big money in the '50s.

The odd thing about her employment was that she never knew in advance when she would be called on for a song. She was always rehearsing. Arthur usually asked her to sing on a whim. She always had two or three numbers ready.

Jim Murray: The person she married later was named Styles. I wonder if she might still be performing?

Bob: I would love to see her again. She might still be alive.

Q: Did your mom know Arleen?

Bob: Yes. She liked Arleen. She was very natural and behaved like a little tomboy.

Q: Did you have any magical moments with Corky?

Bob: When he came to New York with the Pistons, I visited him along with a couple of my high school friends. We went out to dinner with the players. I was very proud of Walter. This was before he got into trouble.

Q: Which players joined you at dinner?

Bob: I remember Ray Felix from the Knicks, and Mel Hutchins and George Yardley from the Pistons.

Q: Have you saved any clippings or pictures?

Bob: I don't know where they are.

Jim Murray: You are so different from Corky. You appreciate everything you have. Corky didn't. He was an unhappy human being who grabbed at everything. You have given me hope. When you last saw him, he had found peace. But he was still Corky.

Q: Can Corky help us all into heaven?

Bob: I'm still angry that we couldn't locate Walter after my mother died.

Jim Murray: It was typical of Corky to manipulate that situation. He turned it around, then used the distorted version. It was sad. He played the offended party after disappearing.

* * *

"Watch out. Here he comes again." That became the family mantra during Corky sightings. Home is where the family is. Home, the place of our beginnings, and the place where we do not need to impress. Corky never felt safe enough to lay down his show and hustle. By hiding, he missed feeling loved. His family never understood nor embraced the boy who couldn't come out. Corky never risked exposure. Fears made it too difficult to express his longings and weakness especially to his family. His mother, a fearful hesitant introvert, lived life as an endurance contest. Bob admired his father. Even at an early age, Bob valued rewards for hard work and self-sacrifice.

Where did this leave Corky? His family acknowledged that he was tall, handsome, smart, and blessed with superior abilities. But he squandered it all. His mother craved stability. His brother emulated his father. Joe Corcoran could guide Corky towards a happy life. What legacy did Joe Corcoran leave young Corky?

- No son of mine runs out on George Washington University.
- I never missed a day's work.
- Nothing good comes easy. Reward only comes to the strong.
- I only had one job—Security is everything.
- I'm terrified to take a loan from the suits.
- All risk is to be avoided, especially revealing yourself to anyone.
- Always honor your mother, or leave.
- Struggle all your life for money.

During my search for Corky, I have attempted to understand. I do not wish to judge him. Rejection of his family values launched him along a lonely path. He recognized what he didn't want without a clear understanding that winning could ever be enough. Satisfaction was reduced to the thrill of winning. Corky won, then lost fortunes. He never identified an amount that could satisfy his undefined goal. Corky dissipated his life's energy through hopeless obsession over a pearl without identity.

We all struggle with a common primary question in adulthood: "What is happiness?" We must discover our unique answer. Those who define personal happiness early in life apply more energy to finding the answer. Others wait until later in life before they identify their goal. Corky never identified what he wanted. Like a nomad, he stumbled between experiences. "I cannot eat. I cannot sleep. I spend my days searching for what I do not know."

There is great wisdom in the story of "The Wizard of Oz." The four characters search the entire story looking for what they believe is missing. Happiness flourishes after they realize that what they desire has been hidden inside of them from the beginning. Corky and the Oz characters are similar. He kept moving, searching for what was missing. He never looked inside for the answer. Since he never identified happiness, I can only guess at what a successful search would have produced.

Assemble the clues, and then project what a happy Corky might have found. He possessed a likeable outgoing personality. He was clever and intuitive. At times, he was attracted to hard work and passion.

What would Corky have discovered while daring to uncover real meaning in his life? The answer lay well hidden. Romantics called it love. I call it service. Corky lived consumed by a desperate need to be served. Any behavior, no matter how cruel, could be justified through his quest to be served. His thieving acts were misunderstood. He loathed himself. Why? Because he was driven. He never realized that he needed only to adjust his view. Reject: "How can I get over on you to get money for gambling?" He could not trust enough to change his thoughts to "How can I be of service to you? How can I live in harmony with you? How can we make your life better?"

Corky led a completely selfish life. Others were mere marks. Corky avoided loving anyone. Nor did so-called friends truly love him. He acquired a few remarkable friends like Jim Murray. Most of us who believed we loved Corky felt pity.

Corky's brother Bob is a sincere person. I watched his demeanor soften as he described Corky's life of privilege and dissipation. Bob loves his half-brother. Remarkable in light of the pain that Corky caused him. Bob and his wife were the only family members who drove to Kentucky for Corky's funeral. During their final visit, he had welcomed Corky home, wanting to believe that he had changed. It was remarkable forgiveness towards one so undeserving. While Corky acted out the Prodigal Son, Bob stayed home and honored his father. He continues to overlook Corky's faults. Bob seems very much at peace. The three of us joined in the hope that Corky finally found peace either here or beyond the veil.

XV

LEAGUE HEADQUARTERS

I pestered Jim Murray for a copy of Corky's Eulogy. The Monks assured me that Jim's words captured Corky's personality. A copy could help me understand Corky.

Jim: I never write anything down. There is no copy. I have pondered an interesting question. In junior college, while Adolph Rupp watched, Corky scored his highest point total against Morris Harvey. I wonder how many points he actually scored. Corky's stories have proven consistently inconsistent. He told me he hit his first 14 shots. I wonder how true that story is.

Q: In search of the truth, I have spoken on the phone with Zelda Spoelstra. In the '50s she was league secretary to Maurice Podoloff, the commissioner of the National Basketball Association. She retired but recently returned to the NBA office in New York City. She is now league archivist. She helped me contact players.

Jim: She was like James Bond's Miss MoneyPenny about whom Ian Fleming wrote. Corky had quite a few. James Bond always relied on Miss MoneyPenny. Hers were cameo appearances. She was secretary to the head of the Secret Service. When James visited, he passed her desk. She put little moves on him. He delighted in teasing her.

Q: She helped Bond. Can Zelda in New York help me?

Jim: Corky took advantage of the NBA's indigent fund. He lied his butt off. In his stories somebody died. Corky bragged. I don't remember the amount.

Q: Here's a related question. Did Corky describe his stepfather during your drives on the Garden State Parkway?

Jim: Other than his mother, Joe Corcoran was most beloved. Joe lived on in him. He worked hard, didn't complain and faced challenges with deep moral conviction. He earned about 80 bucks each week. He was Corky's role model. The book, "The Best of Corky," would include, "The Best of Joe Corcoran." Joe never preached to Corky. His life set his example. Actions outweighed words.

Q: Do you remember anything else about Joe Corcoran?

Jim: Corky communicated through his eyes and mannerisms. Joe Corcoran lived inside of Corky. Of all the people Corky talked about (famous or infamous), I would like to have met Joe.

Q; Was Corky committed to you?

Jim: I don't want to judge. Corky constantly warned, "I'll work you until I find your weakness. Then I'll get you." That was his commitment. I believe I became one of Corky's closest friends. We opened many Ronald McDonald houses. Corky was handsome, well-met, and could be very sociable. He energized when people smiled. He admired people I admired. When he worked with children, he glowed real goodness. He embraced them. Closer than the odd couple, our relationship more resembled the unlikely duo.

* * *

The National Basketball Association Headquarters is in New York City. For over three years, I spoke by phone with Zelda Spoelstra. I valued her basketball experiences. She liked Corky. She also corrected misinformation about him. At first contact, she lamented Corky's troubles. I informed her of the date of his death. It took her by surprise that he died in a monastery in Kentucky.

Zelda, the maternal conscience of the League, keeps in touch with former players. She roots for them while they finish out their lives.

I mentioned Corky's gambling-related NBA rip-off. She corrected me. "That story is not true. I would know." I requested that she meet with me about the book. After some hesitation, she agreed on the importance of getting Corky's record straight.

On a hot summer day, I drove to New York City. I parked my car near the Lincoln Tunnel Authority Building. I walked the 15 blocks to NBA

League Headquarters

headquarters on Fifth Avenue. What an experience. I smiled inside at the sounds and smells of Times Square. I brushed against a seemingly endless swarm of hurrying people jostling between streetlights. Bits of sentences in many languages blended into a confusing buzz. At the center of Times Square I spotted a man dripping with local color. About Corky's height, he strutted golden locks and a golden tan. His arms gestured towards pedestrians as he shoved flyers into their hands. His clothing was a diaper.

I arrived at the headquarters building. Security was tight. I muttered Zelda's name and the guard responded with an affirming wave. "Fifteenth floor."

What would Zelda be like in person? I enjoy New York accents. Hers was impeccable.

When I entered her office, I understood why she directs Alumni Relations. She greeted me with an open manner and kind eyes. I felt at ease, eager to discuss Corky's basketball legend.

Q: Do you remember Corky the player?

Zelda: He came into the league in the fall of 1955. Bronx guys like Elliot Karver, Bobby Maurero, Ernie Watez, and Joe Mascherelli all played with Corky. We all came from James Monroe High School. I was a cheerleader during their senior year. Corky was a Jersey guy. He joined our guys in D.C. at George Washington University. They always were good people. Coach Reinhart was a wonderful person. He was close with Red Auerbach and Arnie Heft. Arnie was one of our officials and he is still active. Eventually, he bought the Washington Bullets after he retired as an active referee.

Q: Corky claimed that he was the only guy who could guard Bob Cousy. He was tall. Could he use his long arms?

Zelda: Did you ever see Cousy's arms and hands? For his height, Cousy had the longest arms and biggest hands.

Q: I saw Cousy play against Philadelphia. I had my heart broken because I was a Philadelphia Warriors fan. His one-hand set shot was devastating.

Zelda: I was a Knicks fan. Trust me, I understand. Before Bob Cousy, there was Bob Davies. He was truly the man who started behind-the-back passing. He played for the old Rochester Royals.

Q: I remember going down to the Philadelphia Arena (at 45th and Market Street) to watch games.

Zelda: I visited Philly all the time because Paul Arizin is a good friend. Corky and Paul played against each other. Paul was a forward and Corky a guard.

Q: Chuck Noble described playing with George Yardley and Paul on the same court. Both wheezed loudly. Wasn't the noise like being in a boiler room?

Zelda: Paul was worse. We always thought that Paul was dying. Then he would shoot and kill you.

Paul and Tom Brennan were teammates at Villanova. Tom and I grew up together in New York. I knew Paul during his college days. Later we were together in the Catskill Mountains. Cousy and George Mikan played for other hotels. All the players were there.

Tom Brennan later worked for the Globetrotters as business manager. He died young. Unfortunately, he contracted a terminal kidney disease in Africa while the Trotters were on a world tour.

Q: Can you tell me about your own career?

Zelda: As a little girl, I followed basketball, football, track and baseball. But basketball was my love. Haskell Cohen was the Public Relations Director for the NBA. He brought players like Chuck Cooper, Fletcher Johnsen and Jim Tucker to the hotel where I stayed in the Catskills. My mother owned a bungalow nearby. I watched every game. Haskell was impressed with me because I knew so much about basketball.

"I can't believe this. You are a girl."

"I know. I have always loved basketball."

Haskell promised, "I'll be needing someone like you to work for me."

A few days later he told me that Mr. Podoloff was looking for a secretary. "He wants someone in public relations who knows the game."

Mr. Podoloff didn't know basketball. He was a hockey man. He had owned the minor league New Haven hockey team. It was 1951. I started the next week. I was still a teenager. To my surprise, they couldn't afford me. Our office was on the 80th floor of the Empire State Building. In order to survive, I found another job on the 73rd floor. I grabbed that other job because our doors opened in the same band of elevators. The owners of the other company visited New York once a month. They never knew that I worked for both. The NBA paid me with tickets. I went to all the rodeos, the horse shows, the dog shows, college double headers, the Knicks and the Rangers games. I was at the Garden every night.

League Headquarters

For a while I took a job in the music business. We worked with Bobby Darin, Neil Sedaka and Connie Francis. I sat in on their recordings, but I never liked the music business.

My social life changed when I started going out with Art (Spoelstra). He had been traded to the Knicks from the Minneapolis Lakers. Previously, he had played three years for the Rochester Royals. The Knicks decided to trade Art to Fort Wayne. Because he refused to go to Indiana, we were farmed out to Allentown, Pa. The Knicks ran an Allentown affiliate in the Eastern League. We stayed there for three years. The Knicks never recalled Art.

When I returned home to New York, Walter Kennedy had become the NBA Commissioner. They still couldn't afford my salary, so I found employment in the garment industry. I stayed involved by helping make arrangements for All-Star weekends.

In 1991 I returned to the league office part-time with the NBA Legends Foundation. Finally, in 1994, I came back full time.

Q: I am grateful for our phone calls over the years.

Zelda: The Philly organization has always been good to me. In the '50s, Eddie Gottlieb put extra seats on the floor for us whenever we came to Philly. I never had to worry about a seat.

I have watched so many college players. In my opinion, Tom Gola, Bill Bradley, Oscar Robertson, Bill Walton and Kareem Abdul Jabbar were the five greatest college players ever. Gola never got much better. The other guys continued to improve in the pros. That does happen. For example, Frank Selvy once scored 100 points in college for Furman. He became only an average pro player.

In the '50s, the typical salary was $5,000. Everyone worked at a summer job. The player's biggest worry was, "What am I going to do after I stop playing?"

Q: What was your recent connection with Corky?

Zelda: I hadn't seen him in years. The only reason I knew that things were not going well for him was through comments by my brother when he was living in Silver Spring, Maryland.

Years ago I had asked Elliot Karver. "How is Corky?"

His response was, "You don't want to know."

But nobody really knew how Corky was doing. Rumor had it that he was into drugs. I didn't know for sure how he was surviving.

My first thought when you said you were writing a book about Corky, was "Why?" When you described how his life ended, I became happy. It is wonderful that the monks took him in and took care of him. What a surprise!

I knew him while he played for the Pistons. His playing days were happy and full of life. I always liked Corky. Many years later we drove to Fort Wayne for a visit with Larry and Joan Foust. We met Chuck Noble and Corky for lunch. Corky was affable and always a very nice person. It was so sad that he became aimless and tragic.

When I read his obituary, it described how the monks took care of him. He became a changed and happy man. He found religion and realized how wrong his life had been. He finally found peace within himself. That was important.

I could have listened to Zelda for hours. She was busy scheduling NBA special events. I shouldn't occupy any more of her time. She emphasized her love for Corky as one of the old gang. Apparently, many players also liked Corky. They empathized with the sadness of his life. They hoped he found peace. Zelda seemed genuinely relieved that his wandering had led to a happy ending.

Q: I had one final question about Corky's Adolph Rupp connection. If Corky had gone to Kentucky and played his inner-city style of basketball, might he have influenced Rupp's attitude towards the game? Could Rupp have avoided intractable defeat in the NCAA Final's of 1966? Could Corky have helped Rupp accept black players?

Zelda: Absolutely not. Adolph Rupp was the consummate disciplinarian. It was either his way or the highway. His practices were completely regimented. If he played for Kentucky, Corky would have had to change.

XVI

REMEMBER THE WARRIORS

I confess to being a gym rat during my teenage years. With my classmates at Malvern Prep (Bill McCormick, Mike Walsh, Don McBride, Bill McConaghy and Emmitt Ward), I haunted basketball courts. We waited endless hours hanging around gymnasiums, searching for the next pickup basketball game. We played shirts versus skins. Our bodies were fatless enough that we didn't mind going shirtless.

My family lived in Wynnewood, PA. It was an easy hitchhike up Lancaster Pike (Route 30) to Villanova's Varsity Hall (now Jake Nevin Field House). Every weekend or holiday, we played basketball all day. Villanova always seemed to have an assortment of indoor and outdoor basketball courts ready for our use. Because we blended with other gym rats, no game was boring.

It was the late '40s when Villanova boasted a great team led by Paul Arizin. Although only 6-foot-5, he played center. His teammates included Wolfe, Hannon, Ricca, Sabol and Brennan. Paul was born to shoot. He perfected an ability to hang in the air longer than any defender. He launched jump shots after waiting until the last moment before releasing his soft line drive. Asthma caused him to wheeze while he struggled up and down the court. Paul's epic gasps for breath preceded hard-earned baskets. We arrived at the gym hours before game time to assure a courtside seat. We never paid admission. College sports were gentle then.

In 1960, I was hired by IBM in its Philadelphia office. Two weeks after my training began, Paul Arizin arrived. We became friends. Paul was always a warm sincere person. At IBM, he cultivated a unique distinction. He agreed with management that he would never accept a transfer to any other office. In those days, the industry joke was that IBM stood for "*I*'ve *B*een *M*oved." Promotions always included a transfer. Paul refused to move his family. He never has. I left IBM six years later. Every year I would run into Paul. Usually, we talked on the beach in Avalon, NJ. He always remembered the details of my life and where I was working. We caught up. Paul finished his career at IBM and retired seven years ago. It is a joy to remember his sincere and soft-spoken manner.

Zelda Spoelstra urged me to contact Paul seeking his memories of Corky. The two players possessed differing skills. Their lives played out as exact opposites. Paul focused on his family. He loved his children and a life devoid of relocation. Paul, a prolific shooter, led the NBA in scoring in 1951 and 1957. He was playing for the Warriors during the year that Corky and Tom Gola were drafted. Corky could only admire Paul's accomplishments.

Paul had sold his house in Avalon. Contacting him could prove difficult. I was attending daily Mass at St. Nicholas Tolentine Church in Atlantic City, NJ. This poor church in affluent Atlantic City once served 3,000 loyal families. The exodus of parishioners from the city had reduced church membership to 100 families. St. Nick's continued to feed 3,000 homeless people each month. I loved the church's Old World beauty.

On a summer Thursday afternoon, I sat listening to the gospel readings. I noticed a man sitting four rows ahead of me. His hair had turned gray. Something nudged me that in front of me sat Paul Arizin. I recognized him by the way he walked to the altar. He walked just like he ran. He hunched his shoulders as if gasping with asthma. I took a chance. After Mass, I slid next to where he was kneeling, still praying his beads.

"Paul?"

He nodded his head, and then recognized me. We went outside to talk about Corky.

Q: When was the last time you saw Corky?

A: I was working at an IBM seminar in Wilmington, Delaware. I don't know how he found out I was there. He confided that he had experienced some bad breaks and that his wife had been killed in an automobile accident.

He asked me for money. I only had $30, so I gave him $20 and saved $10 for lunch. I guess I was lucky to have only $30.

Q: How did he strike you?

A: He looked good. He hadn't gained weight and he seemed upbeat.

Q: Do you remember him as a ball player?

A: I remember him as a good shooter. When he got very hot, he could score at will.

Q: Can you describe playing against Corky?

A: I was a forward and he was a guard. We didn't have too much contact with other teams in those days. As a ballplayer, he was a very good scorer. He was a 6-foot-5 starting guard. We beat the Fort Wayne Pistons in the 1956 finals. He was excellent during that series.

Q: Was he great as a defensive player?

A: I won't judge. He was not in the same class as K.C. Jones, who was known for his defensive ability. Corky never played me, nor I him. So I won't speak about his defense.

Q: Do you remember any specific game against Corky?

A: When the Warriors won the 1955-1956 championship, we beat Fort Wayne, 4-1. We won the first game in Philadelphia. We lost the second game in Fort Wayne. We won the third at home. I considered the fourth game pivotal because it was on their court. We squeezed out a victory by one point. Corky hit a last second shot. The referees ruled that his shot was released after time expired. Had they beaten us that night, the series would have been tied. As critical as that game was, people in Fort Wayne realized that obviously the shot was late.

NOTE: Paul was very close. On April 5, 1956 the Philadelphia Warriors defeated Corky's Pistons 107-105. It proved to be the deciding game in a 4-1 Philadelphia victory. Corky averaged 10 points per game during that playoff.

Q: Corky claimed unique ability to guard Bob Cousy. Did his long arms give him an advantage?

A: After all these years, it is hard to refute Corky's claim. Actually, nobody could stop Cousy.

Q: Do you remember telling me about Al McGuire playing defense against Bob Cousy?

A: There was one game when Al claimed that he held Cousy without a field goal for the entire first half. What he neglected to say was that Cousy scored eight from the foul line, and Al fouled out. You may call that good defense. Then again, you may not.

Q: Didn't Al McGuire hold you down?

A: He played me almost the same way. I had a little height advantage over Al, so I took him into the pivot. I probably didn't get a field goal during the first quarter. Once again, he fouled out. I found myself continually on the foul line.

Q: Were you a good foul shooter?

A: I was well over 80 percent for my career.

Q: Were you the NBA's leading scorer one year?

A: Two years. My second year in the league (1951-1952), I was the leading scorer. Then I went into the Marine Corps for two years. My third year back (1956-1957), I was also the leading scorer. Those scoring titles were not nearly as important as people make them out to be. Somebody has to be the leading scorer. It just happened that it was me. Winning games and playing well were much more important.

Q: Did your team do well?

A: That year, unfortunately not. It was the year after we won the championship. We made the playoffs, but then we lost Tom Gola to the service. The next-to-last regular season game, I got a severe Charlie horse. I was kneed by Walter Dukes. I could only play a total of 20 minutes in our two playoff games against Syracuse. With Tommy and me gone, we couldn't win. It was the year that Boston, with Bill Russell, played extremely well.

Q: Did you know that Corky and Larry Foust were traded to the Lakers for Walter Dukes?

A: I didn't realize that. I did know that Walter was in the trade that sent Corky to Minneapolis.

Q: Did you know that Corky was originally drafted by the Warriors right after Tom Gola?

A: No, I didn't. In that era, it was not uncommon for players to be drafted, then shipped to another team because they didn't fit. Trades were a money-saving proposition. Most people don't know the following story. We had Larry Costello, one of the great players in the league. He played for the Warriors for a year and a half. Eddie Gottlieb didn't think his playing style was helping us that much. Eddie was close friends with Danny Biasone, the owner of the Syracuse Nationals. Larry Costello had been raised in the Syracuse area. In effect, Eddie gave Larry Costello's contract to Syracuse for nothing. No trade was ever announced. Eddie liked Larry and wanted to send him back home. That would never happen in the league today.

Q: *Let me impress you with my memory. Didn't Larry come back to Philly?*

A: When he went home, the team was still in Syracuse. The Nationals later became the Sixers.

Q: *Corky complained to me about how little money he made. Did he fight over his contract with Fred Zollner, owner of the Pistons?*

A: Let me assure you of this. The Pistons were respected as one of the better-paying clubs in our league.

Q: *Corky told me that in his first year, he made $8,000. His contract renewal called for a $1,500 raise. Didn't he send the contract back, wrapped in barbed wire?*

A: That doesn't surprise me at all. Eight thousand dollars in those days was not bad money. While Corky was a good player, he certainly wasn't considered a great player.

Q: *Chuck Noble laughed when I told him that story. I teased him, "From your laugh, I'm guessing you never made that much in your career." Do you agree?*

A: That is probably true, because players always exaggerated their salaries. To illustrate my point about Fort Wayne, in the early '60s George Yardley was traded from Detroit (formally Fort Wayne) to Syracuse. Syracuse had been led forever in scoring by Dolph Schayes. Yardley's contract created inequality in salaries between Yardley and Schayes. Because of the discrepancy, Dolph got a $4,000 raise as compensation.

The way contracts were presented to the players in those days was, "This is what I can afford to pay you. If you don't like it, good luck in finding a job." There was no other league.

The black players could go to the Trotters, but that wasn't the best kind of a life either. Our options were take it or quit.

Q: *As the league's leading scorer, you must have made more than $9,500?*

A: I was very fortunate in that I started at $10,000 my first year. Gottlieb told me, "Because I am paying you $10,000, your salary will probably bankrupt the team." Fortunately, it didn't. After I won the scoring championship, I spent two years in the service. I thought I would receive a big raise. I was given $1,500. I heard the standard story, "We don't know if you can still play."

There was a good reason for not getting paid much. I believe that the money was not available then. There was no television. All games were not on the radio. Admission in Philadelphia for a doubleheader was $2.50 for the best seat in the house. Four NBA teams would appear at Philadelphia's Convention Hall for a doubleheader. The Warriors always played in the nightcap. I firmly believe that we were not treated harshly by the owners. I played because I loved the game, not for the money. When I got tired of playing and the Warriors moved to San Francisco, I fell back on my college degree. That is when I first met you at IBM. It was a good move, because I knew that sooner or later, I would have to get a real job. Too many players today (it's sad to see) hang on too long. They play well past their prime, lingering on solely for the money. I never experienced that challenge. The last year I played, I averaged 22 points per game and logged over 40 minutes per game. I could easily have played longer, but I just didn't want to.

Q: *I remember your playing for the Camden Bullets across the Delaware River. Weren't you retired from the NBA?*

A: It was a dark time in Philadelphia with the Warriors gone. It was comforting to know that I could still play here.

Q: *Why did you play for Camden after leaving the Warriors?*

A: First was the money, which helped. It was an easy way to ease out of basketball. I didn't just abruptly cut my playing days off. I phased out over a three-year period in Camden. I quit Camden because I was working for IBM. That meant that I was working seven days per week. Who needs that? As I got older, the game kept getting harder. At the end I was 37. I had a lot of fun playing with Camden. We had a good team. I have no regrets.

XVII

THE DRAFT THAT SPLIT

Tom Gola is truly a Philadelphia icon. He is arguably the most beloved basketball player the city ever produced. At LaSalle High School, he led the Explorers from 20th and Olney to the City Championship. At LaSalle College, Tom was the head and heart of the most successful teams in LaSalle's history. In 1952, LaSalle won the National Invitation Tournament (NIT). In those days, the NIT was considered the most prestigious college tournament. Virtually the same team triumphed in the NCAA Tournament in 1954. LaSalle was crowned National Champions. The following year Tom and his mates lost in the NCAA finals to San Francisco, anchored by Bill Russell. During his four-year college career, Tom grabbed 2,201 rebounds. This astounding college record remains unbroken 50 years later.

The Philadelphia Warriors drafted Tom with their first pick in 1955. At 6-foot-5, Gola performed as playmaker before the term "point guard" became popular. His all-around talents contributed significantly to another championship, this time at the professional level. When the Warriors left Philadelphia for San Francisco, Tom declined to move. He ended his career playing for the New York Knicks. Tom Gola resides in Philadelphia, still its beloved son. During one successful year, he coached his alma mater. He served two terms as the City of Philadelphia comptroller. I spoke with Tom Gola by phone.

Q: Do you remember Corky?

A: He never played for the Warriors. He went with Fort Wayne and then the Lakers.

Q: How do you most remember Corky?

A: He played with me in the college East-West All-Star game at Madison Square Garden. We were coached by Ken Loeffler, my college coach at LaSalle. It was 1955 and our starting lineup for the East was Dick Ricketts, Maurice Stokes, Eddie Conlin, Corky Devlin and myself. Corky got really hot and sank his first eight shots. He was a streak shooter.

Q: An imposing lineup. Can you remember anything about Corky's life?

A: He became destitute in later life.

Q: He ripped me off. He took money from many others. Can you believe he finished his life at a monastery, a changed person?

A: I was with the city comptroller's office in Philadelphia between 1970 and 1974. Corky came into my office. He spun some tale about his wife getting killed in an accident. He went on from there. I gave him 50 bucks. He was a scam artist. He hit everybody up for money. I don't know what he did for a living. The only time I really got to know him was as a teammate in the 1955 All-Star game.

Q: Who won the game?

A: We did. It wasn't even close.

Q: You performed the greatest single play I ever saw in a basketball game. In the '50s, I was player/coach of a team named "The Travelers" in the Stone Harbor summer basketball league. On a Sunday afternoon in 1954, you appeared at the 96th Street courts. A close friend, Jim Schweidel, and I happened to be walking by. I was invited (the only time in my life) to referee a pickup game. You anchored one team, made up of players I didn't know. On the other team were Blatcher, Maples, Singley and other members of your LaSalle College team.

A: If I am not mistaken, I was working at the Atlantic City Race Track. I was with Frank Blatcher, Frank Finigan and Jimmy McDonald, who also worked at the track. I remember playing in Stone Harbor, but don't ask me for details.

Q: This play is preserved forever in my memory. You were playing center in a two, one, two zone. You pulled down a defensive rebound and, in one reverse windmill motion, lobbed an underhand length of the court pass that landed on the fingertips of your teammate for a lay-up.

A: That was probably Frank Blatcher. He was always a basket hanger.

Q: No. Blatcher was playing against you. This was someone on your team.

A: That would have resulted in a bit of a problem. Many of the LaSalle players played for the lifeguard team. I remember playing against them.

Q: I enjoyed that play, regardless of who scored the field goal. Jim Schweidel and I were recruited to referee. I watched you reach out and push teammates into the passing lanes.

A: Where is Corky now?

Q: He entered Gethsemani in 1993. He died 18 months later. Before joining the monastery, he orchestrated one final fling. He ripped me off along with a few others.

A: Welcome to the club.

Q: You are fortunate that your contribution was $50. Mine was $2,500.

A: I was fortunate that I only had $100 in my pocket, I gave him only $50. I'm really sorry to hear your story. My God.

Q: I came to write his life's story in a strange way. I promised him I would write it before he died. I began the search, and just kept going. I was very happy that his behavior changed while he lived with the monks. Do you believe his personality became joyful?

A: Think of those he left behind.

Q: You might find this story interesting. I interviewed Zelda Spoelstra at NBA Headquarters. She considers you among the top five college players of all time.

A: I met Zelda after I entered pro basketball. In my rookie year (1955-1956) the Warriors won the championship. She worked at the head office. After games against the Knicks in New York, we all met at a bar for hamburgers and a couple of beers before retuning to Philadelphia. She was always there. The Knicks enjoyed a happy reunion after the game.

Q: I watched many of your games. Do you remember playing against Billy French?

A: Billy was the first seven-footer to come into the Catholic League. The poor guy could barely walk. Bobby Schafer also played on that Roman Catholic team. Billy was big, but he couldn't play. His older brother, Jack French, played ahead of me at LaSalle on the NIT championship team.

Q: Do you recall the George Washington team?

A: George Washington had Joe Holup. To this day, he and I are the only two college players who scored 2,000 points and grabbed 2,000 rebounds during our careers. Joe was the year behind me.

Q: Joe has passed away, but I have talked to his older brother, John.

A: I am very sorry that you lost $2,500. It bothers me that Corky would do that. Fifty bucks from me didn't matter. I'm sorry to hear that you lost all that money.

Q: It gets worse. I tried to rehabilitate Corky. I offered him a sales job with my company. He convinced me to give him the money to bail his business clothes out of hock.

A: He could have bought a whole wardrobe with that.

Q: Does it sound strange to you that I would be so gullible?

A: Well, I hope he is at peace wherever he may be.

* * *

The East-West College All-Star game was played in New York on March 26, 1955. My research took me to the *Philadelphia Evening Bulletin* (now defunct).

Corky's team was made up of the very best players in America. His skills were at their peak and his addictions had not yet kicked in. He must have been thrilled to perform as leading scorer in a high-profile game. Fourteen of the 20 players in the game averaged 20 points or more. This experience was the apex of Corky's life. Unfortunately, individual high moments in our lives are rarely recognized for what they are. Corky forfeited the opportunity to savor the occasion.

* * *

Dick Ricketts, Maurice Stokes and Tom Gola—three Pennsylvanians—led the East to an easy 83-68 victory over a West team tonight in the annual All-Star College Basketball game before 18,135 fans at Madison Square Garden. Devlin led the East with 16.

EAST   WEST

	G	F	TP		G	F	TP
Ricketts	5	2	12	Patterson	3	0	6
Gola	2	2	6	Twyman	2	6	10
Conlin	2	2	6	Littleton	1	0	2
Arnelle	2	4	8	Ferrari	0	0	0
Stokes	5	2	12	McKeen	3	1	7
Hemric	3	1	7	Schlundt	3	5	11
Devlin	8	0	16	Lane	1	8	10
Fleming	1	6	8	Mencil	4	0	8
Evans	2	1	5	Ehman	1	3	5
Wilkinson	1	1	3	Garmaker	4	1	9
Total	31	21	83	Totals	22	24	68

Halftime Score—East 54, West 36

XVIII

MINING GUCCI PEARLS

Fr. Joseph Messina was reverenced by people close to Corky. Jim Murray calls him "Fr. Gucci" referring to his impeccable taste in wine, food, clothes, and people. I have known Fr. Joe for 20 years. Sometimes, his epicurean taste makes me laugh. His sermons always inspire me through strong messages. He points me towards the truth. For that reason, I value this priest's spirituality. My primary goal with Fr. Gucci was to focus on Corky's personality. Fr. Joe had received Corky into the Catholic Church. We met for lunch at Lamberti's in Cherry Hill, NJ. Jim Murray sat at our table. His son, Jim Jr., joined us later.

Q: How did you first meet Corky?

Fr. Joe: I met Corky through Bob Healey and Jim Murray. Corky received his First Communion at Jim's house.

Jim Murray: Corky's First Communion was scheduled for a Sunday afternoon. It had to be canceled when Corky fell on the ice and broke his collarbone. We rescheduled the same people at the identical time the following Sunday.

Fr. Joe: Investigate Corky's work with Bob Healey in Mexico. I assisted them. Corky met many political people including El Presidente. At that time, Corky really accomplished good works.

Fr. Dan Rocco exhibited a little more spirituality than Gucci. Corky gravitated towards him. It proved a wise choice. Corky gave 100 percent to whatever endeavor he attempted. I viewed him as one full-out guy.

Q: Could you elaborate on bringing Corky into the Catholic Church?

Fr. Joe: Well, he had been attending most of our Catholic events. One day I asked him if he had considered becoming a Catholic. He asked a few questions. We continued further discussion. Within a month, he entered the Church. He had previously been baptized in another church.

Jim Murray: I remember the day at my house for the baptism.

His feet slipped and he landed on his shoulder. We instituted instant replay the following week.

Fr. Joe: I celebrated a Mass. I baptized him, confirmed him and gave him Communion all in one day.

Q: Do you remember his reaction?

Fr. Joe: He seemed elated. He began attending every available Mass.

Jim Murray: Corky was like the guy in the bubble. He was with you but you could never touch him. An extremely private person, he became instantly attracted to the monks at Gethsemani. Their demeanor tremendously affected him.

Q: Did he join the Church before he left for Gethsemani?

Fr. Joe: Yes. Prior to joining the Church, he experienced a three-day Cursillio Weekend. It greatly affected his spiritual development. The word 'Cursillio' means 'Little course in Christianity.' I explained this Spanish word to Corky. The experience prepared him for his entry into the Church. I did not serve as priest on his weekend. Your friend, Bob Hardy, presented some of the talks.

Q: Did Corky talk about his brother?

Fr. Joe: No. He was estranged from his brother.

So many people in life share weakness about following through. He was the opposite. He was a pit bull who never let go. Corky was deeply sincere about the spiritual things in life. He possessed a sharply developed mind. He brought the same zeal from basketball to spiritual enlightenment. He pursued Gethsemani as if he were already a monk.

Q: When you invited him into the Church, was he searching?

Fr. Joe: Yes. He had pursued other avenues in life without success or satisfaction.

Q: Did he hit you for money?

Fr. Joe: Very little. Twenties, fifties, lunches, and dinners.

Jim Jr.: He gave me money. He never got me. He lived in our house and I knew him pretty well. One night he came into my room. He had just returned to radar (a mysterious disappearance). I was graduating from high school. He laid a couple of hundred bucks on me. Because I had heard all the stories, I was shocked. I'll never forget that visit. He probably hit a horse.

Q: He gave you a graduation present? Do you remember what he said?

Jim Jr.: He mumbled, "I've never given you anything."

I had a good relationship with Corky. A few months after his gift, we visited some distant state. We sat by a pool. He blurted out how deeply he cared about me. That day, he seemed sincere. I enjoyed our conversations about basketball. We were both sports junkies. We attended many Villanova basketball games. Corky drove my father and me to the big one. That night in 1985, we beat Georgetown for the national championship. It was a huge upset. He drove the three of us from Philadelphia straight through to Rupp Arena in Lexington. We continued on to Florida after the game.

Q: My old Kentucky home. Is it ironic how his life seemed drawn to Kentucky?

Jim Murray: Did you know that he always had a way with women? A woman who owned two McDonald franchises attended his First Communion. She drove all the way from Kentucky. Part of his charisma was that he was a natty dresser. He taught me how to stuff handkerchiefs in my suit pockets.

Q: Corky the great dresser and good dancer, but no one got close?

Jim Murray: Now that you mention it, I never really felt close to him. He wore a reverse magnet around him like a shield. If we could see his prison records, he couldn't hide behind his shield there.

Fr. Joe: Corky called me from the monastery. Fr. Dan Rocco coaxed him to go there. Corky was also running away from legal problems. My sense was that he went there to avoid jail. Regardless, he really embraced monastic life. When the Abbot covered his operation, he was deeply touched. He was then one of their own.

Jim Murray: The monastery previously rejected him at least twice. At the time I first met him, he drove to Kentucky hoping to be accepted. Although he lived and worked there, he never officially became a monk.

Q: What did he say when you last spoke?

Fr. Joe: He wanted to check in. A few months later, he visited New Jersey to reconcile with me. At that time, I was chaplain at Underwood Hospital. I had reached the end of my rope with Corky. We met in my office at the hospital. We prayed together. He acted genuinely happy to see me. I believe he also visited Dan Rocco. He attempted to make peace with guys he had hit up. He returned to Gethsemani and died only a few weeks later.

Jim Murray: I visited him shortly after his trip. My son, Brian, drove to Kentucky.

Q: Can you remember anything he said?

Jim Murray: He explained "After my heart attack, I was driving to Jewish Hospital in Louisville. This is really ridiculous. I finally got my act together and I'm now going to die. The doctors observed, "You did too much damage to your heart. You are going to be drinking a glass of iced tea and you'll go." That was exactly how it happened.

Q: Was he ready to go?

Fr. Joe: Oh, yes. I got that sense from his last visit. He wanted to reconcile with everyone he had hurt or abused.

Q: On the day he came into the Church, who was there?

Jim Murray: It was a microcosm of his life. A real assortment of people dropped in. It grew into a celebration. Corky's antics mimicked being a no-show at your own wedding. Rescheduling strained the guests. Even the weather stayed bad. Barbara Deaver (of the New York Metropolitan Opera) sang. In gratitude for her beautiful singing, Corky promised to make her famous.

Q: Corky lived at the Murray house for more than a year?

Jim Jr.: He lived in my room while I attended Villanova.

Q: Do you feel that you knew him?

Jim Jr.: I really believed that I did.

Q: When he wasn't disappearing, how did he spend his time?

Jim Jr.: He upset my mother a few times. She observed him taking advantage of my father. He certainly wasn't give and take. Overwhelmingly he was take. We got along because none of our conversations went very deep. I just enjoyed his stories.

Q: He was searching for a hit.

Jim Jr.: I didn't have money, so he let his guard down. Our relationship was more like a timeout.

Q: What did he take from you?

Fr. Joe: Not much at all. I wouldn't allow that. Mostly, he picked my brain for contacts. He worked those contacts. He was a con artist who said and did things that made me want to die. One day, after he complained about his medications, I put him in touch with Dr. Frank Iula. I think Corky ended up with free medicine.

Q: Did Corky describe a bipolar condition.
Fr. Joe: Yes. He had a way of projecting his disease onto you. For me he prescribed a lithium program. Clinical treatment was only the beginning of his talent. He was a world-class fixer.

Jim Murray: My wife, Dianne, really had problems with Corky's non-degreed diagnoses and treatment plans. Conversely, my kids loved his free medical advice.

Jim Jr.: I could trust that Corky would never tell on us. He stayed home especially at odd hours. No matter what he saw us do, he kept his mouth shut. He kept promising us, "Your secret's safe with me." For us kids, he was a charmer. I did notice, when it suited him, he turned our words against us. Like everything else, his ratting on us was full-out.

* * *

I felt left out upon learning that Corky reconciled with many of those he hurt. I hadn't been included on his tour of reconciliations. Maybe I missed the "A list" of those he wronged. Did he sense that my time would come? Corky thrived at the monastery with access to spiritual guidance. He embraced the endless time to think. A simple "hello" could have made me feel valued. Uniquely, I was snubbed by a con man.

Columbo could have a field day researching Corky's stories. Mark Twain advised that the difference between the right word and the almost right word mirrors the difference between a bolt of lightning and a lightning bug. Corky's stories have been full of bugs. Take, for example, his story about the entry of black players into the National Basketball Association.

He was no champion. The first black player to step on an NBA court was Earl Lloyd. He broke the color barrier as a member of the Washington Capitols against the Rochester Royals on October 31, 1950. That game was played in a high school gym in Rochester, NY. The next night, two other black players debuted. The Boston Celtics had drafted Chuck Cooper. The New York Knicks signed Nat 'Sweetwater' Clifton, who had played with the Harlem Globetrotters. All three players enjoyed multiple seasons in the NBA. They experienced few incidents of racial unrest. Lloyd commented later that most of his experiences were positive. He gained acceptance largely because his white teammates viewed him as just another basketball player. During that era, pro basketball was limited to graduated college players. Earl Lloyd was drafted after an outstanding career for West Virginia State University. He remembers, "The first time the Capitols visited Fort Wayne, Indiana, I was permitted to sleep in the Val Holman Hotel with the rest of my teammates." However, he was not permitted to join his teammates for dinner. The hotel restaurant was designated "Whites Only." Capitols' coach, Horace 'Bones' McKinney, visited Lloyd's room to eat dinner with him. Earl Lloyd never forgot that night. He states, "I love Bones McKinney dearly."

Corky's missed shot record was less exaggerated. His claim was just a little off. The press release: December 25, 1956, Corky Devlin of Fort Wayne goes 0-for-15 from the field against the Minneapolis Lakers to *tie* an NBA record.

Corky bemoaned his treatment by Fred Zollner, owner of the Fort Wayne Pistons. Paul Arizin disagreed: "Mr. Zollner was among the most generous owners in the league."

From their first game on November 3, 1948 through 1957, the Fort Wayne Pistons thrived. The team was named for Fred Zollner, owner of Zollner Machine Works, which manufactured pistons. The team's name changed to the Detroit Pistons during the 1957-58 season.

Corky's boast to the hotel clerk when he arrived in Fort Wayne eventually proved true. The Pistons' only two Division Championships occurred in 1956 and 1957. Fort Wayne's only two trips to the NBA Finals also occurred during those years. Corky promised championships. The only questions that remain are about his contribution.

By 1977, Corky had been out of basketball for two decades. He was trotting our country without a basketball. The success he had foreseen for basketball's future was in full bloom. Sadly, Corky was no longer included.

Corky's story about playing for the College All-Stars against the Trotters apparently was untrue. I researched box scores (especially the game on April 3, 1955 in Philadelphia). Devlin's name did not appear. He did, however, play at Convention Hall for three years against the Philadelphia Warriors.

XIX

MY PARADIGM

Corky had pointed me to Fr. Dan Rocco if I needed a Spiritual Director. I discovered him serving as a parish priest at St. Agnes Church in Blackwood, NJ. I first visited with Fr. Rocco on an August evening in 2001. Traffic was horrendous. So I arrived late. I apologized. He surprised me when he assured me that he would spend as much time as needed. Fr. Rocco speaks with a contemplative gentle demeanor. We settled in his office. As a priest, he needed to discern which parts of Corky's story were not under the seal of confession. Six years had passed since Fr. Dan last spoke with Corky. They had become close friends. Some of Corky's conversations were personal, and some were under the seal of confession. A priest may never repeat anything he hears in confession. I sat comfortably on his couch

Q: Fr. Rocco, will you lead?
A: I must avoid all confessional things, but I'll give you my impressions. There are singular stories that encapsulate Corky. That is the limit about which I can talk.

I attempted to frame our conversation. Fr. Dan did not react when I described how Corky ordered me to continue writing this book. Corky's prompting from the spirit world bothered only me. Most of what I had uncovered had been discouraging.

Q: Fr. Dan, were you surprised by my struggle?

A: I first met Corky when I became interested in Living Bridges (the adoption agency). Fr. Messina invited me to give a talk at Bob Healey's farm. A few months later Corky attended my ordination. He dressed in large boots and a cowboy hat. In 1990, he was a big presence.

Q: Yours was a late calling to the priesthood?

A: I had an early calling. I just responded late. I had been involved in a serious accident and I almost died. Corky became very supportive during my rehabilitation. He called me periodically when he came to town. Each time we went to the same diner for breakfast. Our conversations ranged from God to Corky's understanding of life. One day in 1993, I felt inspired. Corky's usual conversation centered on his past, his family, his exploits and the 128 racetracks in the United States.

I was inspired to ask, "Corky, why don't you go to Gethsemani and become the Gatekeeper?" That was my suggestion. He took me up on it. Off he went to Gethsemani.

Q: Had he visited other monasteries before that?

A: Oh, yes. But he felt a great affinity for Gethsemani. This was the pivotal decision on which you must focus when writing Corky's story. Corky recounted the following story to me after his heart attack. During the attack, he drove himself to the hospital. At that time, he had been serving as Gatekeeper. The doctors told him that he needed surgery in order to live. Corky had never thought to file for Social Security. Even worse, he wasn't eligible for Medicare or Medicaid in Kentucky. He planned to file during the next few weeks. Time ran out. The Abbot at Gethsemani visited Corky's bedside. He whispered the most compassionate and important words Corky had ever heard: "Don't worry about the operation. We will take it out of the cheese." Why was this comforting assurance so important? It meant everything to Corky. After a life of struggles, he finally experienced unconditional acceptance.

Q: Corky and Bro. Alban started a cheese business at Gethsemani. It must have become very successful.

A: It may not have been. But this reassurance turned his life around. I did not know Corky well. I was not his confessor for very long. I only knew him through what he revealed. I never observed the bottom of his soul. This story is critical because he finally found The Place of mutual acceptance. In all probability, he had experienced acceptance in other places. I believe that this was the only time he accepted acceptance.

Q: Forgive me. I feel deep emotion about what you just described. At last I understand that he found a home. He spun so many stories. Yours launches encouragement that he finally found peace and identity.

A: That's the impression I received. I will never know the depth of his peace. But I was truly happy that I had made the suggestion. The Abbot's cheese comment had the flavor of resting in the Lord. Remember that the beloved disciple (John) rested his head on the chest of Jesus. At the Last Supper, John rested on God's Heart. As much as he feared God, Corky allowed himself to be held by Him. Corky suffered his heart attack. It drew him to the heart of God. God's Heart guided him to acceptance at the Abbey. Potentially, Corky acted like the "prodigal son." The son finally returned to his Father. Corky's return initiated his most critical encounter.

Tears welled inside of me. Corky's promise flashed in my heart. "In finding me you will find yourself." Only a few weeks prior, while praying, I had chosen a saint as my role model. My selection anticipated the arrival of Fr. Dan. I chose the apostle John. Now I had hope. Corky also experienced John.

Q: Father, I have interviewed many people. Frankly, evidence of salvation has heavily slanted against Corky. Now, I hear that my reason for choosing John was identical to Corky's. John and Corky were able to accept that they were beloved by Jesus. I was struggling as Corky had. I journeyed to Gethsemani, searching for what he had found. Since Corky opened the gate, I hope to join him.

A: If you don't have Gethsemani, you can't envision a saint. You have only a sinner. If you don't find out what happened in Kentucky, Corky's life makes little sense. That is why his story is so important. It explains the hinge between confrontation and final acceptance. Without Corky's acceptance, our prodigal son never returns home.

I have never visited Gethsemani. I was supposed to go, but his heart attack cancelled my trip.

Q: On my first trip, we drove all night. The next day, I sat talking with Bro. Alban. I blurted out, "Let me cut to the chase. If God created a saint for our times, it probably would be someone like Corky."

Bro. Alban answered affirmatively. He stared and said, "I couldn't agree with you more. I will do all I can to help you write his book." He described how Corky experienced great happiness at the monastery. Until your explanation, I couldn't conceptualize what Bro. Alban meant.

My Paradigm

A: You could never guess why he became happy? That's what I gather. Have you researched his past?

Q: *I am searching.*

A: Do you know his half-brother? I think he lives in New Jersey.

Q: *Here is what I learned from him. Elaborate when you can. His mother died in Atlantic City of Alzheimer's. His sister wouldn't speak to him. He had a brother-in-law bartender in Atlantic City. His brother attended Corky's funeral. Corky also had a daughter.*

A: Have you talked to her?

Q: *No. Jim Murray is not sure she is still alive. All I know is that she experienced substance abuse problems and that she had an excellent singing voice.*

A: So you don't know what happened to her? There are some things that I cannot divulge. There are things I know but I cannot talk about. I don't want to get into the area of his daughter. Corky always searched for her.

Q: *You know that he found her?*

A: Yes.

Q: *Are there any other people you think I should talk to?*

A: Have you talked to anyone who knew him when in California?

Q: *No. He told me that on the day he found his wife, Arleen, with his best friend, he also learned that his stepfather, Joe Corcoran, had died. That launched him off the deep end. He declared himself homeless before the term became popular.*

A: Ok. Let me work with you, for the sake of enlightenment. If what you just said happened with his stepfather, do you see any connection to what happened with the cheese?

Q: *I'm not that quick. Let me think about it.*

A: Think it out.

Q: *He was looking for a home? Is that the connection?*

A: Do you see how the day of his father's death foreshadowed crucial moments in his later life?

Q: *Yes, the prodigal son jumped into the world so that he could finally find his way home. Both Jim Murray and Bro. Alban are convinced that Corky finally found peace.*

A: Again, I'll lead you. I want to stimulate your thought process. Why do you think he played the bad boy role so well?

Q: *I was about to ask the same question. It appears that he hid a genuine missing link. This defect kept others from knowing him. He described you as* his closest confidant. Should I ever need a spiritual director, he wanted me to find you. But you have admitted, "I didn't know him very well." Jim Murray referred to Corky as a man of many caves. No one will ever enter some of them. He was a devious multi-masked person. Throughout his life, he hid suffering.

A: Why?

Q: My guess is that he did not trust himself. He didn't know whether any good remained inside of him.

A: That's possible. Did he trust you enough?

Q: *Apparently not.*

A: Look at what you have told me. I will only go by what you tell me. I will not go by what I know. Can you follow me?

Q: *I understand that many of the things you know, you can never reveal. If I tell you something, you can work with it. Ok. Let me ask you this. We spent a day at the beach. He told me stories about himself that I considered very deep. We were leaving the beach when I asked, "Why me?" I sensed that somehow he examined my being. His look was remarkable for someone who didn't have much going for him. If he was a mystic like Padre Pio, I could understand. His response seemed strange. "I am seeing your soul. I believe that it is safe for me to tell you the truth."*

A: Let me ask you a question. Was this before or after he took your money?

Q: *Before. He added, "I have always been able to read people. This is the one gift I never doubt."*

Corky spent his life wandering. He convinced me that he tried to do the right thing. Almost always he failed. Could someone like Corky possess the ability to read souls?

A: You see, ultimately, he did have goodness. We all do. But, he was fighting great temptation. That happens when you have an addiction. You use your skills in order to survive.

Some people are more gifted than others. The exceptionally gifted fight a tendency to become world-class scoundrels. Their only hope is to cultivate and nurture that aspect in their makeup that is fundamentally good and searching. If they ever stop searching, they lose their humanity. As far as I know, Corky never stopped searching. He continued to battle his demons. If I could read your soul, as the term applies, what would be my temptation?

Q: *To abuse me?*

A: To use or abuse you through what I see.

Q: *Let's say that he could see my soul. He saw that he could rip me off. I was at a financially vulnerable time in my life. I couldn't afford to be reckless. When we left the beach, did he view me as an easy target?*

A: Ok. Now, number one, why would I want to rip you off if I were Corky?

Q: *I just don't understand.*

A: Ok. There are several reasons why I would want to rip you off. One, because I need to. I'm desperate for survival. Two, because I like playing with people. I'm not saying that this was the case. I'm just giving you some options. Three, I'm playing a sadistic game. I am a sociopath. A fourth option, I need to find the person and situation which holds the key to my redemption. His might have been a combination of all four reasons. If you want to understand the totality of his personage, you must deal with him on a deeper level. You could explain away a sociopath because he fits a certain pattern. Is that his pattern? Try to view Corky as a myth. You have been viewing him as a real person. You have been searching for facts about him. You are probably building a chronology of who Corky is. That's interesting, but it will never enable you to understand his story. Read Joseph Campbell's book, "The Death of a Hero". The book explains the concept of the struggle. Campbell examines ways to understand your father, your mother, and the complexities surrounding them both. Corky had a mystical quality about him. He came to my ordination wearing a cowboy hat. At 6-foot-5, he projected bigger than life. He told exceptional stories. He attached himself to very powerful men. He encased himself in the Ronald McDonald House while befriending a generous professor. In the end, he flourished as a monastery gatekeeper. A similar great story was written by Flaubert (a French author). It is a story about the tow master, who pulled people by rope from one side of the river to the other. His life evolved from a life of excess. As a young man, he hunted in excess. He slaughtered animals in excess. Everything he did was in excess. Yet, at the end of his life, he found happiness by towing people from side to side on the river. In this humble employment, he attempted to redeem himself. This man's experience was very similar to Corky's. Corky struggled to redeem himself through great and excessive works. In the end, he settled for simply the gatekeeper. His redemption was not quantitative. Life became a qualitative venture. His redemption required accepting acceptance. Faith is the courage to accept acceptance. This courage points to how the Protestant theologian, Paul Tillich, defines faith.

Q: The tug was familiar. My struggle was drawing so close to Corky's. On July 29, 1975, I experienced a life-changing encounter. My wife and I were participating in a Marriage Encounter. We were sitting talking. Suddenly, I was lifted into the sky. A single small cloud hovered above me. My arm and hand disappeared into the cloud. I was overcome by an overpowering but loving force. This seemingly liquid energy flowed down my arm and into my heart. I started to sob. I had been changed on the spot. All guilt of sin was washed away in that instant. The heavy weight of sin and failure, that I so loathed in my past was instantly forgiven. Tears flowed from my eyes for hours. I had not cried for 14 years. I had been unable to cry since my father's death. I have tried to understand that experience during these past 26 years. I found an explanation in a paper entitled, "You are Accepted," by Paul Tillich. At this moment, you introduce Paul and his paper. My search draws ever closer to Corky and his struggle.

A: Your mystical experience is linked to what I have been talking about with Corky. He, too, was changed after he placed his head on the breast of the Lord. Look at the beginning of the gospel of John. His gospel presents the whole experience of John the writer. He refers to himself as the beloved disciple resting in the bosom of Jesus. Now, listen to the prologue to John's gospel.

"No one has ever seen God, only the Son who is in the bosom of the Father". The relationship between the Son and the Father is that the Son is at the bosom of the Father.

The disciple is at the bosom of Jesus, who rests at the bosom of the Father. So, this resting is the predisposition for faith and for union with God. We observe the beloved disciple who relinquishes himself before he willfully vows to follow Jesus. This surrender by the beloved disciple makes him unique from the other disciples. The other apostles had not yet arrived at that point of relinquishing. They were on their way. Only the beloved disciple stayed and was steadfast during the Passion. We are attracted to this posture because we have seen the end of the story. So, our degree of surrender undermines the depth of our own redemption. Our closeness with God has nothing to do with paying back for all the things we have done wrong. Restitution appeared to be through works instead of faith for a person like Corky (now this is pure theorizing on my part). If Corky had not gone to Gethsemani, he may never have discovered that he was unconditionally loved. Without proof, but from all you have said and all I have heard about Gethsemani, Corky finally accepted God's love. We all need a contact from the Divine Incarnate before we are able to accept unconditional acceptance. We can't just do it. Acceptance of God is much deeper than the popular belief, "I can think it, therefore it is." Accepting the acceptance is much more counter cultural. To experience it, you have to live in the moment.

Q: It is experiential?

A: Exactly. You told me, "I had not cried for over 14 years. When I had this experience, I cried." What did you deal with? You dealt with your father.

Q: There is one final part of my experience. At the end of the weekend, my wife and I left the retreat house deeply changed. The other 30 couples bubbled with happiness. I felt stunned and profoundly moved. My understanding of life would never be the same. As we passed through the door, I heard an interior voice, "Ask anything and I will give it to you." This was my first experience with an interior voice. Without hesitation, I responded, "I want to stop drinking."

At that time, I was drinking large quantities of bourbon and rarely showing it. On two occasions I couldn't remember details of the previous evening. This worried me. Alcoholism frightened me.

A week later, we headed for a social engagement. I poured my usual double bourbon. I lifted the glass and smelled. I shuddered. The bourbon smelled rancid. I haven't finished a drink since. Occasionally, I try a few swallows. I never finish.

What have I learned? Faith is not bulldog determination. Faith seems to happen. It is not even something that is requested. I wasn't smart enough to ask for faith. It just happened. Acceptance of God's free gift is the only way I can respond to God's grace.

A: There is an enlightening story about the famous Playboy Priest, Fr. Hugh Robertson. In the 50s, his mother purchased a television set and donated it to a convent. TV had just arrived on the scene.

One day one of the nuns called his mother, "We love your gift; come over and have tea with us."

When she entered the room, the TV stood in the center of the room with flowerpots all over the top of it. She asked, "Do you use it?"

They responded. "How can we use it? We don't know how it works."

Do any of us know how to open God's gifts? How many do we leave unopened?

Q: My deepest fear is personified in one line of Francis Thompson's "Hound of Heaven".

The line goes, "Lest having you, I might have naught besides."

If I accept God in His totality, there may be nothing left of me. I find it frightening to accept God, total unknown, as an alternative to my carefully guarded life.

A: That is it. That is my point with Corky. If he had not accepted the invitation to Gethsemani, what would he have? His life would have stayed the same.

Q: What hindered him from God's grace earlier in life?

A: Do you mean Gethsemani?

Q: What kept him from going to where he could experience God?

A: This is pure conjecture. He was afraid. He couldn't give in to the "Hound of Heaven."

Q: Corky often mentioned his father. Bro. Alban described Corky's visit to the University of Kentucky. Adolph Rupp changed Corky's plan.

Joe Corcoran responded, "No son of mine commits to one university and goes back on his word."

I had not given this story high importance. Was he searching for his own father when he was led to The Father?

A: That's where you must look at all his struggles. Why did he come to me?

Q: Because he was hurting?

A: He came to me because I am a father.

Q: Why you?

A: He knew to come to me. Eventually, as we become older, God, in His infinite mercy, opens up different doors. If we don't accept the invitation, that door closes. But He opens other doors. If we don't enter any of them, we remain out in the cold.

Q: Never entering any door would be our worst mistake?

A: Spiritually, yes.

Q: That is what Teilhard de Chardin called, quitting, sitting down in the middle of the road and saying, "No," to life.

A: It would be like Sartre, who said, "Of which the only answer is suicide."

Q: Corky not only contemplated suicide, he tried it.

A: Are you beginning to see the possibilities? That's all we have. You have gathered the data; now you must fill in his story.

Q: I have a more accurate understanding of Corky. During our encounter, you touched my being.

My Paradigm

You answered my own questions.

A: You will discover that Corky's story speaks to what it means to be a human being.

Q: *Not many people discover what Corky did.*

A: Not many human beings arrive where he went. They just never open the door.

Q: *Corky's life seemed doomed to failure. Sadness accompanied him everywhere. I considered discontinuing this book because I projected how his story might end. I wanted the conclusion that was black or white, success or failure. Before your insights, Corky's life appeared almost totally negative. Your vision adjusted my sight.*

Q: There is a book, "Barabbas." which became a movie. See it. It will help you understand Corky. Anthony Quinn plays the title role. Barabbas was the scoundrel freed by Pontius Pilate in place of Jesus. He could not live that down. In vain, he tried to continue his life. The question remained. Could Barabbas be redeemed after the evil he had done?

Q: *He probably does a lot of good things?*

A: No. He doesn't. That's the point. He doesn't even intend to do good things. For him, good things don't amount to a hill of beans. Only his intent does. Ultimately, his challenge with God is acceptance. He receives the grace to accept God's love. His accumulation of good works gains no merit. His life personifies our whole debate about faith and good works.

Q: *Are you advocating the Protestant interpretation of faith versus good works?*

A: No, I'm taking the side of St. Augustine. Unless we are moved by faith to do good works, the good works will never give us faith. That's the point.

Q: *Since we cannot merit grace, how do we get God to move?*

A: We don't. You see, on the flip side, God is continually offering the gift of faith. We live our lives so that out of pride, arrogance and jealousy (all sins against love) we are unwilling to humble ourselves. We never recognize that which is being offered.

Q: *Are you addressing Corky or me?*

A: I am speaking to humanity.

Q: *Return to the moment when you urged Corky to go to Gethsemani. Was he in despair? How did he react to your suggestion?*

A: It came out as dramatic repetition. As we talked, the invitation kept coming back. Whatever Corky had done or had tried made no difference.

None of his ventures had amounted to anything. None of his great plans materialized. "You will know them by their fruits."

Corky had no fruit. Obviously, something was missing.

Q: What entered your mind as you made the suggestion? Did God put Gethsemani in your mind? Or, did you mention Gethsemani out of exasperation?

A: Looking back, I was moved by the Spirit. I had a sense of being prompted. Knowing what I know now, I would have urged his move anyway.

Q: What was his reaction?

A: Corky was a charmer. As such, his thoughts retreated before he came back. I always believed that I had nothing to give Corky. He couldn't steal from me. Probably, my poverty was one reason we got along. I tried to help him. When I learned that he had followed my suggestion, I was really happy. It was more than that. I sensed joy. He finally accepted my prodding.

Q: What did the relationship give to you?

A: We went out for breakfast. He knocked at my door.

Q: You didn't really know him?

A: No. We had nothing other than our talks and our connection to Living Bridges.

Q: Corky claimed to have played a role in Living Bridges. He described a food kitchen in Mexico, which still feeds 35,000 people daily.

A: Yes, the brickyard. I don't know the current status of that organization. In the early days, they flew planes full of food and clothing to Mexico.

Corky was never the driving force. He had no money. He worked for that group. I do not know the extent of his involvement.

Q: Like most people, I wander. At the time I experienced God 26 years ago, I felt like Scrooge on Christmas morning. The joy lasted weeks. Then the euphoria died down. Your insight helps me understand my own experience. Are there any other Corky experiences?

A: No, but I can tell you what today is.

Q: August 6th?

A: Yes. The Church celebrates the Transfiguration. On this day Jesus, was transfigured before Peter, James and John.

Q: Again you mention John. Previously, John's head was on Jesus' bosom. Now you point to Jesus' transfiguration. After the Resurrection, John remained conspicuously silent. Peter did all the talking. Somehow, John understood that he had nothing left to say.

One of my favorite scenes occurred after the Resurrection. Jesus built a charcoal fire on the beach. The apostles had fished all night before they spotted Jesus. Peter jumped into the water and thrashed for shore. John calmly rowed to shore. John had a calm assurance that he was loved. I imagine Corky lying in God's bosom. I envy him. I hope to accept God's love before my last chapter.

A: I hope so.

Q: Recently Jim Murray challenged my understanding of Corky. At first, I repeated platitudes. Corky was hard to grasp. Then Jim fired a litany of bad things. I retreated inside in search of answers.

A: Now you know how Corky felt. You have created your own litany about Corky. His struggles may even lead to sainthood. Corky was fragile. Weakness was always with Corky. Do you want to understand how he felt? You just expressed it. This is conjecture. See if this fits. Corky sought the key to change. He groped for what could free him from being a scoundrel. Gethsemani changed him. Had he not gone to Gethsemani, Corky would have remained simply a scoundrel. That is my point. Add up everything in Corky's life to that point. You have a scoundrel. Your study of his life has been linear as opposed to wraparound time. Only wraparound time will uncover who Corky was in the fullness of his personhood.

But you haven't examined his final chapter. Experience his last chapter and you will be able to make sense of his total life. That last chapter is key.

There is a Greek saying in scholastic thought. "What is the first thing thought of and the last thing achieved?" The answer is your goal. Our goals are the first thing we think of. They are also the last thing we achieve.

His finish bespeaks the movement of Corky's life. That is why we have saints. We become saints not because of how we lived our lives. The key is how we died.

Q: I find our discussion difficult. When Corky died, I suppressed a thought that Corky's struggles might lead him towards sainthood. How can I find out? Can I evaluate his death? What questions should I ask in Kentucky?

A: Ok. We will never know if Corky is a saint in the sense that most people think of a saint. We can confirm that he accepted acceptance. That can be determined. Look for external signs of acceptance.

Great questions would be, "Did he confess before he died? Did he receive the sacraments?"

I'm not judging. I'm giving you things to look for. You must determine whether he came home.

Q: Was he a Catholic when he came to you?

A: Yes. Fr. Messina had received him into the church.

Q: What other questions should I ask?

A: Was anyone there when he died?

Q: They found him on the floor of his room. Pills were spilled all over. He never reached his nitroglycerin. During his last year, Corky experienced peace and happiness.

A: Ask how he spent his last days. Was he happy? Was he content? Was he at peace? More important, did he have a sense of joy? You will never be able to state that he is a saint. His coming home is a positive sign.

Q: You have certainly enhanced my view of Corky's life.

A: I was just a friend, a spiritual friend.

Q: More than once he described you as his spiritual friend. I guess you became the only one he could really talk to. You are smiling?

A: You are welcome to come back. The door is always open. If I can be of any help, just ask.

Q: I serve as a foil to Corky. I have little interest in money or worldly gain. Money has never been a goal in my search for Corky.

A: But be enthusiastic about this project. View him in your mind's eye. There is nothing wrong with that. If your work fuels enthusiasm, that's good. It is only when you let success fuel your judgment that trouble takes hold.

Q: You have pointed me towards a better goal. Did Corky find redemption?

A: Key to your quest is that through Corky you are wrestling with the fundamental question of all ages. That question is, "What is success?"

Q: Most people create their own view of success. Our material world craves stardom, power or money. I have never really attempted to define success.

A: The question of our lives, "What is success?"

Q: I would love to identify success. Is it different for each of us?

A: By any standards, Corky was not successful. Yet he was always in the limelight.

Q: People loved him. Everybody. A few people also hated him.

A: I assume that they hated him because of the situations that transpired. Initially they didn't hate him.

Q: His sister hated him. I haven't tracked her down.

A: Don't make the book a biography of Corky. Make it a historical novel.

Q: *I have gathered information from most of his life. The stories are filled with pathos. I have discovered little virtue. I am headed in the right direction?*

A: Sure. I question your writing a biography because there will be parts of his life that are missing. You could never be completely true to him. Consider a thematic approach. Examine books on Nixon and Watergate. They don't tell Nixon's whole story. They focus only on Nixon at Watergate.

Q: *I'm reaching for the real Corky. Understanding his struggle may lead to meaning in his words to me. I need not examine every detail of his life.*

A: Exactly.

Q: *No one could explore all of Corky's caves. Corky meant a lot to you.*

A: I perceived him as taking a journey. The process caused him to reject the slightest sign of intimacy. For some unknown reason, Corky was guided by a mysterious sense of truth. That is why Gethsemani worked.

Q: *Why did he confide in me? What caused him to open up to me? I did ask, "Why me?" Only his death short-circuited my intent to videotape his story. Did Corky and I really connect? My understanding of life has always seemed childlike. Did my openness attract him or was his purpose deeper? I have become the sole remaining spokesman for his life.*

A: There could be a kindred spirit. One chooses who one thinks can handle the truth.

Q: *We were both attracted to Don Quixote through our many quests. Neither of us attained worldly success. Why? We came close on numerous occasions. Success disappeared at the last moment. Were our goals flawed?*

A: That was Corky. Look at his lifestyle. Look at his basketball dreams or what he wanted from the Ronald McDonald House. All his attempts were grandiose. Corky expected success just around the corner. Near misses permeated his endeavors before Gethsemani. Do we know which pursuits reached fruition after he found a home at the monastery?

* * *

An understanding of Corky's struggle lies hidden in the story of Barabbas. "Barabbas" (the movie) was released in 1957. Anthony Quinn starred in the title role. In the opening scene, Roman guards pull Barabbas from his prison cell to be released by Pontius Pilate. He pays a price for his freedom. He stares into the face of the innocent Jesus struggling to pick up His cross.

Barabbas is a murderer. Once free, he returns to a den of debauchery. He brags about his being released instead of Jesus. Fate convinces him that he is a king, as good as any man. While celebrating, he scans the crowd for Rachel. She is the only woman for whom he feels love. But she has listened to Jesus and is now His ardent follower. Rachel describes Jesus' loving message. She yearns for the spiritual kingdom in heaven. Barabbas doesn't understand. Jesus passes on his way to Golgotha. Rachel's heart breaks. Barabbas only ponders.

Barabbas follows Jesus and watches him hang on the cross. From behind the cross, he observes the sky. Suddenly, an eclipse covers the sun. Darkness terrifies the people. Through an eerie haze, the body of Jesus is removed from the cross. The procession carrying Jesus' body passes in front of Barabbas. The Mother of Jesus gazes at Barabbas in sadness and acceptance. The mourners leave the tomb while a heavy round stone conceals the entrance. Unquestionably, Jesus has died and is buried.

Rachel doesn't return to him. Jesus had promised to rise. Barabbas watches her gather a crowd to assure them of the prophecy.

At dawn on Easter morning, Barabbas awakens to enter the empty tomb. He doesn't understand. He encounters apostles who have been hiding. Peter announces that Jesus has risen. They await his arrival. To Barabbas, they are all crazy. He seeks solace among the den of thieves. To re-establish his authority, he kills two challengers. He plans an assault on the temple guards. In the fight, Barabbas becomes distracted. He is recaptured by Roman soldiers.

He reappears before Pilate, who spares him. By law, he cannot be executed by Rome. His debt has been paid by Jesus. Pilate sentences Barabbas to live out his life in the salt mines of Sicily. His life belongs to Rome. He acquires a medallion and chain identifying him as Roman property.

Barabbas becomes a slave in the mines. When men can no longer work, they are killed on the spot. As time passes, the slaves plunge deeper into the mines. In the deepest holes, sulfur causes blindness. At random, a partner is selected. The two men work chained together. His partner is Christian. Hearing the name "Barabbas", the Christian is horrified. Christians love. So he tries to love Barabbas. His kindness entices Barabbas to love him.

My Paradigm

An earthquake strikes the mine, killing the Christian before Barabbas can claw his way to freedom. Profoundly changed, he returns to Rome, burning in the fires set by Emperor Nero. In the street, citizens are blaming the fires on the Christians. Attracted to the Christians, he decides to join them. He discovers a natural talent for setting fires. The Roman soldiers recapture him. They throw him into a dungeon inhabited by Christians. The Christians fail to recognize him. Barabbas wants desperately to become Christian, but he doesn't know how.

Peter is among the Christians. The two meet. Barabbas converts through their conversation.

Barabbas pleads, "I saw His body. He is dead."

"If you were sure, you wouldn't be here. Fish struggle and gasp then die. They want to live."

Barabbas counters, "I saw the discarded wrappings. The tomb was empty. Why did He lie about himself, knowing He would be killed? I saw the body. I know He is dead."

Peter softens, "Why should you believe? When the Spirit of God beckoned, you refused."

"Why would Jesus choose me? Why can't God make himself plain?" Barabbas groans.

Peter's quiet answer, "What has bothered your soul was not nothing. When you think He is farthest, He is nearest. Wrestling with Him is knowledge of Him."

At the end, Barabbas hangs on a cross beside the other Christians. The old world is falling away, making room for the new. In his heart, Barabbas realizes that he is accepted. Though dying, he is finally living. His last words to God "This is Barabbas."

* * *

A paradigm is an adjustment of vision. Fr. Dan Rocco refocused my understanding of Corky. The book is no longer a biography. It is reaching for a deeper understanding. I pray that my search may reveal the truths that he found.

I claim a vision long since forgotten. During my teenage years, Robert Frost enlightened me through his poem entitled, "A Tuft of Flowers." One morning Frost was troding through a newly-mowed grass field. In the glistening dew, he spotted a tuft of flowers thriving alone and beautiful in the sun. After dawn, the mower cut everything down before he noticed these same flowers. Unaccountably, he spared them. Frost discovered, then cherished, their vibrancy. He felt close to the soul who had preserved the wild flowers. The mower valued a beauty that he would not destroy. During my visit with Fr. Rocco, I sensed that Corky spared truths for me to discover. He hadn't planted the truths. He discovered them, spared them, and left them for me. There was no assurance that I would follow. Where will they lead?

Each of us follows his unique path. Corky beckons, awakening my own yearnings. In traveling, he emulated the prodigal son. He prematurely grabbed his inheritance (basketball skills, ability to read people, and deceptive charm). He squandered his talents on lies and grandiose schemes. He pushed away anyone who threatened intimacy. Nothing worked. He begged and stole to feed his addictions. He sank to the depths of despair before attempting suicide. From a distance, his Father beckoned. Corky ignored every call. Nearing death, at the suggestion of Fr. Rocco, he traveled home to Gethsemani. While I knew him, Corky unsuccessfully tried to join that same monastery. In his Father's time, he accepted acceptance. His heart was finally right. Corky had become desperate enough. Only when Corky despaired did the Father's love prevail. His epic struggle to avoid The Hound finally ended. Home at last! Will I recognize Corky's earthly transformation when I return to Gethsemani? His stealing, compulsive behavior, and half-truths pale when measured against his potential triumph. Had someone fed the prodigal son, he would not have returned to his father. Did Corky's struggles lead him to acceptance? His vision is beginning to glow. How far will his tuft of flowers lead me? Corky and I will join at my sunset. May both of our hearts be filled with joy.

"In finding me, you will find yourself." That is what he said. Before I met Fr. Rocco, my role was the observer in this book. I was comfortable remaining unrecognized. Now I am a participant. Only through pursuing Corky, can I encounter him in depth. We have become connected. I apply Corky's view to my own experience. It is time to open up. There is a universality in Corky's life. He pursued worldly success, stumbled, and despaired, but finally found peace. All men are haunted by similar journeys. Now that I see his struggle clearly, I'll keep my own moccasins.

He promised me, "My life has meaning. I want it written. I will help you." He lured me into joining his walk. I cannot remain an observer. Ebenezer Scrooge vowed when faced by the Spirit of Christmas Yet to Come, "Lead me on, Spirit. I know not where you lead."

XX

TAKING IT OUT OF THE CHEESE

Early one morning in November 2001, I visited Jim Murray. After stops for Mass and breakfast, with great anticipation, we left Villanova, PA, bound for the monastery in Bardstown, KY. I had assumed Corky's place as Jim's driver.

We pushed steadily across the Pennsylvania Turnpike, West Virginia, and Ohio. At last the signs said Kentucky. Before midnight, we turned into the driveway leading up the hill to the slumbering monastery.

Jim had called ahead. One of the monks greeted us at the main door. He pointed to the room reserved for the weary travelers. "Our day begins at 3:15 a.m.," he whispered.

Gulp. We agreed to attend the 6:00 a.m. Mass. Surely, Fr. Timothy Kelly lay sleeping somewhere in the building. He had plans to leave the next morning for Cincinnati. Fr. Kelly was the Abbot who accepted Corky into the community. Most intriguing was why he accepted Corky after previously rejecting him. Hopefully, Fr. Timothy could meet with us. The monks enjoy Jim, so I hoped they would cooperate.

I have never been a morning person, but I shuffled to the chapel to witness 50 monks assembled around their simple altar. Most wore the standard black, gray, and white garb of the monastery. In contrast, assorted men stood in civilian garb. No one on the altar noticed us. Huge steel beams (over 25 feet high) supported the simple chapel. The walls were not ornate and I didn't observe any statues. The monks' singing blended enthusiasm with reverence.

After Mass, I played with a bowl of oatmeal in the cafeteria. Timothy Kelly joined us. I expected a professorial former Abbot. We encountered a humorous, thin, direct and open monk.

Q: It's wonderful to sit here with you and the monks. Recently, I spoke with Fr. Dan Rocco, Corky's Spiritual Director in New Jersey. The Spirit called Corky here.

A: I have heard Fr. Rocco's name, but I don't know him.

Q: Fr. Rocco believes that his invitation pointed Corky towards redemption. He is convinced that Corky finally found happiness and peace.

A: In September 1993, Corky was driving through Kentucky bound for California. He stayed with us for a few days. Then he acted as if he were about to move on. Somehow I sensed that he had no real destination and was without money.

I asked if he wanted to stay. "Our monastery has extra work each autumn. Our mail order business picks up for Christmas. Corky, I can give you three hots and a cot at minimum wage from now 'til the first of January. Are you interested?"

He didn't hesitate, "Yes, I am very interested."

So, he became a member of our Community on that basis. He worked over at the Johns Building, packing cheese and fruitcakes. Although he wasn't overly adept at packing, he was wonderful to be around. He lifted everybody's spirits.

At that time, a group of four or five men lived at the monastery under similar conditions. They came from varying backgrounds. One was a Mexican man who was related to one of our brothers. I'm not sure what he was running from. I suspect it was the law. He couldn't read or write. Corky took him under his wing and helped him to get his drivers' license while counseling him. He also assisted other men. At the same time, Corky kept up with his own work. He was always gracious and attended Mass regularly.

On the first of January, Corky visited me to say good-bye. At that same time, Bro. Alban, who ran the switchboard, became sick. Corky had already filled in as greeter of the public on a few occasions.

I told Corky, "We could use you for another month at the gate if you are interested." He replied that he was very interested and that he had recently applied for a job in Louisville.

From that moment, he became a regular at our gatehouse. He was very gracious. People loved him. He was generous with his time and excelled as a good listener.

When January ended, Corky informed me that he had found a job. He had lined up something in Louisville. Then, he suffered a heart attack. During his attack, he drove himself to our local hospital in Bardstown. Later, we transferred him to Jewish Hospital in Louisville.

He was penniless. He carried no medical coverage. Because he had become one of us, we decided to support him. At the end of his hospital stay, he returned here to live in our infirmary for several weeks. That care for him blew his mind. He became a very cooperative, gracious patient. He always got along very well with all the brothers. Meanwhile, the doctors advised him that the damage to his heart was irreparable. His weakened condition would ultimately kill him. The doctors told me that Corky couldn't work again because of the attack.

Corky became despondent about what to do.

I counseled him, "Stay around here. We'll figure out what to do. There is no reason why you can't do the gatehouse thing. The work isn't really that hard."

He accepted my advice and went back to work as our gatekeeper. We relocated him to our family residence on the hill. He was very appreciative and showed it by acting thoughtfully towards everyone. For over a year, he served as our night watchman, switchboard operator, and greeter. Simultaneously, he reached out to our retreatants. They still ask for him.

He never showed signs that his health was getting worse. One spring day, he was scheduled to run the switchboard at noon. He didn't show up. He had attended Mass that morning. Brother Thomas sent someone out to check on him. He had died while he was watching a video which told the story of Ronald McDonald.

Q: Who paid for his tombstone?
A: We did. It is a nice one.

Q: Fr. Rocco described a life-changing experience while Corky lay in the hospital. You visited his bedside to discuss his medical bills. You leaned over him and whispered, "We'll take it out of the cheese." At that moment, he understood that he belonged here. Your words affirmed his value. Your vehicle was the cheese. Does that sound familiar?

A: Yes. It strikes me funny. But it makes sense.

Q: I have visited Bro. Alban twice. He has been very helpful. In particular, I enjoyed hearing Bro. Alban's laugh.

A: Yes. Bro. Alban was very close to Corky. They both enjoyed athletics. Their friendship reminds me that Corky became present to all people.

Q: Apparently, Corky and Bro. Alban cooked up a better way to sell cheese. Corky approached the retreatants when they were ready to leave. Similar to a duty-free shop at the airport, he took orders and delivered the packages at the gate. This convenience spiked sales.

A: Corky was a very handsome man. The lady retreatants, in particular, loved his attention.

Q: His sales approach thrived in a monastery. Were you monks happy with his financial ingenuity?

A: It must have been the November before he died. We were having our annual common anointing service for the old monks. Corky was there so I called, "Corky come up here." We anointed him, too. He was very well-liked. You might find this hard to understand. It is very difficult to live at the edge of our community without intruding too far. He managed it very well. He kept a good rapport with the brothers, but he never intruded too far.

Q: Why were there men in civilian clothes at Mass this morning?

A: We really don't have anyone in Corky's category right now.

Q: Do you think you ever will?

Jim Murray: The thoughtful balance, which Corky maintained with the brothers, required sensitivity and skill. People genuinely loved Corky. A nun in Philadelphia called me wanting to name a children's playground after Corky. He was loved by people of all ages and stations in life.

Q: Did Corky ever exasperate you?

A: No. He had perfected the art of keeping his distance. As a free spirit, he didn't push to get involved. Yet, he was always here. Although he looked good, his health deteriorated. He no longer needed or wanted to wander. He took his responsibility at the gatehouse seriously.

Q: Was he truly happy?

A: He seemed very content. He told me about terrible bouts with depression in his past. He was coming out of a bipolar encounter at the time he arrived. He never experienced depression while he lived here.

Q: Did you notice Corky's inclination towards gambling?

A: I never observed any. He didn't mention much about his past. Briefly, he admitted that gambling had been his burden. The 12-step program had not proved effective for him. He believed that gambling was unique because it doesn't affect your body. Drinking, drugs, and over-eating affect your body. Instead, gambling attacks your psyche, your heart, and your mind. Most people show little empathy towards those who steal money for gambling.

Q: Were you aware that he ripped everyone off, including Jim and me?

A: I didn't know that until now. Corky did acknowledge many bad debts.

Q: Did he express regret?

A: Not in a showy way. Casually, he mentioned that half the United States wanted their money back.

Q: I have not encountered anyone to whom he expressed a desire to repay.

A: He was working on one reconciliation. He hoped to reconcile with his daughter.

Jim Murray: I believe that Corky remembered every dollar that he had taken. He sized up everyone for the purpose of getting money. His actions were not omissions. His were commissions. Hits were totally premeditated.

Q: His conversion from a life as a gambler to the person you describe is spectacular. Did remnants of his previous life deprive him of total happiness here?

He was very content living here. He acknowledged his past. He talked constantly about God's mercy. He was aware that he had been incapable of living on the outside.

I'm unsure how depressed he had become before he arrived here. I don't know whether he would have driven into an abutment if I had let him leave on that Monday morning.

Jim Murray: Corky wore many masks. Somehow, God gave you insight that he had nowhere to go. I am so thankful that he stayed.

Q: What was his reaction to your questioning his lack of money? Did he understand that you were saying, "I care about you"?

A: It is very hard to say. Corky was not that open.

Q: Why were women visiting Gethsemani so attracted to him?

A: He had charisma. He became totally present. Most people come here looking for something. They need to tell their story. Corky listened without judging. Corky gave them a good word without revealing very much about himself.

Q: Corky was a charismatic person, rarely exposing his true self. Is there a parallel with Jesus? Strangers came to Jesus, and He truly listened. Rarely did He reveal even a small part of Himself.

A: In his humanity, listening was all Corky had to give.

Q: Bro. Alban told me a wonderful story. Years ago, Thomas Merton debated another deep thinking member of your community. Merton stated, "We know that God is omnipotent and omnipresent. He is definitely not a Moral Theologian." The other priest could say nothing. Who was the other priest?

A: Raymond Flanagan.

Q: Apparently Raymond has nothing to add to Merton's summation.

A: No. He is an old Jesuit.

Q: Let's examine your decision to take care of Corky in the hospital. Were expenses balanced by an enormous amount of cheese?

A: There was no doubt in my decision. I could see in his eyes, that he had been deeply moved and changed. The brothers served him every meal. For this, he was grateful. Corky was the second of only two people to ever penetrate our infirmary. The other was Abbot Bernard's brother. Corky became very popular. Many people visit his grave to this day.

Q: Were you Abbot when he died?

A: Yes.

Q: Bro. Alban told me that you discovered his body. Pills were all over the floor.

A: He had reached for his nitroglycerin. Had he been dead long? I anointed him.

Q: Was Corky on his way out at the time of his death? Had he worn out his welcome?

A: No. He was living on the edge of our community very well. No one ever complained about him. He certainly pulled his weight.

Q: Was his stay here the happiest time of his life?

A: That was certainly my impression.

Jim Murray: Corky considered himself a counselor for the monks. He was particularly close with Derick. Corky formed close relationships with many of the monks.

Q: Did Corky have a Spiritual Director while he was here?

A: He used to come and talk to me.

Q: Had he stopped searching?

A: He was very much at peace. He had become aware that he could depend on the mercy of God. Soon he was going to die, but he had no fear of death. Corky had arrived Home at last.

* * *

Fr. Timothy left us smiling as he embarked on his drive to Cincinnati. It was still early morning. We decided to speak with another monk, Fr. Allan Gilmore. But first, Jim and I discussed our experience with the Abbot. Interviews benefit from having more than two people present. While one of us talked, the other observed and pondered. Jim Murray added wisdom to the Abbot's words.

Jim Murray: Corky might be the most wounded soul ever to come here. He had just lost his mother and he was suffering because no one contacted him. Angry and hurt, he ran out of my office. Then, we drove him here looking for healing. His process began here at Gethsemani during Holy Week.

No accident, it was God's timing for him to return here. Fr. Timothy knew Corky well enough to sense that he had nowhere to go. His journey led him here. "I'm heading for the West Coast." What a typical Corky non-answer. Corky always looked so confident. No one ever guessed when he was penniless. Fr. Timothy penetrated his facade. The Lord whispered in his ear, "Ask him."

Fr. Rocco extended the invitation. Corky had accepted the invitation back in New Jersey. His future was down to very few options. Corky wanted to believe that he had alternatives. His non-plan became a plan. "I'm going to the West Coast." Believe me, Corky was already calculating whom he was going to hit. When Fr. Timothy, asked "How about staying here with us?" he ignited a God sent mystical change in Corky's life.

Think about the history of this monastery. After the Second World War, the Trappists expanded Gethsemani and many other monasteries. Retreatants, who had experienced the horrors of war, battled memories. Although Corky never joined the military, he fought internal combat, the demons within himself. The Trappists opened their many monasteries as a refuge for these tortured men. Corky fought his own war. Here his battle ended.

Fr. Timothy (the little general) invited Corky to join his troops. The generosity of St. Benedict's order summons all who venture within these walls. Here they encounter Christ. Here we become children of God.

Q: Fr. Timothy would not say anything negative about Corky. Why?

Jim Murray: You asked him repeatedly. Your questions seemed appropriate. This Abbot never sugar-coats his answers. On the contrary, he assured us that Corky fulfilled a need here. Corky's acceptance passed beyond a welcome. The Abbot whispered, "We'll take it out of the cheese."

That answer expanded the invitation way beyond acceptance. Fr. Timothy helped us realize how much the monks loved Corky. Think about the people who visit Corky's grave. We are just recognizing the astoundingly beautiful ending to Corky's life.

Look at the symbolism. We encountered the Abbot before he, too, left us for his road. He extended himself by giving us an hour. Corky would have done the same. Picture Corky about to jump into his car prior to driving to Bardstown. Corky also would have stopped to sit with us.

Q: I felt comfortable with Fr. Timothy. He was very insightful and bright. Didn't he laugh and enjoy our conversation?

Jim Murray: This man had a very responsible job. Gethsemani is the most renowned Trappist monastery in the United States. Once home to Thomas Merton, the Dahli Lahma visited here. Imagine the people Fr. Timothy has encountered.

Q: Did you see similarities between Fr. Timothy and Corky? They share the gift of reading people. Fr. Timothy experienced no friction with Corky.

Jim Murray: He stated something that he alone could know. Corky was totally accepted here. He never became a member of the community, but he belonged. Corky joined the Cistercians without buying a habit.

Q: Fr. Timothy could have accepted Corky with, "You're covered." Instead, he gifted Corky with his cheese comment. Fr. Timothy laughed when he told that story.

Jim Murray: His response was very Benedictine. It's their rule. Charity is the virtue they are supposed to show. His consistent response followed the mission statement of the Trappist organization. When it comes down to where the rubber hits the road, the Abbot pledged unequivocally, "By your work and your generosity, you have earned our acceptance." No cheese, no bond. His was a typical open monastic reaction.

Q: Does unconditional acceptance happen to many people?

Jim Murray: Fr. Timothy played the role of the Good Samaritan. "Here, take care of what he needs. On the way back, I'll take care of anything else."

Q: Did you realize that so many people visit his grave?

Jim Murray: He matched the perfect job with the perfect gift. He welcomed everyone because he was the greeter. Fr. Timothy assumed responsibility for every soul who approached him. "Father, I have a vocation." "Father, I don't." "Father, I want to leave." "Father, I want another monk to leave." His experience was total. He became aware of everybody and everybody's inner thoughts. This morning, his conversation with us couldn't have been more generous, more open, or more terrific.

Q: And enthusiastic.

Jim Murray: Each monk cultivated a unique relationship with Corky. You will meet Allan and Damien. You need each of these monks' unique view of Corky.

On the day that Corky died, Timothy called my home. I was in Morgantown, West Virginia. He connects with anyone, anywhere.

Q: Who is this Allan? Is he another monk?

Jim Murray: I hope we can talk to him. He was the priest who elevated the chalice at Mass this morning.

You are mistakenly caught up in the mechanics of Corky's travels. Why did he leave Washington? Where was he headed? Was he setting the monks up? We can never know his intent. The Trappists have lived here for over a century. They issued the invitation. His spiritual journey finally reached fruition. We all reject numerous invitations. As a result, we reject God over and over.

Fr. Timothy pursued us. While we sat here having breakfast in the cafeteria, he just appeared. He desired to be with us. Fr. Gilmore might also appear. He doesn't like washing clothes.

* * *

Jim was right. Soon, we were joined by the most joy-filled priest I have ever met. In his late 60s, he spoke openly and childlike. I loved the glint in his eye. He had discovered joy in any topic. He spelled his last name, GILMORE. The name means "Servant of Mary" in Gaelic.

Q: Describe your first encounter with Corky.

Fr. Allan: Well, I thought he was Jim's chauffeur. He was a tall man who seemed to be a nice guy. As time passed, I got to know him quite well. He drove a car named "Thomas Merton". The license plate was "XGM." (Note: Jim's former employer, the Eagles.)

Q: Would you believe that I have not read Thomas Merton?

Fr. Allan: It is not over yet. Nobody can read everything he wrote. Merton lived here for 13 years. The day he left was the only time I spoke to him. At that time, I was working in the bookkeeping office. To date, I have held 20 different jobs. Job changes happen when you don't have any talent. Merton came to me for money to finance his pilgrimage to the east. Louis Norbet (our treasurer) chided him, "Are you going over there to stop the war?"

Merton responded: "No. I'm not going to touch it." That put an end to that subject.

Then he turned to me and said, "I'm sorry I won't be here for your ordination."

I was surprised. He had lived as a hermit for three years. I didn't think he knew who I was. He was always very thoughtful. His comment told me two things. First, he was going to be gone for a while. My ordination was a year or two away. Also, he assured me that he approved of my ordination. I was 39 at that time.

He was a man of no pomposity. He had perfected his own way of creating a distance. He could become very serious, especially during homilies. Of his many homilies, my favorite was presented here on Easter in 1967. It has been printed in a book titled "He is Risen." He compared the stone in front of Jesus' grave with the stone in front of our hearts. I consider it very profound.

Q: Do you recall the last thing Corky said to you?

Fr. Allan: He confided, "Allan, I have never been so happy in my life. I am with people who love me and people whom I love." I could tell that his sentiments were real. He had become so peaceful. Although aware of his dangerous heart condition, he kept pushing himself. I observed him carrying many boxes of cheese and fruitcakes between buildings. Most of our monks wouldn't do that.

Corky was wonderful at the switchboard. Fr. Timothy hoped that he could stay as our greeter for two or three years. But the Lord wanted him more. He was so well liked.

Q: Did your Abbot accept him through a comment about cheese?

Fr. Allan: That was a joke. The Abbot always had the power to include him in our community. Corky needed to become one of us before he could be covered by insurance. The enclosure (or boundaries) of the monastery is framed inside the Abbot's head. His enclosure establishes our geographic limits. Enclosure defines our monastery.

Q: *Then Corky was in?*

Fr. Allan: He entered under a special category. Maybe it was one of a kind. Uniqueness is a good thing. A lot of us are characters.

When I was younger, I made a comment about another monk, "He is a character, isn't he?"

My friend observed, "Yes, but we wouldn't want two of him in this community."

Q: Imagine two Corkys in any community. He developed a unique presentation to the outside world.

Fr. Allan: He could have become a great salesman. He needed only to accept himself. He grew to understand that he was lovable. Through that realization, he became able to love. After he described his background, I considered it a miracle that he was still alive.

Q: What was your most profound interaction with Corky?

Fr. Allan: I had been asked to give him instructions to help him return to the Catholic church. The two of us journeyed to New Haven to purchase the instructional books. By then Corky had become deeply interested. And he was truly convinced.

Q: He is well remembered by the monks. Why is this?

Fr. Allan: His size was one thing. I never witnessed the withdrawn side of him at all. The changed Corky was always outgoing and warm.

Q: Do you know why he was protective of women?

Fr. Allan: He confided to me that he had been trashed many times during his life. He believed that many women also had been trashed.

Q: Did you ever hear him stutter?

Fr. Allan: No.

Q: When he would be around women, would he stutter?

Fr. Allan: We all do that.

Q: He told me about the two times he tried to commit suicide. He could only sit there paralyzed.

Fr. Allan: I couldn't imagine that scene. He was so opposite of depressed when I knew him. Nor did he show bi-polar signs. Everything he did indicated that he had been cured.

Q: What single characteristic personified Corky?

Fr. Allan: Joyful. None of us can fake joy. It bubbles out of us like the head on a beer. Corky exuded joy to everyone. I have no doubt that it was real. Corky enjoyed living here. He spread his heaven-sent joy.

XXI

WORKING RELATIONSHIPS THAT DIDN'T

Mike Mintern, when we spoke, was President of the Malvern Retreat House in Pennsylvania, the largest lay retreat house in the world. It hosts over 20,000 retreatants each year. In younger days, Mike taught at a Catholic high school in Philadelphia. During those summers, he worked for Catholic Charities. 25 years later, Mike's career focused mainly on fundraising. Coincidentally, he was participating in a major fundraising campaign for the Kentucky Trappists when he met Corky.

Q: How were you connected to Gethsemani?

A: I attended my first retreat when I was 17 at a Trappist monastery in Conyers, Georgia. That initial retreat opened my mind to value the Catholic spiritual life. Now I embrace the dimension of me that will always be a Trappist. Although I have never been attracted to the life of the monks, deep inside lies a contemplative spirit. Over the years, I have visited most of the Trappist monasteries in the United States. I have missed Utah and Northern California. Each monastery afforded me a little spot to rest my head. During the days, I made my way to chapel. I enjoy discovering special places to pray on my own. It seems primordial. I get up at 3:00 a.m. to join the monks for prayer. To me, that awakening calls the earth into existence. The monks' worship is called Lauds. Later, in the afternoon, we experience Vespers. Our day follows the way of the birds. I once observed some roosters beginning to crow. The sun had not yet risen. About a half hour before the sun rises, roosters feel the heat.

It is not the light that makes them crow. When the monks get up in the middle of the night, they desire to keep vigil with Our Lord. They respond to the call of the One True God. By their presence they are saying "Lord, help me with my existence."

Professionally, I was assigned to the Trappist monastery in Kentucky. For over a year, I served as their fundraiser. The year was 1985.

Q: *When did you meet Corky?*

A: Also in 1985. The fundraising project had just started. The monks assigned me the room next to Jim Murray and Corky. We were all Philly guys. A few days earlier, I had placed a phone call urging Jim to get involved with the Trappists. We drove to Kentucky. Along came Corky. As we rode, I listened to endless talk about the Michael Jackson Tour. I noted that they had christened their van "Thomas Merton."

Q: *Was Corky quiet during the trip?*

A: No. He talked all the time. My intuition warned me that Corky was funny business. I didn't know Jim well enough to grasp what he was doing with this character. Jim's assessment of Corky was the opposite. To him, Corky was the real thing. Little by little, I learned about their connection through Leonard Tose and gambling. Corky and Jim had become close friends through helping gambling addicts.

Q: *Was Jim helping Corky?*

A: Early on, I observed Jim's many helping relationships. Jim was an accomplished helper. Many people hung around him hoping to regain their equilibrium.

Q: *Was Corky Jim's project?*

A: I never saw Jim take anyone on as a project. Jim's response to Corky was authentic. At that time, I didn't expect Corky to become very important in my life. As time went on, I grew closer to Jim. Corky became an increasingly important part of the equation.

One morning, Corky decided to psychoanalyze me. My reaction was immediate. Corky was full of shit. I was able to identify the difference between a guy trying to resolve his own stuff and someone trying to gain an advantage. My college degree is in Philosophy.

Q: *Was he talking to the wrong guy?*

A: Yes. I need guidance as much as anyone. But I don't value it from Corky. I spent weeks in his company. I studied his act. At first, I found him likeable. I loved listening to his colorful sports stories. He was entertaining and likeable. He was not a guy with whom I could feel simpatico.

Q: Did he play you? Did he try to discover your vulnerabilities?
A: I don't think I was that significant to him. There was a jadedness about Corky. He assumed everyone else was searching for an angle.

Q: Get them before they get you?
A: Something like that. He truly believed that "Everyone is looking for his own deal." I haven't met many people with his philosophy. Corky acted street smart. His "wise guy" dimension became apparent to me. I am reasonably aware of the ways of the street. But I would never work people over the way he did. I balanced our ways with the spirituality of St. Francis de Sales. We aspired to be a gentlemen, which prevailed over street smarts. Corky lacked gentlemanly spirituality. He viewed life closer to that of an alley cat.

Q: What particular experiences caused you to know Corky?
A: Later that same year, Jim and Corky revisited the monastery. Corky began keeping company with some woman. They made googlie eyes at each other. Corky's lady friend directed a Ronald McDonald House in Kentucky. Corky had become sweet on her. Corky and I were sitting in a Louisville hotel lobby with a couple of hours to kill. Jim had wandered off. Corky decided to psychoanalyze me. In a few minutes I grasped what he was doing. Dr. Sigmund Devlin was gifting me with answers to the questions of my life. All I could think was, "Who the hell is this guy?" Conversely, there was something very compelling about Corky. He talked openly about his own demons. I was 32 years old. But I could see that he was searching for conversion in his own life, yearning to be something better than who he was.

I asked him when he became aware of his gambling problem. He responded with a story, also centered around sitting in a hotel lobby. Corky had lost $200,000. Obsessed with grabbing more money, he stopped because he couldn't figure out a way to mooch more money.

Those numbers seemed huge in my world. Later, I observed how he embellished stories. I also noticed that his stories were laced with inaccuracies. I worried that Corky was taking advantage of Jim. Because Jim was a good soul, he was vulnerable to predators. My instincts convinced me that Jim was good, so I wanted to trust his judgment of Corky.

As time passed, I questioned the reconciliation story with his daughter. I detected distortions. I cannot imagine a child, missing for most of her life, reconciling in one visit. All that he could reasonably accomplish during that first visit was an openness to reconciliation. There is no instant intimacy. Corky was 50 and strung out. I believe that while traveling with Jim, Corky searched for that safe place which links heaven and earth. The searcher finds answers through a person reflecting the best of who he is. Jim became that person for Corky.

Jim is protective and loving towards Corky. He and I view Corky differently. Although I respect Jim's view, I don't get it. For example, take Jim's attachment to Leonard Tose. Jim was recently interviewed about Leonard's life on *NBC Nightline*. I told Jim my opinion: "Jimmy, why would anyone watch a movie about a guy who abused everyone? Tose abused himself and ultimately lost the Philadelphia Eagles along with his fortune."

To a lesser degree, I feel similarly about your book. That the book has evolved into a story about conversion, makes me think entirely differently. I don't understand, but I realize that you may be uncovering a message. While I served as Director at Malvern, I have discovered that all our lives are linked through similar struggles. Each weekend I observe guys struggle with reality and commitment. Some have been off track for 25 years. They have lost any sense of how to get back. With God's grace, they find a way to ask, "Help me." One guy confided, "I haven't been able to get out of bed in the morning for three months." After each retreat weekend, I whisper to my wife: "With the problems I have heard, not only couldn't I get out of bed, I couldn't face the rest of my life." Some tragedies retreatants create. Others just happened. Yet, God's grace beckons to them, "Come back." When you introduced Corky's possible conversion, I became excited. Had I missed that dimension in his life? I had not seen that. I would love to learn more about your work. Corky's change would be a wonderful result of hanging with Jim.

Q: You don't believe that Corky changed?

A: I visited him before he died; I didn't see it. I traveled to Kentucky in September of 1994 (seven months before he died.) I always enjoyed visiting Gethsemani. Fr. Allan Gilmore told me that Corky was living in the guesthouse. We walked up the hill in the late afternoon. I remember our conversation on the new outside patio. Corky had recently written some negative letters. He sent one to Jim. He did not want to discuss the letters.

Q: Did he seem healthy and happy?

A: He told me that he was recovering from his heart attack. God had been good to him. I thanked God for putting Trappists on this earth.

Q: Can you expand?

A: Even rascals need a place to go. All evil traits and understanding of weaknesses acquired during our lives are crap. Some of us accumulate more than others. We start believing that each person is defined by his traits. It's not true. Addiction and illness are dysfunctions. Left to our worst devices, each of us acquires negative traits and habits. Left to our best devices (Gethsemani), we are nurtured enough to let go of the nonsense in our life. The more weakness we understand and jettison, the closer we draw to our goal: the realization that we are children of God. Each of us craves to be affirmed. The Trappist monastery is one place where affirmation is possible. It is important that the monastery became Corky's place. About half the monastery's visitors are guys who have become confused. Many souls find a life at the monastery. Others, after discovery, go back into the world. Thomas Merton was a great example. He was once a lost person, who found himself among the Trappists.

Q: *I was intimidated by the monks on that first morning. They appeared so distant. You're saying they are approachable.*

A: Your experience is common. Most of the monks are simple open men. They want to help in any way. Their lives are as human as ours.

Q: *Do you understand Corky's struggle to be good? Success came as a result of his acceptance at Gethsemani.*

A: People do bad things. Do not confuse them with bad people. It wasn't easy to see, but Corky did have a fundamental goodness. The eyes of God saw him better than I. Corky may have been a good person who had done bad things.

In 1994, I did not comprehend any big conversion. He seemed less troubled. He had benefited from grace freely given at the monastery. His change didn't strike me as dramatic. Fr. Allan Gilmore assured me that he had seen a conversion in Corky. When I think back, Allan makes sense. Corky had joined the monks and he became one of them.

Monasteries over the world include merciful exceptions to their rule. The monks accept guys living around the fringes. These guys just can't quite enter through the front door or the back door. The term is, "They are not regularized." Monasteries make room for these souls. Observe their civilian clothes when you attend services.

Q: *The wannabe's?*

A: Yes. The wannabes. Emotional or canonical reasons keep them from entering all the way into the community. Unofficially, the monks make a place for them.

In our confusing world, conversion appears to be a parting of the clouds. It's not a gift that any of us grasp or merit. The key is our disposition to let God do it.

As we mature, we realize that our demons are similar to everyone else's. None of us is capable of avoiding demons. This realization draws us towards dealing with them. No one is good enough or better than anyone else. We learn that we have no reason to feel superior simply because our demons don't appear to be as bad as another person's.

Here is a story about the meaning of conversion. In the '20s, Simone Weil, a brilliant Jewish girl, was born. She earned a Doctorate in Philosophy in the early '40s in France. In those days, a female doctor was unusual.

Simone discovered Jesus. Although she believed in him, she never converted. She never reconciled her Jewish roots. She practiced the Jewish traditions (staying Jewish), while she believed that she could be faithful to both faiths. She agonized all her life about the religion to which she should belong.

A book entitled 'Waiting for God' tells her story. In 1942, French President General de Gaulle brought Simone to England to be part of the French government in exile. She authored the new constitution for the Fourth Republic. This brilliant young woman actually rewrote the French constitution. While in England, she decided not to live any differently than her fellow Jews, imprisoned in concentration camps. She ate only portions of food similar to those who were suffering. Subsequently, her health declined and she died. She was buried in a Catholic cemetery in Canterbury, England. I have visited her grave.

At the end of her book, she describes her experience of conversion. In her view, conversion starts with embracing our world with all its tragedy. The God we worship is not a God of holy pictures. He is the God of brokenness who embraces the total human experience. If we refuse to embrace this God, we delude ourselves, wasting our entire lives.

* * *

Mike gave his view on Jim Murray's oceanfront deck in Sea Isle City, NJ. That day I talked to another of Corky's co-workers.

Carol Johnston is a pretty, middle-aged woman with an outgoing personality and a warm smile. She served as Jim Murray's office manager for over 20 years. Her adversarial interaction with Corky was continuous.

Q: How did you see Corky Devlin?

A: Everyone has a good side and a dark side. I encountered more of Corky's dark side. I grew uneasy in his presence. At first, I wasn't sure why. The day Corky sauntered into our office, I read him. I watched him work Jim and his wife, Diane. They have hearts of gold. Corky's manipulation frustrated me. I felt very guilty. I berated myself for being judgmental. All the while, I really believed he was manipulative. Because I didn't like sitting in judgment, I remained silent for a very long time. Corky was a user. Jim and Diane were blind to his act. For me, it has been a tremendous experience knowing them. Corky thrived with his hidden agenda.

Q: Give me an example.

A: The Murray's own a beach house in Sea Isle City, NJ. Corky disappeared one winter. In January, we discovered him living in the beach house without the Murrays' knowledge. He had run up phone bills of over $700 every month. He pried open a door and made himself at home. This was not the first time. He had been firmly instructed not to come back.

One Thursday, Diane and I drove down to prepare the house for a retreat weekend. We were shocked when we found Corky asleep in the Master bedroom.

Diane screamed, "Get out."

He picked up his clothes and walked right past us without saying a word. Diane was furious. Corky remained nonchalant.

Q: What gall! Do you remember any good times?

A: I was happy to see Corky enter the Church. I had prayed that he would turn his will over to God. I was confident that, if Corky surrendered, he could change. I was very excited when, apparently, he changed. We all celebrated with him. Unfortunately, before long I recognized the same old Corky.

Q: He played the role of coming into the Church well.

A: Extremely well. There were times when he and I prayed together. Corky acted humble, even asking forgiveness in certain situations. We enjoyed numerous conversations about spiritual things. Corky was warmly welcomed into our spiritual circles. We supported him in trying to change his life. We cared about him. We became his family because we knew how hard it is to change. My friends had helped me over and over during the time I tried to change my life.

But pretty soon, the same old lies and distortions slipped out of Corky's mouth. I couldn't understand why Corky took advantage of those who had been so open to him. They had grown oblivious to the evils of worldly possessions and earthly knowledge. For Jim and Diane, relationships were far more important than worldly goods. They loved Corky where he was. Increasingly, I saw him take advantage of Jim and Diane Murray.

Q: Once you observed his behavior, what did you do?

A: I set a new goal. It was to keep Corky out of our lives at any cost. I went to Jim and Diane to explain what I had seen and heard.

Q: What had you seen and heard?

A: Corky talked to me about Jimmy in very negative terms. We worked together. When Jimmy was away at meetings, Corky began 15-minute diatribes about how Jimmy was getting on his last nerve.

I finally asked Corky: "Have you said any of this to Jimmy? Why don't you talk to him like a man? Explain your difficulties to him. You travel together."

Corky never faced Jimmy. One day, Corky called me at the office from the road. I challenged him that now was the time to air his gripes. When they returned, I learned that he had not uttered a word.

Some of his actions were underhanded. Corky solicited friends of Jimmy. He should never have approached them.

They contacted Diane and me. "Who is this Corky guy? Why is he saying such things about Jim behind his back?"

One day, Corky slithered into the office. Jimmy was sitting in the back office.

I challenged Corky: "Have you confronted Jimmy about the things that bother you?"

Corky had not. So, I told Jimmy what Corky was saying. Most of his comments were hurtful. When I returned the following day, Jimmy had confronted him. That was the last day Corky visited our office. He left with his tail between his legs. Corky was a typical con man. He felt uncomfortable around those who had his number. I had his number.

Q: What did Corky say about Jim that was untrue?

A: Some things were personal. Whatever Jimmy was doing, Corky put it down. He was tired of walking in Jimmy's shadow. Everywhere they went, Corky took second place. Jim Murray co-founded The Ronald McDonald House. Corky was jealous.

Corky approached some of Jimmy's friends behind his back. He asked for money. That money was supposedly for Jimmy (who had no knowledge of what Corky was doing.)

Q: Did he actually get money and pocket it?

A: I do not know. Jimmy received phone calls a year apart from friends wanting to know what was going on. They did not want to embarrass Jimmy. After much hemming and hawing, Corky admitted that he had asked for money because Jimmy needed it. That was completely untrue.

It was rare for Corky to have any relationship without trying to con the other person. Corky never trusted people enough to allow them to love him.

Q: Corky was a coward?

A: I said that to him. I challenged him that he bitched to me, but he lacked the courage to face Jimmy. I ordered him never to say one more word about Jimmy. I called him a coward to his face. His lack of a response surprised me. He never argued. He did not know what to do with me. The con man had never been confronted.

Q: Did he pick on women while honoring them at the same time?

A: I never saw him interact with women. His phone bills resulted from calling women friends.

Q: Corky was the classic louse. Would you agree?

A: Corky owned no vehicle at the time. He used the Murray's van, which he always borrowed. One day after borrowing Diane's van, he called her from some place in New Jersey. He complained that the van ran out of gas and described where he had parked it. Then he disappeared. Diane called me and I drove her to Jersey. We filled the van with gas before she could drive it home. I was furious. He took advantage of people who cared most about him.

Q: Did he push the former NBA player role?

A: Not in my presence.

Q: Image was everything. What people thought of him was paramount?

A: Yes. He came off as the ladies' man. His persona never impressed me. Once he dated Marion Gibson. She seemed like a nice person. This was 20 years ago. Corky never married her.

Q: Did you meet Dr. Sylvan Tompkins?

A: I visited his place a number of times. He and Jim hung out at the racetracks. Sylvan was one of the most unusual men I ever met. He was brilliant and he had written many books.

Jim and I visited Professor Tompkins in Strathmere, NJ. He was an accomplished horseplayer. Rocky usually met us there.

Q: What was your impression of Rocky?

A: I'm getting in trouble. Birds of a feather flock together.

Q: Who were the other feathers?

A: Corky and Rocky. Con men to the ninth power. I loved Rocky. I even loved Corky, although I didn't like him. Rocky was a smooth little Italian guy who, in his prime, was something hot. He had an alcohol problem which propelled him into a tough life. The four amigos spent wonderful times together. Jim was the stable force for the group. They loved each other to the degree that each was capable.

Q: Corky was not capable of deep love?

A: To the degree that he was able, he loved Jim. Corky was gifted with every capability he could possibly want. I watched him hell-bent on destroying himself.

Q: Did he feel worthy of their love?

A: He had a good thing and he succeeded in destroying it.

Q: On projects, did Corky recognize his own meager contributions?

A: He was a hanger-oner. He never did much work. On numerous occasions, he dropped Jim Murray's name to raise his value with those he met. Along with Jim's name went McDonalds. If you are a con man and a bullshitter (Corky was superior at both), you know how to work people. Near the end, con was all that remained. When I looked at him, he knew that I was on to him. Not Jimmy, however. The Murrays were generous to a fault. Their forgiveness knew no bounds. Corky became extremely arrogant. On the night we found him in the Murray's bed, he was not contrite. I doubt if he thought to apologize.

Q: That is unbelievable!

A: Diane sent me to the bathroom to start cleaning. I was on the verge of exploding. That was who Corky was. He never considered cleaning the bathroom.

XXII

FOR HIM THE BELL TOLD

"Master Greenhalgh is too tall for kindergarten. Put him in the line of first graders."

Those words, expelled me from the first-day kindergarten line of boys at Waldron Academy. My promotion prevented me from being a classmate of Bert Bell Jr. It was September, 1941. Pearl Harbor would be bombed in three months. The world slumbered on the brink of change. At five, I was preoccupied with blending in a line of boys who were vertically compatible. That was my introduction to the Mercy nuns of Waldron in Merion, PA.

Bert Bell's father founded the National Football League. Everyone knew him as Bert Bell. His real first name was DeBenneville. In the '30s, DeBenneville married Frances Upton. On her wedding day, Mrs. Bell was lead singer and dancer with Flo Ziegfield's Follies. In shows of the day, Frances acted opposite the great Eddie Cantor. In 1933, DeBenneville purchased the defunct Frankford Yellow Jackets football team (defunct, a polite way to say they were out of money.) He renamed his team the Philadelphia Eagles. The Great Depression ended shortly after his purchase. DeBenneville and Frances resided with their two boys (Bert and Upton) and daughter (Janie) at the family-owned Ritz Carlton in Philadelphia. DeBenneville breathed life and vision into his Eagles. He assumed the title, "First Commissioner of the National Football League."

During those years, professional football struggled as a novelty. Television was not yet available in family homes. Pro football provided stimulation for players who needed to bang more heads beyond college. Heads were protected by leather helmets, not by today's highly protective cages. DeBenneville sensed what pro football could become. His league now resembles Roller Ball in many ways. Teams represent American cities in a passionate struggle to claim supremacy (the Super Bowl.) He instituted revenue sharing and introduced sudden death to the playoffs. Most profitable was his marketing of team jerseys. Today, revenue from merchandise is shared (except by Jerry Jones) by each NFL franchise. Professional football is now the most beloved sports attraction in our country. Weekly clashes attract has-beens, never-wases and wannabes, rekindling childhood dreams by cramming into stadiums. DeBenneville chose Sunday as game day because, at that time, professional football didn't dare compete with college games. Now the opposite is true.

As pro football grew, DeBenneville moved Frances, Bert Jr., Upton and Janie to Narberth, PA. He wanted to avoid the Philadelphia city wage tax. National Football League headquarters was relocated to nearby Bala Cynwyd. A growing number of league employees avoided that same tax.

The Eagles grew in popularity throughout the '40s. Bert and I sat in opposite stands of Shibe Park on a snowy afternoon while the Eagles defeated the Chicago Cardinals for the league championship (1949.) Sr. sold his Eagles to a group of 100 Philadelphia businessmen, headed by Jim Clark. In 1959, Bert Sr. negotiated a deal to buy back the team. He wanted to have his sons own and operate the Eagles. The deal came within days of being completed. On a crisp November afternoon, while watching his Eagles play the Pittsburgh Steelers at Franklin Field, Bert Sr. suffered a heart attack. Sons Bert and Upton had come within three days of owning the Philadelphia Eagles.

Bert and Upton enrolled at Waldron. For eight years, the boys' lives were shaped by the Mercy nuns. No other influence in those early years matched that of the nuns. The nuns' values have never really dimmed for me. My brother, Peter, sells industrial real estate in Philadelphia. He often refers to "The curse of his Waldron conscience." He cannot lie. For better or worse, our values were engrained in us.

After Waldron, Bert and Upton enrolled at Malvern Prep where we spent four more years. I had not seen Bert in 49 years. I learned from Jim Murray that Bert and Corky had been rivals. Bert, once business manager of the Baltimore Colts football team, had written sports for a newspaper in Baltimore. More recently (since 1978), he had been a dealer at Bally's Casino in Atlantic City.

Corky hung out with Bert Bell. They became friends in Baltimore in the '60s and continued their rivalry in Atlantic City. Corky claimed to have maneuvered more than one girlfriend away from Bert. Could the rivalry between Corky and Bert shed light on Corky's methods and motivations?

I left messages at Bally's Casino. One morning, Bert returned my call. Bert worked only on the evening shift. We reunited the following Monday morning at Hanna Gs restaurant in Ventnor, NJ.

As I entered Hanna Gs, I was intrigued by Bert's resemblance to his father. Bert's appearance and facial expressions are identical to my memory of DeBenneville. His newspaper background and relationships with sports personalities made Bert humorous and insightful. His description of Corky's selfish behavior provided refreshing insights. Bert places high value on honesty. He observes people's personalities. I found it natural to trust his judgment.

Q: Is there a single characteristic of Corky's personality that stands out?

A: Corky was obsessed about winning. For the rest of us, after a pickup basketball game, we forgot the score. I easily forgot details of completed games. I focused on the next game. Not Corky. He lost often during his life. When things didn't go his way, he reacted immaturely.

Q: Being fatherless left scars. Could that have caused his need to keep proving himself?

A: Maybe he felt competitively inferior to men. That's why he picked on women.

Q: He picked on women?

A: After failing among his peers, both in basketball and with women, Corky needed to compete with me. I provided a chance to prove himself. Even today, I dismiss Corky through comments like "Yes, I knew Corky, but I never needed him." I was never in competition with him. I didn't care how successful he felt. His women were usually those with whom the flame had died.

Corky was never abusive towards women. He picked on them to feel better about himself. He courted many women. I sensed that he wanted to prove something to himself.

Corky was a ROUE, always on the make. Name-dropping was a big part of his act. Corky perfected his role as the consummate con artist. NBA guys like Bob Ferry warned me not to loan Corky money. To me, he was enjoyable company. Whenever the two of us hung out alone, I enjoyed being with him. He was verbal and we enjoyed similar things.

I returned to Margate from Baltimore in 1978, during the process of a divorce. I agreed to give my ex-wife our Beatles records. They have since become priceless. I got our washer and dryer. The condo I bought in Margate already had a washer and dryer. I ended up giving the old ones to Ratso. She was a slithery, lovable little creep from Hoboken. We worked together at Resorts.

Q: Did Corky hit on Ratso?

A: No. She was too smart for him. She was a street urchin who told him to get lost with his charm. In the end, she ran off with a girl.

Q: Is that why she didn't dig Corky?

A: No. At the time, she was doing guys. If Corky had pursued her, she would have ignored him. She ran off about five years ago. When it first opened, we all worked together at Resorts.

Q: Let's suppose Corky believed that Ratso liked you. Would he have tried to win her away from you?

A: Probably not. With Corky, a woman had to be halfway decent looking. Ratso looked like a Ratso.

Q: Did she hear the name you called her?

A: Certainly. At any venue, I enjoyed yelling across the room, "Hey, Ratso." Most of the women Corky and I were involved with were reasonably attractive.

One of my favorites was Awkward Annie (Corky did not know her.) She was very attractive in a different way. We were friends when I lived in Baltimore. She wore eight or nine grades of bleach in her hair. The colors made her easy to spot. Alex Hawkins, a former Baltimore Colt, wrote stories about Awkward Annie. His name for her was "Awkwardness." The Orioles hired her from an agency. She was one of those people who couldn't do anything right. She cultivated habits like knocking things over or falling down. Unfortunately, Annie was in love with me. Because she observed that I was somewhat religious, she lied and told me that she was attending church every Sunday.

One night, the two of us headed for The Bear's Den Bar, in Baltimore. I insisted that she enter alone, because I didn't want anybody to see me with her. I watched her enter the bar. It had a reputation for being pretty dark. I went in and searched for her, but I couldn't find her. Then I spotted a guy scuffling in the corner. It seems he had hung his coat on Annie. He mistook her for a coat tree.

Q: Did she say, "I'm sorry, I'm waiting for Bert"?

A: No. She couldn't get any words out. After her coat scene, she never heard the end of it. If she had met Corky, we probably would have competed for her. I welcomed his competitive nature.

Q: Was Corky a low-life?

A: Yes, but he was covered with a nice veneer. Some guys rob you and you hate them. Even though he hit me up now and then, Corky didn't bother me. I sensed what he was. Ultimately, I felt sorry for him.

Q: He wore a good mask. Describe his mask.

A: I found him very unattractive. His carefully-orchestrated appearance included the hair and the jittery movement. He even affected a Joe Cocker hitch. This street-smart character's gotta be on the go. "I gotta go to Indianapolis to close out this deal." His schemes were always designed to impress. He did it well. He acted out his schemes as if they really existed.

Q: When he first met anyone, he sized him up. He revised his data to determine when and how much he could get. Does this fit?

A: Not to me. He was smart, but he used skills in the wrong direction. Many of his scams were creative and inventive. His experiences on the basketball court mirrored those of later life. He knew instinctively that I would never be a fertile field. He probably sized me up for exactly what he got—$200.

Q: Did you get any of the $200 back?

A: I think he returned $50.

Q: Was the money returned to plant seeds for a bigger hit?

A: Yes. I decided to be careful about lending him money again. I stuck to that decision because he never fully repaid the original amount. He sensed that I was on to him. But I never let him know what I was thinking. If he walked in here right now, Corky could probably entertain both of us with stories about his exploits.

Since Corky had worn out his welcome with NBA players, he was reduced to impressing non-players with his supposed prowess. Have you discovered whom he hit for the largest amount of money?

Q: Supposedly, Corky stole around $50,000 from a jewelry company. Could he have wanted to be caught?

A: Many gamblers come to the Casino to lose. They behave similar to racetrack bettors. Losing consistently creates a "Cause Celeb." Their stories sound something like "You should have seen that jockey. He stood up in the saddle 20 feet from the finish. Do you believe that?" Without some colorful story, Corky's peers wouldn't listen to him. The big loss served as an attention-getter. Otherwise, who would bother with Corky on the corner?

Q: *He was proud that he had visited every racetrack in the United States.*

A: I doubt if he knew about every track. Just another boast of our Runyonesque friend. His impressive array of tracks embellished his losses.

Q: *He punctuated stories with names of losing horses. Now that I remember, he never mentioned a winner.*

A: Corky knew of my past success as a handicapper. In the '50s, I placed bets for Art Rooney, owner of the Pittsburgh Steelers. He regularly fed me $2,000 to place $100 bets. No one noticed when I went to the window. My father told me that Art was the most successful handicapper he ever knew.

Due to betting, my relationship with Corky deteriorated. His senses warned him that I might be getting too close. I knew the rules. After I demonstrated that I understood his tactics, he never tried to con me.

Q: *When Corky played at the casinos, what games attracted him?*

A: Blackjack and sometimes Roulette. Deep inside, he wanted to lose. He cultivated reasons to protest, a psychological need. Gamblers defeat themselves. They need some tale which appears to begin with winning. Suddenly their fortunes turn, and they make themselves martyrs. Their stories ooze with irony.

Q: *So victim Corky punishes the gambling Corky.*

A: His tale transforms defeat into Runyonesque irony. In later life, he parlayed his experiences on to the payroll of Gambler's Anonymous. He claimed his reward for a lifetime of self-deceit. You advocate that Corky's journey finished peacefully in a monastery. Free of addiction, he accepted the truth. I warn you, Corky remained theatrical and capable of deception.

Corky was this kind of guy. If he walked into this restaurant today and said, "Good Morning," I would put on my pajamas and go to bed. That is how little I trust anything he said. If he found salvation, that transformation would propel me to my favorite poem, "The Hound of Heaven" by Francis Thompson. The hound would have exhausted himself in the relentless chase of Corky.

I have been around people like Corky all my life. I put up with Corky's masquerade because he could never hurt me. Sure, I gave him $200. That amount was acceptable to me because I knew that he wouldn't take it any further.

Q: Are you shocked that he ended up in a monastery?

A: His transformation anticipated his death. Beneath pretenses of being religious, Corky feared that he might be wrong. He agonized over heaven and hell as his final breath drew nearer.

Q: He never stopped trying to be good?

A: His contrition came at such opportune moments. Think back to the time he had himself committed. He orchestrated a convincing act to gain favor with the court. Later in life, he perfected the gambling. Corky calculated: "How many years can I get out of gambling?" He craved excitement. Capitalizing on his ex-player image, relentlessly he kept stealing and playing.

Q: Corky had exhausted all sources of money for gambling. At the time of his exodus to Gethsemani, was there nowhere else to go?

A: He could have come back to live with me. I might have put handcuffs on him. I understood his sickness. He could have lived with me.

Q: Did you know that Corky discovered a diagnosis for compulsive gambling?

A: Corky became a helpless victim of himself. He belonged in leg irons. I talked to him like that. I kidded a guy on the square. What I said was the truth.

Q: Describe the day in Baltimore when Corky disgraced himself during the Gunfight at Lock Raven.

A: Corky (ex-basketball star) began appearing at the playground to join our pickup games. We played five-on-five full court. Lock Raven was a typical inner-city playground at 32nd and Greenmount. Corky acted the ex-professional star role to the hilt. His entrances were loud and showy. His act reached its apex when the girls were watching.

One afternoon in 1970, a 25-year-old kid named Allan Dial ignited his game, producing an offensive show. I had dated Allan's sister (that interested Corky). On defense, Corky guarded Allan, who displayed superior foot speed. Seven jump shots in a row rained over Corky's condescending defense. Corky applied pressure. Allan spun around him for easy lay-ups. No one said a word. Allan, 6-foot-3 and 13 years younger, made Corky look terrible. Even worse than being owned by Dial, Corky was no longer being fed the ball on offense. To a point, Corky acted as though being out-shown wasn't bothering him.

I stood on the sideline. When I glanced away, Corky went off. He grabbed Allan around the neck and began to choke him. Corky always maintained his cool. Not this time. His mystique as the legendary basketball player was in jeopardy. His self-image depended on winning. He regressed to a child. Without reserve, he attempted to strangle Dial. The other players pulled him off. I can't remember whether Corky shouted. Hollering wouldn't have been cool. When life didn't go his way, Corky couldn't manage himself. This infantile pattern remained consistent throughout his life.

Later that morning, Allan reappeared with a weapon. Another noisy melee broke out before Allan could be restrained. Corky relegated the story to cave status. Occasionally, I couldn't resist needling him, "What's new in choking." He never responded. He couldn't acknowledge that incident.

Q: When Corky appeared in Atlantic City, you were working at the casinos. How did he strike you?

A: He had married a casino worker named Brownween. We called her Brownie. I'm not sure whether they actually married. They might have only been engaged, typical of his splashy lifestyle.

Q: Did you ever watch Corky gamble?

A: I never did. Corky cultivated the image of an accomplished gambler. He wanted everyone to know that he was the real deal.

Q: Do you know why Corky told so many lies?

A: He depended on his celebrity status. His self-esteem danced between what he really wanted to be and who he was. We had many conversations, (particularly about gambling). He was compelled to tell a good story (even if the story was denigrating to him.) He craved attention.

Q: After he studied you, would he act out what you wanted him to be?

A: He didn't have to think about it. His reading people was instinctive.

Q: Did he lose touch with his real identity?

A: He didn't care. Someone so committed to his way of life knows where his life is headed.

Q: Where was his life headed?

A: He lived, always slithering out of the sun's rays. His was a succession of cons. He feared that he might get caught. During his time before the judge, he pleaded insanity. He diagnosed his own illness. His arrogance landed him in an institution. That's getting caught.

Q: *Is that the real Corky?*

A: Yes. Dumb.

Q: *I once asked Corky to describe the NBA. He claimed that his unique weapon was razor-sharp-elbows. Did he intimidate opposing players?*

A: Corky invented pro-basketball stories. He swore to me that the first time he played against Bill Russell's Celtics, his first four shots were blocked. That's a story he would tell me, but not you. He only told you fairy tales.

Q: *Why would he choose me to write his story?*

A: You might be the only person interested in researching. Who else cared enough to even listen? Today, Corky has less appeal than he had 10 years ago. Every aspect of our world, our priests, rabbis, bankers, business leaders, even our presidents have become increasingly corrupt.

Q: *Help me understand your world.*

A: Look at my friends. Corky is close to the norm in my world. I always seem to meet his type. I enjoy them and hang around with them. In their colorful way, they prove interesting to writers. Damon Runyon wrote volumes about guys like Corky.

Q: *Do you have trouble accepting that he could change?*

A: At the end, he may have acquired some redeeming value. But if someone convinced him he had another three years to live, he would have gone right back to business. Absolutely, I'm convinced that he started out trying to con the monks at Gethsemani.

XXIII

THIS, THE AUTUMN OF HIS LIFE

Fr. Dan Rocco's insights propelled me to write "My Paradigm." It took months to absorb his words. He prompted me to refocus on Corky. Corky's struggle acquired an expanded spiritual dimension. Fr. Dan had changed parishes to become the pastor of St. Jude's Church in Blackwood, NJ. Again, he serenely awaited my arrival.

Q: When I approached you a year ago, I had reached the end of my rope with Corky.

A: I understood that from what you wrote.

Q: I have limited control over the sequence in which I encounter those who knew Corky. Immediately after I visited you, I interviewed Fr. Timothy Kelly. He accepted Corky after your invitation. I tried in vain to lure Fr. Kelly into saying anything negative about Corky's stay. As many people visit Corky's grave as Thomas Merton's.

A: That's cute. It is very funny.

Q: After the '90s, I want to speak with Fr. Damien, Corky's closest friend. My focus will be on Redemption. Perhaps he will shed light on the last year and a half of Corky's life. I have pursued Corky through the eyes of many people. He lied and fabricated across the board. I interviewed his brother, Bob.

A: Good. That is important.

Q: Bob's recollections exposed Corky's biggest lies. For example, Corky did not admit himself to the mental institute in Arlington, Virginia. Corky pleaded insanity to avoid time in jail. He had been caught embezzling. So he contrived to claim temporary insanity. He bragged to his family about his clever move. Slick Walter has lied about everything. His conversion to Catholicism surprised everyone. Can I confirm any truth imbedded in Corky's life experiences?

A: You may have to become an artist.

Q: *Corky has created an ever-deepening effect on me. Will I ever understand?*

A: No longer is the book about Corky. It is a book about Paul. Your book reminds me of a movie in which the author learns from, then grows through, examining the life of someone else.

Q: *"Immortal Beloved," the life of Beethoven.*

A: Close. I was thinking about "The Third Man." We don't realize what really is moving the author until the story is finished. The viewer must grasp the whole picture. He must experience the conclusion before he can understand all the movements towards the end.

Your story also reminds me of the worst pirate who ever roamed the seas. All that pirate needed to do to gain salvation was to look at a child and fall in love. A simple act changed his life. Do you understand? I'm talking about Corky's kind of living and how acceptance could change him.

Q: *I felt pain when you described the pirate. I am hesitant to accept a role in Corky's story. When I first heard his voice, Corky said, "In finding me, you will find yourself." His words are making more sense.*

A: Corky deeply hurt you. It is not important to figure out why. Did he really intend to do it? That is the subtle change in your view of Corky.

Q: *Numerous coincidences transpire as I write this book. Two occurred when I encountered Jim Murray and Paul Arizin. Corky seemed to be urging me to continue. I began by writing a secular book. The book is becoming increasingly spiritual.*

A: The current trials of the Church, including pedophilia and defections, remind me of your experience. We need to remain open to forgiveness and redemption. This doesn't mean that we condone what is being done. But we must never close the doors. We must live in an environment which allows each wounded person to reach out for forgiveness.

There is a real estate man in my parish who has helped us on numerous occasions. He owns many buildings. One day, a very disheveled bag lady wandered into his office and asked to use the bathroom. He told her to go ahead.

After she left, one of the secretaries scolded, "How could you let her use our bathroom? Didn't you see the needle marks on her arm?"

He replied, "It's not your bathroom. It is my bathroom. I don't see a problem, and I'll clean the bathroom." He did.

We have to nurture that openness to receive the downtrodden. We may be the only hope for those like Corky and the fallen priests who have done horrible things.

These moments of compassion assure us that people can change. Through God's intervention, there can be movement and correction in life. For us, we must be willing to really listen to the downtrodden. Yesterday was your favorite feast day, the feast of the Transfiguration. We met on that day one year ago.

Q: Do you think me dense to have waited an entire year to return?

A: I see it as quite a coincidence.

Q: I ponder what will be the last thoughts of this book. At times the clouds briefly part, hinting at the future. I think of your words. "There is hope for everyone. No matter how awful our lives have been, there is always hope."

A: That is why I have started talking about the saint of the day when I say daily Mass. The large majority of saints were scoundrels at one time in their lives. Every one experienced problems, which could have kept them from holiness.

Q: We don't hear about their struggle.

A: Exactly. There is a difference between being good and being holy. Holiness deals mainly with openness to God. It progresses out of being in union with the Lord God. People who are good may not necessarily be holy. Some holy people are good. This does not mean that holy people are always viewed as good by society. The Church has a wide capacity for acceptance of holy people. Many were not necessarily good.

Q: You remind me of my conversation with Bert Bell, a friend since childhood. Out of the blue, he introduced "The Hound of Heaven." He pointed me towards my most painful line in all poetry, "Lest having you, I might have naught besides." Thompson shrinks from The Hound. I have struggled with this concept since childhood. I fear having nothing if I totally surrender to God.

A: Self-absorption. You fear being absorbed into the Divine.

Q: Yes. Otherwise, I might have the courage to let go.

A: That insight is so important about the Transfiguration. We are told that Moses and Elijah were visibly identifiable in the scene. Although

Jesus was transfigured, the other two were not absorbed into Him. This is a basic presupposition about God. The early Greeks fell into the trap of seeing God only as the Almighty God. From there, they found it difficult to understand how God could let there be weakness and suffering.

God always starts with Love. John repeats over and over, "God is Love." With that understanding, what is God's motivation? If God loves, what does God want? He wants Redemption because only through that can we be incorporated into Him.

Q: What is Redemption?

A: Go back to the very beginning of scripture. Examine the Overture of the Bible, the first chapter of Genesis. In this chapter, the Bible reveals how the world was created. Four basic truths are stated. These four basic truths are themes that repeat themselves throughout the Bible. The truths God reveals remain unchanged so that we will follow.

The first truth is that there is one God. The second is that creation is good. The third is that God has ordered the universe. The last and greatest truth is that we are made in God's image. Understand that Jesus had such passionate love for us, that it compelled Him to the cross. He was surrendering His will. That is not action. The whole dynamic of surrender allows us to trust. We can only trust when we rely on an inner sense of what is right and good. As long as we can discern what is good and holy, we are on the way to redemption.

Q: Is that what you saw in Corky?

A: Yes. I saw that he possessed all the key ingredients which allowed him to make the connection to knowing that God loves him.

Q: Many have said, "No." They did not believe that Corky could change. They saw no connection remaining. Are you assuring me that he still had that connective capability?

When I started this search, I could not see the struggle in Corky. I saw only his glamorous veneer. As I uncovered his weakness and evil tendencies, I grew disgusted with his life. Now you reveal beneath the hypocrisy and fear, Corky's light of hope. He had not become totally corrupted. You compel me to dig deeper. Again you introduce a new view.

* * *

Could it be that Fr. Dan Rocco, more than anyone, embraces the real Corky? I grope for the spiritual Corky trapped within a painful decadent physical life. Is he guiding me through Fr. Dan to the truth, which no one else can see? Certainly, there have been no coincidences in my search. To Corky I promise, "I'll keep going." To the source of all Truth, I plead, "Lead Thou me on."

XXIV

HEALEY'S BRIDGE TO CORKY

Bob Healey, a very successful businessman, had Corky living on his farm. Bob met me in his office in Lumberton, NJ. His affection for Corky was apparent. He was eager to discuss Corky—the good and the less good.

Q: The diplomas on your wall tell me that you are a lawyer. Are you also a yachtsman?

A: I am Chairman and CEO of five different companies. One is a yacht manufacturing company. We manufacture most of our boats in New Jersey. Foreign boats are built for us by a boat manufacturer in Plymouth, England. Other yachts are built for us in Italy. We own a real estate redevelopment company and a telecommunications company, which provides digital satellite television, high-speed internet, and telephone services. We also have an oil production, gas exploration, and gas production group in the Appalachian Basin. My brother and I are equal partners. My brother specializes in the boat building. On the side, I operate five charities.

Q: How did you meet Corky?

A: I was practicing law. I was developing the last major case of my legal career. My client was a compulsive gambler, a businessman from Philadelphia.

I needed to understand whether compulsive gambling was a psychiatric disorder or bad acting. If my client was suffering from a psychiatric disorder, he would not be able to enter into a legal contract (to gamble.) If we could sustain that theory, we could negate many gambler transactions. My client had lost $500,000 at the casinos. He owed another $300,000.

During preliminary development, Corky came to me. He offered to help with my investigatory work. He contributed experience working for national organizations helping gamblers. He contacted experts to assist us in putting together a case. He was very knowledgeable about compulsive gamblers. I welcomed his understanding of all aspects of gambling. Both sides brought experts to strengthen their argument. As a compulsive gambler, Corky contributed considerable psychological and technical insight into how the casinos operate. I studied gambling so I could deal with the casino lawyer's arguments. I utilized Corky in all aspects of our case. Corky was a very dynamic person and a tremendous charmer. Over time, Corky introduced his repertoire. He described playing professional basketball, which made him interesting and likeable.

Andrew Carnegie once said: "You can take away my fortune, but don't take away my people. With my people, I will earn back my fortune." So I have a tremendous appreciation for the value of people. When I meet a talented person, I usually feel in sync. Corky mesmerized me. I gave him a job with a salary. He came to live on my farm. I also bought him an automobile. Jim Murray and I attempted to rehabilitate Corky. I referred to him as nuclear energy. If we could control him, he would light up the world. If we couldn't control him, he would blow up the world. My own experience with rehabilitating people has a three-to-five percent success rate. Realism never deterred me from trying. It would have been a tremendous accomplishment to rehabilitate Corky. The reward would be great.

Q: *I tried to do the same.*

A: So many people tried to help Corky. To one extent, he was a con man. To another, he really tried. The truth lay somewhere between extremes. In my view, he just ran out of people. He hit bottom. He arrived where he was destitute, without money or friends.

I bought him a car. It eventually wore down. So I decided to buy him a newer car. I bought him a really fine car. After I paid for the car, Corky left to pick it up. For some reason, he told me he had been unable to trade in his old car. I told him to sell the old car and give me the check. You guessed it. He sold the old car, but he never gave me the money. His deceit irritated the hell out of me. He wore out his welcome here. In the end, he became really down and destitute. One of my friends spotted him walking along the road. Corky owned no transportation.

While in that situation, he approached me. He wanted money for a bus ticket to go to Gethsemani. I told him I wanted to accompany him when he bought the ticket. His response was, "Okay, I'll be back." He never returned.

He desired to do the right thing, but he carried so much emotional baggage. A great number of people are unable to overcome addictions. His problems seemed overpowering when compared to our problems. Sadly, he believed that his problems prohibited him from overcoming them. The sad truth of his life: Corky was never a bad guy. He tried his heart out, wasting great talent. I hope that he found peace in his heart. The challenge for someone with great talent and deep psychological problems is the tendency to self-destruct. Judy Garland was one of those people. She achieved great success. It only increased her pain. Great highs from super success swung back to painful lows. Extremes become a pattern. Corky's success fueled his pain. I felt great sadness when I learned of Corky's death. I pray for his peace at Gethsemani and peace with God.

Q: What year did you try your last case?

A: The Gamblers Anonymous case was in 1974. We sued Resorts International in Ocean County, NJ. We avoided the political climate in Atlantic County, where the casinos were located. We were headed for a jury trial. I had accumulated a filing cabinet of research material. Through Corky, I met Dr. Robert Custer, the country's leading psychiatrist and expert on gambling. He certified our analysis. His work established compulsive gambling as a psychiatric disorder. He became my key witness.

The trial approached, attracting more and more national publicity. Wire services picked up our story. Our approach to gambling was truly unique. Our case ignited opposition from Resorts Casino. If we established compulsive gambling as a psychiatric disorder, the implications were enormous. Pandora's Box would open. The case was destined to be heard by a jury. A legion of Resorts' lawyers attacked. They succeeded in their intimidation of my client. He lost his nerve.

Q: Do you feel free to tell me your client's name?

A: I don't feel free to tell you that. It would not be ethical because he stopped. At that point, I decided to bluff that I intended to pursue the case. My client received psychiatric help and succeeded in overcoming his problem. I could no longer pursue my goal of helping compulsive gamblers. My client was my only means. Atlantic City was becoming the Sodom and Gomorra of our day.

We discovered, during those investigations, how aware the casinos were of each compulsive gambler. Casinos deliberately target compulsive gamblers.

After we lost our victim, we attempted to negotiate a settlement. We could not succeed through direct negotiations. Jim Murray helped. He knew Leonard Tose's ex-wife. She had married the President of Resorts Casino. Jim convinced her that Resorts should settle our case.

Corky found himself driving through the pinelands area of South Jersey. He encountered a mayor in a bar. The mayor told him about a grant request for $500,000 by Corbin City. The grant established a school catering to special children. To obtain the grant, the town needed matching funds of $500,000. The town ran out of extensions, so the state was about to shift their money to someone else. The deadline was December 31st of that year.

Corky strode into the bar. He met the Chairman of the Board of this little school. This Chairman owned the gas station in Corbin City. Corky met with many of the local people. No one had the slightest idea how to raise that kind of money.

Corky returned to my farm and described the plight of the Corbin City School. We urged Jim Murray to get involved. Jim takes on causes as long as they are good. The Corbin City School was a worthy project. We developed a scheme: Resorts refused to pay any money to a compulsive gambler. They would not agree to a settlement that included a potentially damaging psychological connection. We negotiated for the amount that matched the Corbin City school need. On December 31st, Corky grabbed the casino's check and drove it to Trenton just ahead of the three o'clock deadline. The school was awarded the grant. Their dream of building an addition became a reality.

Corky Devlin endured teasing after he returned home. He orchestrated the deal. Through that case, I came to know Corky. Many other men around here came to know and respect him. Fr. Joe Messina and Dr. Frank Iula became his friends. One thing never changed, he stayed on the make for our money.

Q: Could you have won the case that you settled?
A: I think we would. When we agreed to a settlement, we agreed with prejudice. This agreement stipulates that we can never again bring it up. There was also a gag order involved.

The diagnosis of compulsive gambling establishes it as a psychiatric disorder. Compulsive gambling has been well documented. They pose the question "Does this disorder prohibit a person from his ability to enter into a contact under the law? Can this person rationally enter into a contract?" Gambling is a contract. Thus, the question comes under the rule of contracts. I say, "No." If I offer to pay you for going to the store to purchase a pair of pants for me, that becomes an oral contract. When I visit the casinos and I place a $10 bet on a specific number, if I win they pay me $30. That becomes a contract between the casino and me. I agree to put up my money. If I lose, the casino takes my $10. If I win, the casino gives me $30. The question posed through a compulsive gambler is: "Do I possess legal competency to enter into that contract? Am I compelled to do it? Do I possess the ability not to do it?" My analysis tells me that, when I am sitting at the table, I do not possess the ability to stop. I must continue. Even if I win a million dollars, I become unable to stop. I just keep going. I cannot leave. The only way I become able to stop occurs at the moment that I am out of money. As I sit, there is no rationality in my gambling. There are two major reasons why people gamble. Either they want a sense of drama or they want to win money. The person who is not a compulsive gambler wins, picks up his money, and leaves. The compulsive gambler is unable to do that. For this reason, the psychological impairment diagnosis becomes an accurate one. This affliction is a compulsive disorder similar to drugs and alcohol addiction. Heroin is a combined physical and psychological disorder. This is also true of alcoholics. Under the law, a drug addict who cannot control his use of drugs and shoots someone is held responsible. The law assumes that he does have control over shooting someone. I am not talking about the stealing of $20 to gamble. I am talking about the act of gambling itself. Based on this argument, I was able to clear the motion.

Q: Did Corky ever tell you that Dr. Robert Custer treated him for a bipolar disease?

A: No, he never told me that. Now that you mention it, strange things happened to him. He once spent days locked in a motel unable to talk to anyone. He had those experiences periodically.

Q: Can we explore your project with Corky in Mexico? What happened?

A: Jim Murray called me to inform me that his friend was starting an international adoption program. He adopted children from Mexico and placed them in the United States. The project needed funding. Jim escorted Bob Iatesta to my farm. Bob and his wife were spiritual religious Catholics. They were experiencing logistical problems bringing children here. In

Mexico, unwanted children live in orphanages. In the U.S., couples want children. Internationally, he struggled with government red tape to obtain visas and citizenship. The Mexican government, embarrassed because they were unable to care for their own children, fermented psychological problems with the United States. I agreed to fund Bob Iatesta's project.

Q: Was this Living Bridges?

A: In the late '70s, Bob returned to my farm, and described the poverty he had witnessed in Mexico. He focused on a village named Landrillera, about 30 miles south of Mexico City. In English, *Landrillera* means "brickyards." Their closest town was named Extapaluga. The people existed in huge gravel pits. To survive, they dug clay, filled wooden boxes and added water to make building bricks. The bricks were then baked in a kiln. Truckers visited each day, transporting the bricks to the city to be sold. After the brickyard owners and the truckers extracted their shares, little money remained.

So many people in Mexico suffered from poverty that the government could no longer help everyone. The brickyards were cut off. The government no longer acknowledged that brickyard people existed. They were stripped of all identity (including birth certificates and census records). When a brickyard person successfully spliced into an unguarded electric wire, the loss of power was totally ignored.

Q: This sounds like communism.

A: No. That decision was pragmatic. The government admitted that it could no longer help. The decision was not evil in itself. It was the result of a political situation.

Bob urged me to visit Mexico. I pleaded that I was very busy. One day, I found an ad describing four and a half-hour flights from Philadelphia to Mexico City. I flew alone to Mexico. When I landed, I was greeted by Bob and his Mexican friends. Our first stop was the shrine of Our Lady of Guadalupe in Mexico City. I experienced the Holy Tilma. This cloth contains an image of the Blessed Mother painted with unearthly material. As a result of her appearance on December 31, 1531, human sacrifice among Mexican Indians ended. Millions of Aztecs converted to Catholicism. At the shrine, Mexican women crawl on their knees up the steps. I have always had devotion to the Blessed Mother. I wear the miraculous medal (he showed me). During the Depression, my family prayed the rosary together. We asked that my father could make enough money to pay our bills. Our Blessed Mother took care of us.

After visiting the shrine, I was escorted to the brickyard. I never imagined such poverty. In Mexico, there are really two classes, the poor and the rich. The middle class is very small.

The brickyard had one little school. It had been constructed from pieces of propped-up huts. The owner of the brickyard intended to evict the children from the schoolhouse. When I met her, she referred to me as "The Gringo." Through an interpreter, I told her that I wished to purchase her land to build a new school. After much prayer, I promised to return to help build the school. Two weeks later, I returned. She had changed her approach. "The Gringo will not buy the land. I will keep the school for the children of Mexico."

Her comments increased my determination to build a new school. At that same time, I encountered a Jesuit priest, Padre Enrique Gonzalez Torres. Immediately after the big earthquake, he had been assigned by the Cardinal of Mexico to use money donated by people around the world to rebuild housing. He organized engineers, estimators, and builders, a very elaborate operation. Enrique had been born into a well-to-do Mexican family.

Miguel de La Madrid was President of Mexico. Miguel was the first Harvard-trained economist President. Prior to Madrid, Mexican Presidents had accumulated bundles of money before leaving as billionaires. This president acquired wealth through courting American interests. His attitude was "Pay me and I will give you what you want." Madrid was the first honest president. His wife was Paloma de La Madrid. In Mexico, the wife of the President took responsibility for all human services.

I obtained permission to buy bonds (Mexican debt). In our country, local banks had been granting loans to the Mexican government in an attempt to build an infrastructure. They nurtured third-world countries to stimulate their growth. In the past, they had been unable to repay the loans. Their growing debt now represented a major political and financial problem. A gray market in third world debt just kept growing. I learned that I could buy Mexican debt from our banks at 35 cents on the dollar.

I made a deal with the Mexican government. I spent $350,000 to buy $1,000,000 of Mexican debt. The Government paid me $1,000,000 to redeem the debt. We used the money to build two schools. Then, we turned them over to the government. The government agreed to operate the schools. Mexico still operates the schools. At that time, the Catholic Church could not own property in Mexico. Subsequent to the revolution of VIVA ZAPATTA, when the Church sided with the owners of the haciendas, restrictions were placed on all priests. Priests couldn't wear Roman collars. It was an oppressive climate. I had to be convinced that the schools would not be used as forts or armories.

Padre Enrique worked closely with us. The architects worked without pay. Enrique also cajoled bidders for services to work at cost. I priced reinforced concrete schools in New Jersey. Our schools would have cost $3,000,000 to $4,000,000 dollars to build.

Q: Was your agreement in writing?

A: The bond transaction was handled by Citibank. I trusted Enrique Gonzales Torres, a very good person. The million dollars was in an account for Living Bridges. Our money was spent as needed. You might think it crazy to make a deal like that, but I prayed constantly to the Blessed Mother for guidance.

I installed my operating guy in Mexico. He and the Mexican woman in charge developed serious differences. She became an egomaniac. I removed my manager. After that, I worked exclusively with Enrique and the Mexican woman. The project succeeded because everyone was very honest.

A serious problem arose in acquiring ownership of the land to build the schools. A woman on our committee was a cousin of Paloma de La Madrid. She arranged our visit to the Presidential Palace. As we paraded past the Palace guards with their guns, Corky Devlin strode confidently at my side.

We waited, having coffee. In comes Paloma with her entourage of five people. In very clear English, she questioned: "Why do you, an American, come to Mexico?"

I knew, from studying the history of Mexico, that she was really asking why an American businessman wanted to come to Mexico. I was probably a crook. In a reflex reaction, I reached under my collar to display my Miraculous Medal.

At the same time, I said, "I've come to answer the call of Our Lady." I replaced the medal and waited.

The silence seemed like years. She and the other women conversed rapidly in Spanish.

She responded; "Whatever you need, you shall have. Whatever assistance I can give you, it will be given."

Back in the days of the revolution, the great haciendas became no more. Everyone had been given a piece of ground. The small portions of ground were known as "Ahito."

"The ground for our school is Ahito?"

Paloma's response was, "Abrogado" (lawyer.)

When the abogado appeared, they conversed in Spanish.

Paloma turned to me and announced: "We will clear the ground for you in 30 days."

We left smiling. Corky rode shotgun.

Q: Not literally?

A: No, no, he didn't have a gun. Paloma scheduled a ground-breaking for the day that we started building the schools. Paloma would join us in a big helicopter. She wanted to greet all of the children. Mexicans are great for pomp and ceremony. I was excited about the ground-breaking. I arrived two days early to review the plans. Corky and I happily anticipated the grand event. I examined the drawings, and I noticed no provision for water. One Mexican spokesman planned to transport water in by truck. All the water I had seen was filthy. Brickyard people washed in it among other things. My experience in other businesses helped me understand that water is vital for schools.

"No. That is not going to work. Where is the nearest source of water?"

That water was in an adjacent town, Extapaluga, run by its mayor.

My next question was, "Is he going to be at the ground breaking?"

"No. He does not get along with the Federal Government politicians. He has not been invited."

It became imperative that I contact the mayor of Extapaluga. We scheduled our meeting with the mayor for the same time as the ground breaking. When I spoke with him, I emphasized that I chose to be with the mayor rather than at the groundbreaking. He was intrigued by why I visited him, ignoring the ceremony. Because he had not been invited, I decided to be with him. We began to talk. He revealed his profession, a schoolteacher. To him, schools were very important. I told him that later in the afternoon, after the groundbreaking, I would like to take him to the brickyard.

He asked me: "Why are you doing this?"

It had worked once, so I pulled out the medal. "It is for Our Lady."

When he saw the medal, he asked, "What do you need?"

I said: "We need the water. We have no water."

He replied: "The brickyards are not part of my town. I cannot give you water because it is supplied by the Water Authority."

I pleaded "We have to solve this problem."

The mayor's final comment was, "Let me think about it."

When I returned two weeks later, he told me: "I have talked to my cousin, Louie. He is the Water Commissioner in Mexico City. I told him that it was very important that we provide water for the schools. Louie asked me why de La Madrid wasn't going to provide water."

"This man is very good. We have to provide the water."

We decided that I would take over the brickyards and incorporate them into my town. Since they would become part of my town, Louie would then be able to provide the water.

Then we built the schools. Corky rode with me. He became my confidant.

Q: What was Corky's mood at that time?

A: He was very supportive. There were times when he couldn't travel with me. Whenever I took him with me, he urged me on. He was convinced that we were doing a great thing.

The schools eventually got built. Two sessions were taught in each school. Those joint sessions educated eleven hundred children. Enrique orchestrated the project for the Mexican government. Corky and I flew down for the Grand Opening.

Months later, I hosted some of the Mexican people at my farm. Accompanying them were two Bishops from Mexico. Our local Bishop McHugh of Camden joined us. At one point, Bishop McHugh whispered to me, "Why not the city of Camden? Why Mexico?" Corky grew very close to me through all of that. He lived here. He served as a great inspiration to me.

I have never returned to Mexico. The U.S. government passed a luxury tax on our yachts, which nearly put us out of business. I grew very concerned at the home front. Corky became an integral part of our outreach food program in Mexico. We fed poor Mexicans 2,300 hot meals each day. Meals cost us eight cents American. To make that work, they contacted a Dominican priest who lived on the West Coast. He drew up a deal with the U.S. government, exporting stored surplus food. The food had to be distributed outside of the U.S. If it were released here, the surplus would defeat the purpose of the program. The food consisted of large quantities of powdered milk, flour, cornmeal, and other basic commodities. The Dominican priest shipped the food around the world. We paid the cost of freight. I paid eight cents per meal. Our program far exceeded the Mexican government's Meal Program. The government ran the schools. I never went back. Many letters have urged me to visit. Someday I will return.

Bob Iatesta still runs his Mexican adoption agency called Living Bridges. I direct my Living Bridges Foundation. Both organizations have the same name.

Q: Two Living Bridges?

A: Yes, they are two separate entities. When I stopped funding the adoptions, the luxury tax on yachts had almost put us out of business. I was without funds to further assist Bob Iatesta. He has successfully continued the adoption program.

Q: Corky embellished the story. He said the food bank feeds 35,000 people.

A: He claimed 35,000 people? The Mexican women feed 2,300. Corky was certainly involved. On many occasions, he traveled there by himself. But I am sure of my number.

Q: Did he have dinner with the President of Mexico?.

A: That would be Miguel de la Madrid. I don't believe so. Corky and I met with Paloma de la Madrid. After the groundbreaking, she was always available to us.

Q: This question is not easy. Corky claimed to have shepherded your involvement in Mexico. He called the local paper to announce that you were going to give the money. His announcement stuck you with the project.

A: No. I became involved in Mexico through Jimmy Murray and the adoption program. The paper had nothing to do with my involvement. When committing to buy the ground, I became completely involved.

Corky never helped me with any business problems. Most of the Mexican problems required that I go down there by myself. The Blessed Mother worked out all our problems. How else could one guy like myself fly to Mexico and build two schools? My companies up here have whole staffs of construction people. Each time I returned home, I was high because all of our problems had been solved.

Q: What are the names of the schools?

A: I don't remember. They simply referred to them as the schools in the brickyard. On the day of our dedication, Enrique cried. The contractor cried. We all cried. Corky took part in all our efforts. He was a consummate cheerleader. He could never be a businessman. As someone who had suffered great pain, he felt compassion and understanding for poor people. Those who experience great tragedies are either destroyed or become warped. Or they survive to become greater people. Corky, through all of his problems, had compassion for others. He understood pain.

Q: You kicked Corky out of your farm. Why?

A: It was during the car deal. When he took the money, I lost trust. Our break occurred in the late '80s.

XXV

THANKFULLY, ONLY *LIKE* A THIEF IN THE NIGHT

Corbin City, NJ, is five miles due west (inland) of Ocean City, NJ. Bob Healey pointed me towards a school for special children. I drove down Route 50 and turned left on Carl Road, finally locating the Helmbold School. Would Corky's story prove true? Was he a benefactor of the school?

Corky guided me. I found myself sitting at the desk of Debbie Hostler, the daughter of the former mayor of Corbin City. The same mayor Corky met years before in a Corbin City bar.

Debbie, now in her 40s, still serves as secretary at the school. She remembered Corky well. She referred to him as Walt.

Q: Is your father still living?
A: Yes. He owned our gas station on Route 50. He lives in the house immediately behind the station. Walt also dealt with our superintendent of the Helmbold School, Dr. Peter Finley.

Walt was a question mark for us. He was always in the midst of some deal.

Q: *He was always moving?*
A: Exactly. Years ago, I was taken sick with multiple sclerosis. I awoke one morning to see Walt Devlin on my television set. I thought I was dreaming. He was being interviewed on a Philadelphia talk show. There he sat smiling.

Q: Corky claimed he obtained money to build your school.
A: That is this building (Hostler Hall). We were conducting a referendum to build this school. That was 1978. Corbin City has not built anything since then.
Q: Where did you get the name Helmbold?
A: Our school was named after the Atlantic County Superintendent of Schools, John S. Helmbold. Today Atlantic County has additional schools in Absecon and in Mays Landing. Our campus educates about 150 students. Hostler Hall provides service to 45 of those students.

Debbie called her father and arranged a meeting with Corky's old friend, the mayor. I waited on his winterized porch before being joined by Dorcey Hostler. He is in his 80th year.
Q: How do you remember Corky?
A: Walt was extremely personable. At the time we met, I understood his intentions. He became very involved with the school. He interacted more heavily with our school people.
Q: Would Pete Finley be a good person to interview?
A: Yes. He knew Walt best. Pete was very involved in the construction of the current building. He supervised the contractors at the time they built Hostler Hall.
My son, Dwight, would also remember Walt. He was killed in an automobile accident. The School is named after Dwight.
Q: The school wasn't named after you?
A: No, it was my son, Dwight. He worked as an aide at the school when he was attending college. He earned his degree in Special Education. Dwight was a great kid. He learned to play the guitar, which proved to be a unique avenue to reach the kids. After graduation, the board signed him to a teacher's contract. During that summer of 1976 before he started teaching, he was killed.
Q: Was Corky at the dedication?
A: No. He had left the area.
Q: Probably on the lam.
A: Could have been. He was a very excitable likeable guy.
Q: Would you trust him?
A: At that time, we all did. He appeared out of nowhere. He left just as suddenly. When he decided to leave, he just disappeared.
Q: You introduced him to the school?

A: I guess so. Today, I am so far removed. I was born in Philadelphia. I still find it strange that a small town like Corbin City accepted Walt with all his showmanship. Ours is a friendly little town. Each of us knows everybody's problems. But Walt entered our lives like the Lone Ranger. He came. He saw. He conquered. Then he left. All this Lone Ranger lacked was his mask.

* * *

Dr. Peter Finley remembered Corky fondly.
Q: Do you remember how you first met Corky?
A: Yes I do, Paul. While Jim Murray and Corky were driving through Mays Landing, they stopped at our local watering hole. There they met faculty from the Helmbold School. The teachers were celebrating a birthday. Corky and Jim joined the celebration, probably bought a round. After they listened to our teachers, Corky asked them if he could visit their school.

I arrived at the school on the following Monday morning. Corky was sitting on the front steps. Who was this guy? He was 6-foot-6 topped by a shock of white hair. Dressed very nattily, he introduced himself and wondered if we could talk. He sincerely wanted to visit our school.

We had coffee. An athletics connection between LaSalle (where I went) and George Washington was established. Corky knew Tom Gola, Frank Blatcher, and many other LaSalle players. We chatted about sports before we talked about the school. I wasn't terribly busy at the time so I took him on a brief tour. Immediately, our children were fascinated by him. He was so tall, outgoing, and friendly.

The first tour proved to be a resounding success. He acted very gracious toward our staff. When the tour was over, Corky asked if he could come back. I assured him that a return visit would be fine, and then he left.

A week or two passed before he returned. This time he asked if he could find his own way around the school. He wanted to attend classes to get to know the students and teachers. He wanted to understand the handicapped. I gave him my permission. Off he went on his own.

He returned on a regular basis (once every two weeks.) Sometimes, I accompanied him to the gym. He was still able to dunk and do tricks with the ball. The children found him fascinating. Our Physical Education teacher was delighted.

Summer arrived. Corky showed up a couple of times. Then he disappeared for a while. He had been working for two brothers who owned a boat works. He repossessed boats. This employment relocated him to Florida for a few months. Upon his return, he started visiting again. One day he entered my office with an unusual request. He asked me if there was anything the school needed. I told him there were a lot of things.

He replied, "Like what?"

I wasn't sure where to start, so I said, "I'd like to have a television set for each classroom in the district."

We didn't have a big school—only 200 kids. Each student was severely handicapped. We were educating the low-incident handicapped. Our students included the deaf, the autistic, and the neurologically impaired. They came to us from 50 school districts in six counties. Our children's needs were unusual. They included physical and educational needs requiring diverse supportive services.

Q: Pete, explain "low incident."

A: "Low incident" refers to a handicapped condition that doesn't have a high frequency. Autistic children are classified as low incidence handicapped. Higher incident includes mentally retarded and emotionally disturbed children. Originally we had serviced only about a half dozen students in our three county area. Because their home schools could not provide adequate services, our school became regionalized. The Helmbold School was built for these students during the 1982-1983 school year.

Q: Why did Corky show an interest in your kids?

A: We never talked about why. He had never worked in education. Our qualified group of professionals accomplished fascinating things with these kids. Their work interested Corky. On the other hand, Corky liked the adulation he was receiving. The kids grew to love this tall athletic person who played basketball with them. I believe Corky developed a genuine interest in handicapped children and a love for their educators.

Q: I am touched.

A: I have no other explanation. He came regularly and most of the time he brought them treats.

Q: Return to your request for television sets.

A: Corky coaxed, "Maybe a little more than that."

My next suggestion involved a 90-acre area of Corbin City where I fantasized building an athletic field. I envisioned an athletic complex that would meet the special needs of the handicapped.

Corky asked, "How much would that cost?"

I estimated: "Between $10,000 and $15,000." The total depended on the amount of equipment we installed.

Corky prodded, "What would be next on your wish list?"

I told him the following story: In 1967, a survey was conducted in Atlantic, Cape May, and Cumberland counties to determine the frequency of hearing-impaired children who were victims of the rubella epidemic in 1964. Only a half dozen were identified. That number tripled in the following years. The children's school districts did not know they existed. With no education program, the City Board of Education agreed to take responsibility for a new program. The John S. Helmbold Education Center came into existence. Programs and services were expanded and became regionalized. During the 1980s, the federal government gave us a grant to build a vocational building. The school was only half finished. The Board of Education had no way to acquire our share of the needed money. Corky Devlin and Bob Healey came to our rescue.

Coincidentally, New Jersey issued a Request for Proposal (RFP) inviting school districts to request funds for programs targeting special education students. The original children enrolled at our Helmbold School were getting older. They had reached high school age but we had no high school. We needed a vocational program. Federal government money was available through the state for the programs we needed. I submitted a proposal. We were granted $480,000 to build an educational complex. We were assisted by the Helmbold Foundation Board. The Foundation included interested citizens who tried to raise enough money to build a school. Our vocational wing would be one pod in the school complex.

In New Jersey, getting a school built was very complicated. The planning boards, zoning boards, the county and state and the Pinelands had to sign off. Between the time that we received the initial grant and the time that we gathered approvals, the cost doubled. Our new total had swelled to well over $900,000. We could not tax the residents of Corbin City because our school children were not residents. We had no taxation powers with our school districts. Our only way to obtain any money was through grants. The money we did have was sitting in a bank. I told our story to Corky. We lacked $500,000 to build the school.

Corky lit up, "Now you're talking. I think I can get you some help."

In my mind, I thought, "Talk is cheap. Showing up with the money would be another matter."

Well, Corky left on another trip. A month later, he called to ask if he could bring another visitor to the school. "I want you to show him the works."

One of my favorite programs was a restaurant, the Carl Room (named after the original property owners). One of our teachers opened the restaurant in her classroom every Wednesday. Our children prepared the food, waited on tables, and did the bussing.

Corky brought Mr. Healey the following Wednesday for lunch.

Q: Bob Healey described you and the school.
A: The two arrived early. Like Corky, Bob was taken by the students. Visiting our school can be a very emotional experience. I have seen more than one guy in tears after he witnessed the handicaps these children are bearing. It is our process that touches them. Bob became deeply moved by our children.

They left. I didn't hear from Corky for a couple of months. Then he asked to return for another visit. Again I thanked him, but didn't give his request much credibility.

Bob and Corky arrived for lunch in the Carl Room.

Bob Healey confided, "We have been very intrigued by your school and the work your teachers are accomplishing. We want to get involved in moving your goal along. We will assist you in getting this vocational building off the ground."

He handed me a check for a half million dollars.

I could have dropped dead, Paul. I wasn't sure how many zeros that was. Bob just said, "Here. Put this to the use that you want. Finish your building." That was it. I asked where it came from. He said he would prefer not to tell me. To this day, I don't know where that money came from.

Q: Was the check written to Bob's personal account?
A: I don't remember. It was too long ago. The money enabled us to finish the school. Upon completion, we scheduled the dedication. Neither Bob Healey nor Corky responded to our invitation. Neither attended the dedication nor the opening of the school. I never saw Bob again. Corky Devlin also disappeared. Several months passed before the school finally opened in the fall of 1984. We named it "Dwight Hostler Hall." It was named after a teacher who behaved like Corky in many ways. His life was that of a ne're-do-well. At 19, he didn't seem to be headed anywhere. By coincidence, he, too, visited Helmbold where he became fascinated by the children who in turn found *him* fascinating.

Dwight was a free spirit. He walked our grounds with bare feet in jeans with no shirt, a guitar slung over his shoulder. The guitar accentuated his long blond hair. The kids adopted him as their Pied Piper. He spent an increasing amount of time with the students. Dwight experienced difficulty holding a job. I decided to offer him a job as an aide. We wanted to pay him for work he was already doing. He accepted. The job motivated him to return to Stockton College where he earned his degree in Special Education in record time. Dwight wanted very much to teach. We were planning the first class (in New Jersey) exclusively for communication-handicapped children. I offered the teacher's job to Dwight. He signed our contract.

I'm not sure I can get through this, Paul. Two weeks before our school was to open, Dwight was killed in an automobile accident. That created a most difficult time for everyone, especially the children and the teachers. We were devastated. We named the building after Dwight and his family. His father had been very committed to the handicapped. He piloted The Helmbold Center through difficult times.

One morning Corky reappeared. He drove a big maroon-colored van. As I remember, he was on his way to Gethsemani. That visit proved to be the last I ever saw of him.

Over the years, I have pondered about Corky and Bob. I ran into Jim Murray five years ago. He told me about Corky's demise.

Q: Before this interview, you described Corky as "Like a thief in the Night." Did you know he was a thief?

A: I find that hard to imagine. He never gave me any inkling of dishonesty. Of course, he never had an occasion to be dishonest with us. Corky was Snow White pure. When I used the thief term, I was referring to how he came and went. He visited us unannounced. I encouraged him to come anytime. He was free to roam. That was the meaning of my comment.

Q: When he arrived, he was not planning to donate money to the school. Did he change because he fell in love with the kids?

A: I have to say, "Yes." He evaluated our Foundation Board. The board had no money and Corky knew that. He could never have hit them for funds. I find it hard to imagine that Corky was not an honest person.

Q: *Did he share anything about himself?*

A: He never revealed himself. Now that I think back, he got personal once. At that time, I was teaching Christian Doctrine (CCD) at our parish. We wanted to reach adolescents, but attendance was abominable.

We couldn't drag the children to class. I decided to try speakers who had experienced some crisis of faith. Corky talked to the kids about his struggles as an athlete. He stressed honesty and doing what is right. Unfortunately, we didn't have many kids that night. But his talk was excellent.

Q: He stressed honesty? Did he describe his playing career?

A: He talked about the invigoration of playing on the court. He loved hollering spectators. He chose to leave basketball while he was still on a high. He didn't want to experience the letdown of the has-been athlete. After his career, he sold school rings.

Q: Did you sense that Corky might be a compulsive gambler?

A: No. I had no reason to suspect that.

Q: You could have saved Corky enormous pain had he revealed himself. I met him in 1992. Your background offered needed help, but he could not ask.

A: I am very indebted to Corky and Bob Healey. There was considerable discussion about naming the school after one or both of them. At the time, the Board members were acutely aware of how Dorsey Hostler and his family were suffering over the death of their son. The Board voted to go with the name Dwight Hostler Hall. But we felt very positively about Bob and Corky. We suspected they walked on water.

XXVI

CORKY DEAREST

Would I ever be able to talk to Corky's older sister? Corky hurt her most. She was his full sister. Joan was born to Bill and Anna Mae Devlin in 1930. She helped raise and watch over Corky. She yearned to see his best, almost always experiencing his worst. Corky generated experiences, which remain hard to describe. For good reason, Joan washed her hands of Corky. Reopening old wounds could prove painful. Still, it was important to approach her. Bob called in hopes of preparing her for my questions. He left cooperation up to her.

Joan, a small extroverted woman, had lived as a widow for eight years. She seemed almost anxious to talk about Corky. I visited her home near Atlantic City. We sat comfortably at her kitchen table. When she began talking, she expressed honest opinions of her wayward brother, Walter.

Q: Why did you stop seeing Corky?

A: Walter had reached the point where he was unable to differentiate fact from fiction. He was in the habit of lying about everything. He became truly tragic. He made a total mess of his life, and he hurt so many. He lied about all his relationships, including both of his marriages.

Q: Only two marriages?

A: Only twice. He was capable of messing up many more. His first marriage occurred while he was playing basketball for the Pistons. He met a farm girl from Fort Wayne. She aspired to become a singer. She was very cute, but she only stood 4-foot-11. They looked like Mutt and Jeff.

Walter introduced Arleen on the Arthur Godfrey Talent Scout program. During the competition, she finished second. She was awarded a contract on Arthur Godfrey's television show. She also sang on the radio show. During that time, Walter and Arleen married at Godfrey's home in Virginia. No one in our family was invited to the wedding.

Q: Tell me about Arleen Adams.

A: At the time she signed the contract, the show included personalities such as Pat Boone and the McGuire Sisters. She earned $1,500 per week, but didn't know how to cash a check. I accompanied her to the bank. I tried to convince her to open an account. She insisted on sending cash to Walter and to her parents, who lived on a farm in Indiana.

One day Arthur advised her to dress better for appearances on the show. Shortly before that day, Walter had bought her a beautiful cashmere coat for Christmas. Coincidentally, I had bought a gray imitation fur coat. Arleen stood barely 4-foot-11. I towered at 5'6". She admired my coat and asked to wear it. My coat dragged along the ground. She looked bizarre. Our switch forced me to adopt her cashmere coat. A week later, Walter returned home. He threw a fit. She wore that imitation fur coat. I told him I was wearing her cashmere coat to work. He complained bitterly. I simply advised him to talk to his bride.

Arleen and I went shopping often. She bought 20 blouses or 20 skirts at a time. She chose the cheapest ones she could find. Her clothes-horse husband prodded her to buy something expensive. She believed that spending a lot of money was ridiculous. In the same day, we could watch her on television singing a blues number and be out front shooting marbles or swinging a hula hoop with the kids. Her tomboy behavior made her very funny. At that time, we lived in Newark. The neighborhood kids loved her. One day, she announced to my mother that she had decided to do some food shopping. She returned home with five pounds of bologna.

Q: Sliced?

A: Thick.

We laughed. "Arleen, please, this could feed an army of people."

"I didn't know. I thought Pop might want it for lunch."

She laughed a lot. We enjoyed laughing at her.

Q: What did Corky think of her behavior?

A: Walter loved her. But he refused to change his life to accommodate her. When she embarrassed him, he thought it was cute. She was cute. At the beginning, they were all right together. He had trouble in discussions with her because she could not understand. Walter used big words. Many people couldn't understand what he was saying.

Q: Did Corky introduce you or your brother to the glamour of basketball?
A: No. He loved the game because playing was something he was good at. He wasn't good at many things.

Walter and Arleen gave birth to a beautiful little girl. Dawn became the only person whom Corky truly loved without reservation. Their marriage broke up because of Walter's antics (mostly writing bad checks.) Arleen met someone else before she divorced him. Dawn was adopted by her stepfather, Bill Skiles. Bill, with his partner Henderson, worked for the Disney organization. Arleen and Bill settled in Costa Mesa, California. They had two other children. Before Walter died, Dawn came east to live with him. At that time, he was living in Sea Isle. He had not seen Dawn for many years.

Q: Was he living with Professor Tomkins?
A: I never knew the name. Walter claimed to be house-sitting. It was the late '70s when Dawn stayed with him. Walter took Dawn to see a doctor because she was experiencing a drug problem. Arleen was attempting to take Dawn's child away from her. Walter hired a lawyer and escorted her to court. Dawn won her case against her mother. Walter only provided me with sketchy information about Dawn. I had not seen her since she was three. She looked the same, even though she was now in her 20s. Through her trials and tribulations, Walter was thrilled to have her with him. She returned to California and promised to keep in touch. I don't think she did. She used Walter before turning her back on him. It was sad. Walter couldn't believe how the relationship ended. I reminded him that this was how his friends felt about him.

Q: What effect did Dawn have on Corky? Did he cry?
A: Yes, he cried. He was always able to cry. As a child, he was a crybaby. If he bumped his arm, he would put band-aids all over his arm. Just to be safe, he would wear a sling. Basketball was a fairly rough sport, but he played. My mother experienced the end of the world each time he stubbed his toe.

Q: Would you call him narcissistic?
A: Oh, yes. I am three years older than Walter. Although I loved him dearly, I never liked him. I couldn't understand why everyone thought he was such a great guy. He displayed the persona he wanted them to see.

In later years, he confessed that he had gambled as far back as his days at George Washington. In college, it was card playing. He found college life difficult. He played on scholarship, which forced him to follow the regimen of the team. He aced any test without much study. He always put basketball ahead of academics. He assured us that the coach wouldn't permit him to hold a job.

I bought all of his clothes during the time he attended school. I took him twice each year to buy clothes for the following semester. I also sent him money each week during the school year. I wrote Walter letters at school and enclosed a card with a stamp. All he had to do was sign the card and mail it. Most of the time he forgot. When he did mail one, my mother showed it all over the neighborhood. She adored Walter. She sensed his special need.

Q: Why did you do special things for Corky?
A: Because my parents couldn't. My father never made a lot of money. I helped out financially because I really loved my step-dad.

Q: Joe Corcoran?
A: He became the best friend I ever had. I adored him. Walter concocted lies about Joe. Walter claimed that my father was mean to him and hit him. That was never true. My dad never touched any of us. He hollered at times. But he was the straightest arrow I've ever known. He would be pleased to learn that Walter joined the Catholic Church. Dad was born and raised a Catholic. He was excommunicated because he married my mother. He never got over his pain. He attended church regularly, which caused him to yearn for the sacraments greatly. He approached numerous priests about returning to the Church. He encountered discouragement at every turn. If ever a person deserved to practice his religion, it was my dad.

After he graduated from college, The U.S. State Department sent Walter to Turkey for three months to teach basketball. He was paid $10,000. Walter spent $7,000 on clothes for himself. He returned to our house carrying his new wardrobe. I'll never forget that day. My dad, who only owned one suit in his life, couldn't believe that his son owned all those new American clothes. Walter's coming-home present was a television set. In 1955 that TV was the only gift he ever gave my parents.

Walter became very sick with dysentery while in Turkey. He grew very gaunt. His commission was to teach the Olympic basketball team the intricacies of our game. Of course, the average Turkish player stood

5-foot-4. Picture them with their giant coach charging onto the court—a funny scene.

Q: Was there anything significant about his childhood?
A: He entered daycare as a four-year old. We moved around. My natural father no longer wanted to be married. He made that announcement while she was in labor with Walter in the labor room of Atlantic City Hospital. For the next year, my mother lived in shock. We constantly visited her parents in Scranton, PA. She had two sisters who lived in Atlantic City. They also helped us. We lived in the Inlet section of Atlantic City. My mother held numerous jobs. During one job, she worked at The Dude Ranch on the boardwalk.

Joe Corcoran's sister was our neighbor in Atlantic City. Joe lived in Harrison, NJ. He wanted someone to care for his elderly parents. My mother accepted that job, so we moved up to Harrison. Later, we moved to Newark where Walter discovered basketball. He played in another neighborhood because the kids around our home were all my age. We hardly ever saw a black face in our neighborhood. Walter's school (Newark Central) was primarily black. I don't remember why he attended Central. It must have been for basketball.

I once asked my father why he never adopted us. He replied, "It has nothing to do with loving you. You will marry one day and take your husband's name. With Walter, I believe that every man is entitled to his own name. He will encounter his father again."

His prediction came true. Walter saw his father again. My father died in 1962. We moved back to Atlantic City to be near my mother's sisters. On the day my dad died, we could not find Walter. We only knew that he was on the run after writing bad checks. Our landlord's son (a lawyer) flew out to California. He located Walter serving a jail term. It was May of 1962 and the inmates loved him. Walter cooked gourmet meals for them. Walter Ashley (the lawyer) got Walter released and brought him back on a plane. Walter hung around until my mother got the insurance checks. From the $25,000 insurance policy, Mom gave Walter $10,000. My other brother received $10,000. She gave me nothing. My mother believed that I would always be able to support myself. She would always have to help Walter.

I pleaded with her. "We are not helping Walter by giving him money."

He grabbed the cash and raced to the nearest track. He returned in less than a week's time. He wanted to know if there was anything more coming.

About a year before he died, my father had been injured in an accident at work. He became disabled. The checks started arriving six weeks before he died. With that money, my father put a $1,000 deposit down on a new car for me. My job required that I travel. I worked as a sales representative for Lanvin perfumes. That car made me happy. After my father's death, my mother and I moved into a three-bedroom apartment in Ventnor, NJ. We were enjoying life. Then Walter arrived. He strutted into the apartment holding a notepad and began writing. My mother fell for his antic.

He confided, "Lyndon Johnson has asked me to work up a program."

I saw through his scheme. I warned my mother not to give Walter money. I was confident we had nothing to give him. I guessed wrong. My car disappeared for eight weeks. Not satisfied, he abandoned it in a snowstorm on the Ohio Turnpike. The engine started to rust out because it sat abandoned. Then he reclaimed the car, drove it back to Ventnor, and left it in front of our home. He never gave us an explanation. He called my mother and told her to look out her window.

Q: Where were the keys?

A: In the car. Someone could have re-stolen it. Shortly after getting the car back, I met my husband and we decided to get married. We wanted to go away on our honeymoon. Walter agreed to drive my mother to Bob's house for the week. Well, he disappeared for both the wedding and the drive. We spent our honeymoon weekend with my mother sleeping in the next room.

Q: Did he ever explain why he didn't show up?

A: No, he never did. He had been living in D.C., where he was being treated by Dr. Custer. At one point, Dr. Custer requested a meeting with Walter's family. Walter had just appeared on the Today Show hosted by Dave Garroway. That show focused on compulsive gambling. Later that year, Walter appeared on the Phil Donahue Show. He described his thoughts leading up to an attempted suicide. Dr. Custer had saved his life. His success story was a flat-out lie. Walter was still gambling. He hurried from the program to the nearest track. Dr. Custer seemed very sincere. He continually tried to help Walter, who continually lied to him. I questioned Walter about why he was lying. Not even Dr. Custer could help a liar.

Q: Could Walter ever go straight?
A: I don't think he could. He had progressed over the edge. Granted, Walter experienced some bad situations during his life. His real father and his stepmother signed him into a mental institution for 90 days. In 1962, they arrived in Margate, NJ armed with questions for us to answer so that Walter could be committed. My mother couldn't understand what was happening. They refused to talk to me.

Something was very wrong when I walked back into the room. Bill and Louise Devlin, both alcoholics, re-entered our lives after my marriage. They started following me to work. They demanded a family reunion. I didn't want to get involved. Bill claimed that Walter had gotten into trouble and that we all must help him. They plotted to have Walter declared mentally incompetent. They targeted an institution in West Virginia. Eventually, they succeeded in sending Walter away. Walter told horror stories about being dropped on the floor and receiving shock treatments for 90 days. He stayed just long enough to get rid of a troublesome court case. The Devlins were only interested in protecting their reputation. Walter had written several bad checks which they successfully kept out of the newspaper. Louise had been a legal secretary. She had worked as secretary in the office of Harold Ickies, Secretary of the Interior. Bill sold shoes all his life.

In the Atlantic City area, Walter habitually passed bad checks. He assumed many names. Usually, he called himself Corky. Another alias was Corky Adams. He also took out a string of Social Security numbers. What amazed me was that he walked into any bank and came out with a loan.

Q: How did he do that?
A: Honestly, I don't know. After we purchased our house, we were turned down for a home improvement loan. My husband and I were both employed. Walter went to the same bank the following week and came out carrying a personal loan and a car loan. He used our address and our telephone number. Later, the bank called us, demanding the money back. It was ridiculous. He ran out on every loan he ever received. He used phony names and pulled references out of a hat. He also approached many sports figures. Most of them didn't appreciate getting involved.

Walter became notorious in the Washington D.C. area. He claimed to hold George Washington's single game scoring record for over 20 years. His picture appeared on the cover of *Life* Magazine playing at Madison Square Garden. I was proud of his accomplishments in college. After he turned pro, he could never make enough money. I don't know how many cars he owned over the years. After he was traded to the Minneapolis Lakers, he started new shenanigans.

Q: Did he gamble while he was playing?

A: I don't know. He claimed that he didn't. Compulsive gambling started after his playing days. His specialty was horses.

Q: Corky told me that he came home one day and found Arleen and Bill Skiles together. The next day he learned that his stepfather was dead. Those two events set him off.

A: Not true. On the day his father died, Walter was in jail.

Q: How many times was he in jail?

A: Several times. Usually Walter was jailed for a bad check, but he never served much time.

Q: He once occupied a cell with a guy who had murdered his previous cellmate.

A: I never heard that story. Walter cultivated his very vivid imagination. He specialized in county jails. He never served hard time.

Q: He acted like a trustee cooking for his friends?

A: He laughed and joked about his jail experiences. His uncle, Billy Jones, lived the life of a hobo. He wanted to get thrown in jail periodically. His services were in demand because he could cook their favorite meals.

Sadly, Walter's life was wasted. He was given an education, but he never used it. He followed no life plan. Very talented, he could sell anything.

Q: Including himself?

A: Mostly, he sold himself.

Q: Do you remember anything about his second marriage?

A: His bride was quite a bit younger than Walter. Her father served in the US Foreign Service. She was a student when he met her in D.C. They lived together in Maryland before they married. It was 1965. None of our family was invited to that wedding, either. She was pregnant, and he was in jail (sentenced for six months.) Eventually, she gave the baby up for adoption.

Q: Was this after the wedding?

A: Yes. She gave the baby up. Walter learned that the baby was being put up for adoption. A court hearing was scheduled in Richmond, Virginia. Walter called, begging me to try to adopt the baby. He couldn't bear to lose another child. I told him I would not front for him. My husband and I did drive to Richmond for the proceedings. We were not admitted into the courtroom. We retained a lawyer, but Walter's wife realized we might be representing Walter. She argued that my husband and I were unqualified to raise her child because we were not college-educated. That marriage lasted about a year. Her parents were horrified that their daughter had become involved with someone like Walter. We never heard anything more from her.

Q: After that marriage, he became a nomad?

A: He drifted from place to place. He moved to Atlantic City and worked as a gardener's helper. He was never permitted to work in any casino.

Q: When did your husband die?

A: Seven years ago.

Q: Around the time Corky died?

A: Yes. I remember receiving a call from my sister-in-law. She and Bob were planning to attend Walter's funeral and they offered to take me. I declined. I can't understand why they went. Walter once promised to put Bob through school. They never enjoyed a real relationship. Walter didn't even attend Bob's graduation from high school.

Q: Was Corky a close friend of your husband's?

A: Not at all. He once threatened to beat my husband up. He was always trying to grab money from my husband. Walter hung out at The Rugby Inn where the bartender permitted him to run up a large tab. My husband worked as a bartender at The Tilton Inn. He avoided The Rugby Inn because the owners asked about Walter. They wanted their money back.

Once, we assumed the payments on a car owned by Walter. Our agreement was drawn up legally. During Walter's college days, Louise, Walter, and I attended basketball games. We enjoyed taking team members to dinner on weekends. Bill and Louise lived in Annandale, Virginia. After my father died, Louise moved to California. After she died, her lawyer notified me that I had been named the sole heir to her estate. My husband and I sold her house. The will stipulated that Walter was left $100 (for reasons known to him). Not surprisingly, he approached me, demanding an increased share of the money. I gave him $7,000 (the amount we had paid off for his car). After he realized that he wasn't getting any more from me, he approached my husband at his place of employment. Walter towered over him. Walter was 6-foot-5. My husband stood barely 5-foot-9. He glowered menacingly, demanding money.

My husband looked up, "Get the hell out of here and don't come back." Walter skulked away.

That attempted shakedown occurred in the '80s. I saw Walter one more time. He arrived at my house while I was getting ready for work. Walter was wearing a pair of old shorts and no shoes. His appearance scared me. He requested money to visit Dr. Custer. He had finally realized that he needed help.

"I am at my wit's end, and I must visit Bob Custer."

I had $20 in my purse, I handed him the $20 to pay for a bus or train. I loaned him a pair of my son's jeans that were way too short for him. I also gave him a pair of small sneakers. He jammed his feet into them (he wore size 12.) Walter limped through my door for the last time. He looked pathetic, hobbling to the corner. He disappeared in the setting sun.

I have tried constantly to think kind thoughts about him over the years. Sometimes I do. But more times I remember the way he treated my mom. He never mistreated my dad, only because he left home when he was 17.

Q: He mistreated your mother?

A: He used her. He was never nasty to her. He just played on how much she loved him.

Q: Didn't she die of Alzheimer's?

A: We didn't call it Alzheimer's then. We called it hardening of the arteries. Near the end, Walter took responsibility for getting her admitted into the hospital. Through a friend, who headed an institution in Atlantic County, he got her a bed. I had nursed her here in my home for nine years. I still feel guilty about allowing her to enter a nursing home. I just couldn't take care of her anymore. She no longer knew any of us. Anna Mae had been kind to so many people. Walter didn't show up the day that we admitted her. He never visited her until she finally died in 1991.

Q: Jim Murray described visiting Anna Mae with Walter. He cradled his mother in his arms. At that moment he wept.

A: He loved her as much as he was capable of loving.

Q: He wasn't capable of love?

A: I really believe that. The only person he ever truly loved was his daughter, Dawn. He just never stopped talking about her. He exuded happiness when she visited him. I told him how much I wanted their relationship to work out for him.

Q: During Corky's final days at Gethsemani, he accepted God's forgiveness. Apparently, Corky lived his last 18 months in joy and free of his addictions.

A: I find that very difficult to believe. He used them in the same way he used everyone else. His life had closed in on him. He used them to escape. He had nowhere else to run.

Q: The Abbot and some other monks believe his conversion was genuine.

A: They are good people, so they don't want to think badly of him. Accepting Walter was the result of their beliefs.

Q: So, you don't buy conversion?

A: I honestly don't. Over the years, he took advantage of everyone. That includes the Professor in Sea Isle. Walter stole his car. Months later, Walter contacted my son in D.C. He admitted that the car had been stolen. He asked my son to intercede with the police. I did not want Walter involving my kids. My son called the police. He convinced Walter to abandon the professor's car on a specified street. It was up to Walter whether he stayed to face the police. Walter didn't. The car had been driven to and from Kentucky. He sensed the end of his life. My son gave him $250 with assurance that it was his last.

Q: All doors had closed.

A: My son ordered Walter never to visit his father or mother. Walter accepted, "I know not to go there."

Q: The monks believe that throughout his life Corky struggled to be good. Did he ever lose his sense of conscience? Did it consistently pain him to do the wrong thing?

A: When he was an inmate at the mental institution, the doctors diagnosed him as completely amoral. Their diagnosis always stuck with me. I don't believe he ever changed.

Q: Do you know where he lost all morals?

A: I have no idea.

Q: Because he spent time in a day care center, did life owe him something?

A: That was one excuse he gave. Certainly, he could not have felt unloved by our parents. We were three kids. They treated us all the same. My mother bent over backwards for Walter.

Q: Are you happy that he became a Catholic?

A: Because of my dad. We were raised as Presbyterians. I don't think Walter ever stepped into a church after he reached the age when he could do what he wanted.

Q: Did you ever feel close to him?

A: No. When he was very young, I wasn't very nice to him. I made him dress up in my doll clothes. When he was two, he had to sit at my tea parties. Our family was always moving. I acted in a play in second grade at the Massachusetts Ave. School in Atlantic City. My mother convinced me that Walter was a very cute little boy with dimples and blond curly hair. Even then, he wanted to be a clothes-horse. He once skipped school because he didn't like the socks my mother put on him. He hid all day outside the schoolyard.

Q: *No one is totally bad. Didn't he wish to be remembered kindly by anyone in this world?*

A: I try to look at his life in a fair way. A few years ago, I could not have talked to you. He was my brother. I loved him, but I didn't like him. I never liked him. He could never be trusted. He never told a plain simple story.

Q: *If he found redemption, how would you feel?*

A; I would be happy for him. I just don't believe that it could happen. He was incapable of being honest with himself, let alone with anyone else.

Q: *Did he know himself?*

A: Better than anyone else. I never understood what he wanted out of life. He never identified what he wanted. He was always very good with children. That talent grew because he acted like a child himself. Increasingly, he felt more at ease with children than with adults. He behaved like a kid showing off. I laughed at him. He was sad.

Q: *How his family sees him is devastating.*

A: Well, my not attending the funeral created a strain with my brother. I was 12 when Bob was born. I assumed the role of substitute mother to my youngest brother.

Q: *Why did your brother go to Corky's funeral?*

A: When my brother married for the second time, he married a great woman. They have three children. He also maintains a good relationship with the children from his first marriage. Bob is a family man. After he and Nancy married, my brother entered the Catholic Church. Our father would have been pleased. The Church worked very well in my brother's family. I truly think that my brother wanted to be kind to Walter. He overlooked Walter's mistakes. I never felt strongly enough about Walter to hate him.

Q: *Your struggle reminds me of "The Sopranos."*

A: It's true. It's not very logical. It would be a big surprise to me if I ever started liking Walter.

XXVII

THE BIGGEST KID IN THE YARDS

Living Bridges, an international adoption assistance organization, links U.S. families to impoverished children in developing countries. I encountered co-founder Bob Iatesta in his office in Rosemont, PA. In his 60s, Bob remains CEO of Living Bridges. He talked about Corky's involvement with the Living Bridges children.

The project began with Corky's accompanying Bob Healey to Mexico. They uncovered a desolate area, the Ladrillera (La-dree-year-ah). Corky's compassion was shown when he spent time with the inhabitants who survived by baking bricks from the clay that lay at their feet.

Q: What was Corky's involvement during those beginning days in Mexico? Bob Healey advised me that there are now two Living Bridges.

A: Later in our ministry, Bob and I chose different directions. Bob focused primarily on making the area financially viable through Living Bridges International (NJ.) I envisioned our ministry being mostly people-oriented. Living Bridges (PA) predominantly assists in adopting, hosting, and educating children.

Corky traveled with us during our first tour. He became very involved after observing the brickyards. Bob Healey and Corky collaborated to build the Vocational Tech Schools.

Q: You badgered Bob Healy into visiting the brickyards?

A: Oh, yes. At first, he and I traveled alone. Bob had quite an experience.

The day we arrived in Mexico City, we visited the famous Tilma Cloak. It contains an image of Our Blessed Mother as she appeared to peasant, Juan Diego, in the 15th century. The cloak is highly venerated throughout Mexico and most places in the world.

Q: The Tilma Cloak was your first stop in Mexico City?

A: The church housing was holy ground. What really blew us both away occurred later that day. We drove to the operating brickyards (30 miles south of Mexico City.) The Ladrilleras were literally 'brick-making ghettos.' These inhabitants dried bricks in the identical way that the ancient captive Hebrews made bricks for the Egyptians. They mixed straw, mud, and water in wooden molds, which they baked in the sun. Then the bricks were kiln-dried and trucked into the city to be used for construction. Today, concrete has replaced bricks in the construction of high-rise buildings. In those villages, people survived in bond slavery—much like the Jews when they were slaves. To make things worse, they were forced to buy the water essential for making the bricks. Bob was introduced to women eating food gleaned from a leprosarium (leper community.) These poor souls picked through garbage discarded by the leper community. When you sink below the lepers, you have fallen pretty low.

Q: Didn't these people catch leprosy from eating the garbage?

A: I don't think so. Leprosy is primarily a congenital disease. Whole families live together as lepers. The disease is not as widespread as it once was in Mexico.

We first visited The Ladrillera in 1986. Women volunteers had already been trying to assist in the brickyards for six years. My wife accompanied me right after the earthquake of 1985. A year later, with Bob Healey, we discovered a place where the women had built a chapel. The men in the community were essentially dysfunctional, defeated by severe unemployment and alcohol problems. The women cemented the community.

Q: A matriarchal society?

A: Very much so. Witnessing these people surviving overwhelmed us both. Bob Healey concentrated on helping un-adoptable children. He built the schools, which still help a lot of kids. I chose a narrower approach, assisting in adoptions.

Q: Do the schools have names?

A: The community is Santa Barbara. The schools are vocational technical high schools. I 'm not aware of any specific name. The plaques on their wall honor Bob Healey.

Q: What was your impression of Corky?

A: I met Corky traveling with Bob Healey. Corky impressed me as a Damon Runyon character—a really special person with a great heart. He avoided doing anything the way most people did. He demonstrated empathy towards the broken-hearted. He had been so broken himself. He entertained me with unbelievable stories. From the beginning, I considered him a beautiful person. Later, I was at Jim Murray's house when Corky received the Sacraments of the Church. We reconnected through Tom McGarrity at the Trappist monastery. Corky's acceptance at Gethsemani demonstrated God's sense of humor.

Q: Corky also conned the Trappists?

A: There was a little of that. There has never been a pure human conversion. Conversions can never be perfect. A little bit of self always remains.

Q: Did you know that he was a compulsive gambler?

A: I know his whole rap.

Q: He gambled for the sake of gambling?

A: Gambling was his weakness. He was aware. I did not observe his early gambling with Leonard Tose. Corky experienced great brokenness during his life. He was humble when trying to help others, effective within his own limitations.

Q: So he accompanied Bob on your second trip?

A: Yes. We conducted a tour for about 20 people.

Q: Was Corky quiet on tour?

A: Corky was never quiet. On our trip, he and another single guy engaged in active competitive passes on the same single woman-friend of ours. Corky always wore red sweaters. His rival wore green. The intriguing question became, "Is Joanne going to go green or red?" Finally, she made the right choice. She went green.

Corky was always on the move, working a deal. His deals did not concern empire building. They were always about helping others.

Q: Did he mix well with the children in Mexico?

A: He behaved like a kid himself. In a lot of ways, he acted like a big adolescent.

Q: Would the kids jump on his lap?

A: Sure. They had never seen a human being that big.

Q: He was a curiosity?

A: He brought a lot of fun. Corky had an electricity about him that lit up wherever he went. He was very charismatic.

Q: Did he speak Spanish?
A: Oh, no.
Q: He didn't even bluff?
A: No. He just smiled.
Q: When you and Bob talked business, was Corky present?
A: Bob Healey tried to help Corky straighten out his life. In return, Corky tried to become an operative on some of Bob's projects. It didn't work. Corky wasn't cut out for business. Bob Healey was very generous in helping Corky.
Q: What did Corky contribute? Was he the gopher?
A: More than that. Bob Healey was preoccupied with his businesses back in the States. Corky lived alone in Mexico a lot. Bob kept an open heart. He assigned Corky responsibilities he could handle. Corky always landed on his feet. He had a skill for escaping bad situations.
Q: Do you remember any particular moment in Mexico?
A: He really worked hard to encourage Bob's generosity towards the kids. After Bob realized the gravity of the children's plight, his heart was right there.
Q: Did he rip you?
A: He tried at the very end. Corky was always desperate. I don't know how many options he had left when I knew him. He always considered himself a deal-maker. That was his personality. But his deals clouded the surface. Underneath was a good heart. As an addicted person always in debt, his was the usual profile.
Q: I'm fascinated by the dichotomy. He was always on the make, but kids loved him.
A: He was a big kid himself. Peter Pan never grew up. Kids saw him the way God saw him. There was nothing malicious about Corky. Sure, he took advantage of people. I never trusted him. He maneuvered into convoluted situations. On the surface, he acted the role of a scoundrel. Underneath, he was warm-hearted and really cared about other people. That is why he was invited to join the Trappists. He lived searching for security and a place to belong. He needed a family. I really believe that.
Q: How much do you know about his family?
A: Only that it experienced a lot of brokenness.
Q: Caused by Corky?

A: I've never found a broken relationship that didn't have two sides. People are human. He wasn't malicious. He constantly groped for stability. When he put on his blue suit, he could really sell.

Q: *Not so when he wore red in front of Joanne.*

A: You should have watched the two of them trying to impress Joanne. It was comical. As the competition escalated, it became increasingly important to both suitors. Each carried a deep desire for a companion. She did, too. Her decision was to go straight. Maybe her life wouldn't be as exciting, but her choice was certainly more stable.

Q: *Her life wouldn't be as much of a gamble.*

A: Great play on words.

Q: *Would it surprise you that he was gambling at the time you knew him?*

A: Corky was always gambling. Jim Murray described his level of addiction as "exceeding drugs." It was obscene. We all deal with money during our lives. When gambling is your addiction, you are tempted every day.

Corky lived the quintessential mixture of darkness and light. When his light was on, he could do wonderful things. When darkness ruled, he was capable of almost anything negative. He was like all of us. Only he exaggerated both extremes.

Q: *I hope to revisit Gethsemani.*

A: What have they told you?

Q: *The monks loved him. In the end, I will have to form an opinion about his life. Many people loved him. Others despised him. I uncovered summary statements that describe who this man was. Sometimes I feel as though I haven't looked in the right direction. He fractured into so many pieces during his life. Corky's life never experienced solid foundation. His slippery journey unraveled, devoid of any sense of home. The pain of wandering masked his biggest ache. I have wandered after him. I have been absorbed into his excitingly senseless life. Corky never set goals. Consequently, he never accomplished defined goals. In childhood, we were taught that motivated people set goals. As an adult, I'm pursuing a man without goals. He lived his life totally experiential. A nomad (homeless before the word was invented), he stumbled into his final home. Brigadoon was in Kentucky. His destiny appeared by accident. Surely, he had been guided. His only contribution to the process was his "yes" to a call. He owned nothing for long. What profound message did he hear? Does our world include many Corkys? How much of me is living in Corky?*

A: What is the objective of your book? What are you trying to accomplish?

Q: *The search lures me onward. Why, I'm not sure. During my first trip to Gethsemani, I found Bro. Alban. I had never spoken to a Trappist.*

Something deep inside said, "If God created a saint today, he wouldn't be converting thousands of people in a football stadium. He would be a sinner in our broken world, trying but failing, to find God on his own. God would have to help him become a saint."

Bro. Alban's words were simple: "I couldn't agree with you more. I'll do anything I can to help you write the book."

I spent time with Abbot Kelly. Would you believe that Corky's grave receives more visitors than Thomas Merton?

A: Are they mostly women?

I have a belief. Throughout history, most of the goofy things individuals do fade. The really solid moments endure. We are all a mix. I'm 66 years old and I haven't found a perfect person. I have met many good people, but all are a mix of darkness and light. We misunderstand God. He is not looking for perfection. He knows our heart and our capacity to grow. The sin in our lives is really deplorable weakness. Once we try to cover up our weakness, we substitute problems of integrity. Corky was always an open vessel. Despite his weaknesses, he always strove to accomplish some great good.

Q: *Did you pray with him?*

A: I prayed with him a lot. None of us is perfect in our prayers or intentions. Does any one of us experience perfect integrity? No. We all try. Saint Francis wore a hair shirt. His goal was to integrate the inside and outside of his person. He never got there. His hair shirt reminded him that he needed to clean the inside along with the outside of his being.

Q: *Judgment is reserved for the end of our lives. Corky fell often, but you assure me that he always got up. Crawling back to our feet seems really important. If we rise, is there always hope?*

A: Exactly right. He got up. Corky inconvenienced himself for other people. Our conversations always got around to how he tried to help some person. The schools were big deals to Corky. He was capable of hitting home runs.

I want to encourage you to write about this truly remarkable character. You know, every book becomes more about the author than about anyone.

XXVIII

GEORGE WASHINGTON SPEAKS

Ed McKee of George Washington periodically checked on the progress of this search. He provided names and telephone numbers. Ed truly cared about Corky. I valued his insights. I called Ed McKee and turned on the tape recorder.

Q: Corky was up and down. Could you describe his moods?

A: When I first met him, Corky shared that his personality was extreme. When up, he loved mixing with people. When on the way down, he did not want to show that personality to the public. He gave me his local telephone number so we could talk. Sometimes months and years went by when we didn't talk. I wished Corky well at these times because I could only say some prayers for him. He was acutely aware of his condition. People who suffer from depression experience similarities to drug addicts or alcoholics.

Corky had been married years before. He felt very badly that he had not been successful. At that time, Corky didn't know why he was the way he was. He progressed into compulsive gambling. He learned the tricks and all the cons that resulted from lying to himself. He described many efforts to help other gamblers.

Q: How did you first meet Corky?

A: Actually, I found him. I keep rosters of former George Washington basketball players. I wanted to locate him because he played on such great teams. Absolutely by accident, a family visited my office. They had a daughter who wanted to work in our sports information office. I reminisced with her father about George Washington basketball. Out of the blue, he described Corky Devlin in Florida. Red flags went up. What a stroke of luck! I asked the father to send me Corky's phone number. I received the number and dialed up Corky in Pennsylvania.

I started: "Is this Corky Devlin, who played basketball at George Washington?" He was taken aback. He assured me that he was. I told him how delighted I was to make his acquaintance by phone. I had been searching for him for years. We talked and he told me that he visited Washington from time to time. He promised to visit the campus the next time he was in town.

Soon he came by. His mood was up and friendly. He was smiling and happy to meet anyone who wanted to listen to his stories. His reasons were two-fold. He enjoyed talking about his life and his NBA career. He also presented himself as a scorer, not a shooter.

"Look it up. I hold the NBA record for the most consecutive misses in a game. If I went zero for fifteen and the coach didn't take me out, you know that he thought I was pretty good."

When the Milwaukee Hawks moved to St. Louis (1955-1956), I was a 10-year-old basketball fan. There were only eight teams in the league. Fort Wayne, Minneapolis, St. Louis and Rochester made up the Western Division. In those days, NBA teams didn't fly very much. The train came through town. Corky was a rookie assigned the job of standing in front of the station with a big red lantern to signal the oncoming engineer that the Pistons wanted to get on. Corky stood in the middle of the night waving a big red lantern, hoping the train would stop. Glamorous current NBA travel plans include charter flights from coast to coast. This was only one great change since the mid-'50s. Corky was proud to participate in the growth of the league. He was a character. There were a lot of characters on both the Pistons and the Lakers.

Q: When did you become friends with Corky?
A: During the eight-year coaching reign of Mike Jarvis (1991-1998), the Colonials went to the NIT and NCAA tournaments several times.

Q: What made you really like Corky?
A: He was genuine. He didn't mince words. He told me how he felt. He was truly happy to be alive. Being a young sports fan in the '50s, I served as an attentive audience.

George Washington's most famous basketball alumnus is Red Auerbach. I enjoy sitting in a room with Red listening to endless NBA stories. Although I have heard Red's stories two or three times, I never tire of hearing them.

While my time with Corky was limited by his health, I sensed that he was a genuinely good guy. He sincerely apologized for his bad behavior. When he was under depression, alcohol, or compulsive gambling, he disappointed himself. He was very ashamed of many things. But the Corky Devlin I knew was first-rate.

Q: Were many of Corky's stories exaggerations?

A: We never discussed Corky's performances at George Washington. He never bragged. He acknowledged he had been good, but stressed that he had played on a good team. He assured me that Joe Holup was the star of the team.

Players from other eras complained. We had a center who still accuses his guard of hogging the ball. Many players were convinced that they deserved more credit. That was never the case with our '50s team or Corky. He never dwelled on himself. He accentuated the team and how happy he felt to be part of it. He also applauded our '90s teams for their closeness. He believed that our coach was getting the most out of his players.

Corky told me that the Pistons' star was George Yardley, a collegiate standout from Stanford. George became the first player in NBA history to score 2,000 points in a season. The following year, Bob Pettit (my hero) also scored 2,000 points. George Yardley was balding and very thin. He looked much older than he was, but he could really play.

Corky was part of my youthful memories. It was a pleasure to befriend him as an adult. I never observed him down. After that last visit, he never resurfaced. Brief as our time together was, I am happy I knew Corky.

Q: Through it all, Corky had a good heart?

A: I have no doubt about that. He was ashamed of his early life and very apologetic. I remember his sitting in my office and opening up. Sometimes, it is easier to confide in a relative stranger. He saw me as an extension of the university he loved.

Q: Corky had a very fractured relationship with his family. Could George Washington University have become his family?

A: I suppose that could be the case. I have seen pictures of Coach Bill Reinhart at various stages during his coaching career. Whether in the '60s, '50s or '40s, he looked old. Bill Reinhart found Corky, placed him at Potomac State, and brought him to George Washington. Corky played during the coach's glory years. G.W. won many games with players from diverse backgrounds (mostly from Pennsylvania and New Jersey.) I would not be surprised that Corky viewed his coach as a father figure. In those days, George Washington was a different institution and Washington was a different city. Washington was a sleepy Southern town. We were nestled at the north end of our country's South. Today it has become cosmopolitan and connected with Baltimore, Philadelphia and New York. We are considered more Eastern or Mid-Atlantic than Southern.

Corky adjusted to the slower pace of the South. Our university primarily enrolled Washingtonians and Southerners. Our best football team played at that same time (1956.) We won the 1957 Sun Bowl in El Paso. That football team was primarily Pennsylvania and New Jersey players. Our student body remained very local and Southern-oriented.

Because he was from New Jersey, Corky injected his sarcasm and personality into our Southern town. Players from all sports lived in Welling Hall. That dorm is not here any more. Currently, G.W. sponsors 22 varsity athletic teams. In Corky's time, we had just five varsity sports. All were men's sports. Most of our scholarship players lived in Welling Hall. Those players blended into Corky's family. Psychologically, your theory about Corky's adopted family is true.

* * *

Q: What highlighted your relationship with Corky?
A: It was during the time in George Washington University's history when basketball was rolling along well, the Mike Jarvis era. We had improved from never being in the NCAA Tournament (except 1954 and 1961) into the national limelight. Corky played on the 1954 team. One afternoon, our athletic department hosted a coaches' luncheon here on campus. Coach Jarvis attended with some of our players and many fans. The event was very upbeat because we were preparing to enter the Atlantic 10 Conference Tournament and the NCAA Tournament. Corky was in town and up psychologically. Corky's teammate, John Holup, (from Alexandria, VA) also attended the luncheon. We gathered at the Marvin Center (our Student Union building.) Each former player was introduced and encouraged to share a few stories. John and Corky attracted considerable attention. People really enjoyed hearing about the good old days.

On a sports talk radio station in town, WTEM, James Brown hosted a noontime show. He had been an outstanding basketball player at

DeMatha High School where he played for legendary Coach Morgan Wooten. Subsequently, he starred at Harvard before being drafted by the Atlanta Hawks. After college, James became the television color analyst for the Washington Bullets. He now hosts the National Fox AFC Sunday doubleheader football show. I called James to inform him that we had two players from our 1954 team. He asked for them as guests. Following lunch, we escorted John and Corky to a room with a telephone hookup to the radio station. John and Corky were really enthusiastic on the show.

The following comments speak to us from the past on tape from the radio interview on WTEM. The conversation was punctuated by much laughter. Corky describes his last game, retelling his story about the West Virginia game. Pay close attention to his final comment.

James Brown   I have heard so much about these guys. I am at a disadvantage because I did not follow the team back in 1953-1954. I was two years old at the time. I have heard so much about Corky Devlin and the Holups. Now we have them. Is it John or Joe we have now?

John Holup   This is John Holup.

James Brown   You guys were at the coach's banquet today at G. W.?

Corky Devlin   Yes, it was our second coach's banquet.

James Brown   Recognizing that this year's team record stands at 10-2 (after the West Virginia loss), it is off to the best start since your team that went 11-0 and finished the season at 23-3. Let me start first with Corky Devlin—class of 1955. He was the fourth all-time leading scorer and played professionally with Fort Wayne and Minneapolis. When you look at the guys today, were you hoping that they would challenge your team's record, or were you hoping that your record would stay intact? Be honest about it.

Corky Devlin   Being honest about it, I didn't want anybody to break my record.

James Brown That's calling it like it is.

Corky Devlin The kids playing today are 10 times the players that we were.

James Brown You have to be pleased that these guys are putting G. W. back on the map as you guys did back then.

Corky Devlin There is almost a parallel, James. Back when John and Joe and I were playing, the university was in a building phase. It was a great opportunity to help the university, help ourselves, and help the program become more nationally recognized.

James Brown I'm hearing that the Atlantic Ten Conference is now rated as sixth best in the country. George Washington was picked in the preseason as number three. I've got to believe that if these young guys continue to develop, John, they can compete for the title.

John Holup Yes. The biggest advantage I see is that they have a big man. You are always competitive when you have a big man. They do have a lot of good ball players. As coach said, he plays his bench. I agree with Corky. Today's players do a lot more than we did in our day.

James Brown John, take us back. What made that 23-3 squad so good? You went to the NCAA tournament.

John Holup As I see it, Coach Reinhart was very good at recognizing talent and putting his team together. He hand-picked players. Eliot Karver and I started on the freshman team. Corky joined us from junior college. My brother, Joe, came in later and probably outdid us all. We needed a point guard which we found in George Klein. We usually went with six players. Corky played both front and backcourt.

James Brown Let me see, Joe, you were drafted by the Boston Celtics.

Corky Devlin   James. It's John.

James Brown   Did I say Joe?

John Holup   I'm the good-looking brother.

James Brown   The safest thing for me to say is J. Holup.

Corky Devlin   Remember it this way, James. It's the accordion player, not the drummer.

James Brown   I was going to say Joe was drafted by the Celtics back in 1953.

John Holup   I was drafted by the Celtics.

Corky Devlin   We'll get this right.

James Brown   Why don't you guys conduct the conversation? Ask me some questions.

Corky Devlin   Actually, Joe was drafted in 1955-1956 by the Syracuse Nationals.

James Brown   I love it. Did you hear the disclaimer at the beginning? I was two years old.

Corky Devlin   And you're living up to it.

James Brown   Corky, I've got my notes from when I was two years of age and I can't read them.

Corky Devlin   I remember you and your daddy sitting right there in the front row.

John Holup   In later years, I was the school administrator at Roosevelt High School in D.C. Occasionally, I would have a parent come in and recognize me as the ball player they watched at Uline Arena.

James Brown   I love it. Uline Arena. There's a name from the past.

John Holup   Uline was a nice place compared to some of the other places we played.

Corky Devlin   John, tell the truth. Uline was never a nice place. It was like being in The Boston Gardens. We put the boards down over the ice. We froze them out. We had the greatest baskets in the world. I wish I owned them today.

James Brown   Let me ask, John. Didn't you lead the team in 1952 in scoring, averaging close to 14 points per game?

John Holup   Right.

James Brown   All right! I got one fact correct. Now before I let you guys go, Corky did I hear a story correctly about a game you guys played at West Virginia? Hot Rod Hundley was playing. Was there a fight at the end when you actually punched the guy?

Corky Devlin   Yeah. I punched Hot Rod.

James Brown   Tell the story. What actually happened?

Corky Devlin   Here is the shorthand version. Double overtime game. It was the Southern Conference Tournament at a time when most of the ACC teams were members—Duke, Maryland, North Carolina State, etc. West Virginia got ahead of us by five or six points. Rod went into his act of spinning the ball and hot-dogging; I wasn't going to let him embarrass me in my last college game. I said to him as he went to the foul line "Knock it off or I'm going to belt you." He laughed at me, and he threw one behind his back. He took a left-handed hook shot on the other foul shot. I chased him for about

	15 feet and threw a punch at him. He stood up and wanted to shake hands. I punched him again. The crowd started booing. They threw everything that wasn't nailed down on to the court.
James Brown	Wow!
Corky Devlin	We had to stand there while they went through the awards ceremony. As the fourth, third, and second place teams received their awards, people are walking by and slapping me on the head and telling me what a clown I am. I'm crying like a baby. That's very tough for an Irish guy like me to do.
James Brown	What a dangerous thing to do in West Virginia!
Corky Devlin	Actually, it was down in Richmond. During the awards ceremony, I got up and had to walk the length of the court. The crowd was hollering and screaming. By the time I got to half court, they began to realize that I was going to apologize. It went from booing to silence to a standing ovation.
James Brown	Outstanding. You know how to work a crowd.
Corky Devlin	What I remember most was that Rod Brown, who was the A.D. at West Virginia, actually came into our shower to hug me and tell me that it was a classy thing for me to do.
James Brown	Thank you, guys, for a great interview.
Corky Devlin	It isn't often that you get a chance to lie about yourself 40 years after the fact.

XXIX

ALONE AND ON THE GO

Audrey Karver is the widow of Elliot Karver, who played with Corky for two years at George Washington. Although Elliot died in 1977, Audrey is blessed with clear recollections of her college days, including experiences with Corky. As a Minnesota girl, she began dating Elliot during their sophomore year. Elliot remained at school for an extra semester, coaching the Junior Varsity team. Audrey could evaluate Corky from a woman's perspective.

Q: What did you think of Corky during your college days?
A: He was already into gambling: he was always short of money. Since Elliot's death, I have not heard a thing about him. I remember Corky and Elliot got into a shouting match at Georgetown during a very close game. Corky was not normally that type of player. He told a lot of stories.

Elliot was contacted by the Baltimore Bullets. To show you how times have changed, they offered him a salary of $8,000. I still have the letter presenting their offer.

Elliot's response was, "No way. I could go into private industry with any of the big corporations and make at least $12,000 per year. Why would I play basketball for $8,000 a year?"

That ended his career.

Q: Today, $8,000 doesn't cover the player's meals.
A: Of course not. That wouldn't even pay their electric bill. Pretty funny. The minimum is now $325,000 per year. My youngest son, Mark, was not

good enough to play in the NBA, but he had a nice career playing for 10 years in Europe. He got to see the world and quit playing this year.

Q: Let's get back to Corky. Do you have any memories of how Elliot viewed him?

A: He was a sneaky guy. I watched him at parties in Fraternity Houses. Girls seemed to like him. He was someone Elliot and I never trusted. He never mixed much with his teammates. Instead, he hung out at a couple of fraternities. Beyond that, he was just a gambler. I want to be kind. Elliot never hung with him. Corky never became a part of our group because nobody liked him. I viewed him as kind of strange. He didn't fit in.

Q: Not trustworthy?

A: That would apply. He was always hitting you for money. After college, he bet on a lot of games.

Q: He gambled after college?

A: He went to the racetrack often in college, usually by himself. Elliot and some friends also went to the track. They also hustled pool on 14th Street. Corky always stayed to himself. We never knew what Corky was doing. I just assumed that it wasn't good. We never knew whether his stories were true.

Q: Did Elliot comment on Corky's performance as a player?

A: He was selfish. He competed 100 percent, attempting to outdo the star on the other team. He liked the spotlight. Originally, Coach Reinhart didn't like New York ball players because they were too "smart-assed." After coaching troublesome kids from other states, he came to like New York kids.

Q: Where was Elliot from?

A: The Bronx.

Q: Describe Corky's social life from a woman's perspective.

A: Corky dated a cheerleader for years. The relationship may have been exclusive for her, but it certainly wasn't with him. He constantly moved around, doing his thing. Her last name was Mather.

Audrey proved helpful while painting an unflattering picture. I hadn't realized how little professional basketball players were paid in the middle '50s. Only highly-motivated players joined the NBA. Others, including Elliot Karver, found the pay ludicrous. In essence, playing basketball required a financial sacrifice. Players of that era didn't dream of million-dollar contracts. They had no illusion of the big payoff. Corky's career offered camaraderie and gentler interaction with teammates. Serious fights were the exception. Corky seemed to be a non-fighter to Audrey. He wandered within his world fueled by competitive drive. He needed desperately to prove himself. He understood Elliot's view of professional basketball's limited salary potential. Like a moth, he was attracted to the limelight. Corky was drawn to the thrill. Pro basketball bestowed additional years for glory and fast-paced living. He hung on for three years before his body broke down. Ultimately, he lost control.

* * *

The fight Audrey recalled was more a shouting match. It occurred against Georgetown University at McDonough Memorial Gym during the 1952-1953 season. Coincidentally, that game reunited Corky with Bill Devlin (his father.) In the excitement after George Washington's thrilling overtime victory during which Corky played a key role, he felt a tug on his arm.

"I'm your father," an elderly man yelled.

"Where were you?" Corky growled.

Bill Devlin was ready to inflict pain on his wounded son.

The game story appeared in the Washington Post, written by Herb Heft.

G.W. SNAPS HOYAS STREAK IN OVERTIME 79-65
DEVLIN SAVES COLONIALS ON STEAL AND FIELD GOAL

George Washington University exploded for 21 points in an overtime period and knocked Georgetown out of the ranks of the unbeaten, 79-65 last night at jam-packed McDonough Gym.

Corky Devlin, a 6-foot, 5-inch sophomore from Newark, saved the day for the Colonials 49 seconds before regulation time expired when he stole the ball from Hoya Bill Bolger and drove in for a lay-up that enabled G. W. to pull into a 58-58 tie.

Devlin ... was the high scorer with 22 points. Eight of them came in the important fourth quarter. Elliot Karver, the husky drive-in guard, had 13 before he fouled out seconds before the end of regulation time.

XXX

THE NATURE OF ADDICTION

In February, 2004, I interviewed addictions counselor and former football player, Dennis Umberger. He was born and raised in Palmyra, three miles east of Hershey, PA. His high school team was misnamed the "Palms." Dennis still remembers their favorite cheer, "We sway to the left, we sway to the right, stand up, sit down, fight, fight, fight." Gritty stuff, very intimidating.

Dennis kicked for Adams State College in Alamosa, Colorado. In 1971 he was drafted by the Pittsburgh Steelers, where he kicked for one year. A knee injury forced retirement. Long before professional football, Dennis found himself addicted to kicking.

Q: What does "addicted to kicking" mean?

A: My father was a perfectionist. Mine was an all-consuming need to please him. As early as elementary school, I obsessed over the art of kicking. At 11, I propped a football on the ground and kicked it over light-tension wires. Success prodded me to practice more. I strained for greater distance. I craved love and affection, which I never received from my father. I kicked longer and more accurately. My father told everyone else that I was the best kicker he had ever seen. He never told me. In 1967, I set a Pennsylvania high school record with a 51-yard field goal. In college, I kicked a 57-yard field goal, the result of practice, practice, practice. My longest kick brought national recognition. It was a 94-yard punt (a record that still stands.)

Q: You were also a punter?
A: I punted in high school and in college.
Q: You hold the national punting record?
A: I believe so. During that fateful weekend in 1969, I set the record on a Saturday. The next day the New York Jets played in Denver (200 miles north.) The Jets kicker hit a 99-yard punt. The Denver Post split its front sports page. My picture was on the left and the Jets punter on the right. As far as I know, both records still stand.
Q: What did your father say that day?
A: To me? Nothing.
Q: Not even, "Good kick"?
A: No. He was not there. He witnessed my high school field goal. I attended college 1,800 miles from home. He only came to Colorado for parents' weekends. So he saw none of my record kicks. Ironically, everybody in Palmyra learned about my exploits from him.
Q: You kicked for the Pittsburgh Steelers in 1971. Wasn't that Terry Bradshaw's first year?
A: Yes, it was also Terry Hanratty's first year. When I blew my knee out, I turned to teaching. I taught elementary physical education for 20 years in Elizabethtown, PA, and I also coached football. After I took a sabbatical leave, I never returned to education.

I migrated to the mental-health field working on welfare projects for a Philadelphia-based company. This included four different prisons in the state of Maryland. I specialized in drug-addition counseling and case management. I have been working in drug addiction for the past six years. I have been at my current hospital for two years.
Q: While in the prisons, did you counsel prisoners?
A: At times. Mainly I taught educational classes for vocational services. I prepared prisoners to hold jobs after incarceration.
Q: Are you are currently working in drug addiction?
A: Drug addiction with dual diagnosis (mental health and drug addiction).
Q: Does Corky's story ring true?
A: Oh, my goodness! It's so familiar for so many players. My first connection was with the great offensive lineman who played for the Steelers, Mike Webster. He experienced a similar situation. He digressed from riches to rags. Mike played as a leader of Super Bowl teams. He ended up selling his Super Bowl rings. Over the years, many players tried to help

him. Their efforts accomplished nothing. He kept moving downhill. He died a homeless person on the streets of Pittsburgh.

Q: Was his downfall gambling?

A: I don't know exactly. I'm convinced his addiction was alcohol and drug related.

Q: Corky embraced his homeless lifestyle.

A: Once a person reaches that stage, he gets comfortable The question becomes "Did he have an out?" Some people showed interest in helping Corky out of that lifestyle. Could any one empower Corky to want to be a better person? I work with many people directly off the street. Literally, they have slept in a car that night. Their plight is compounded by becoming comfortable while they see no way out.

Q: How destructive is gambling as an addiction?

A: Addictive gambling is very similar to alcohol, food, shopping, or drugs. One addiction is not better than another. They all require tremendous effort to get out.

Q: What similarities occur among addicts?

A: People enter addiction when they "lose themselves." They embark on a desperate search for something to replace themselves. The outward search (the addiction) is directed towards happiness. They fail to realize that happiness only comes from inside.

Gambling leads to loss of money. Alcohol and drugs result in a loss of health. Who can measure which is a better addition? Addiction begins very early in life. Most of us never had a chance. We were wounded early which builds into our loss of control. Addicts learn to cope. Our final epic is between turning around or falling further down hill. We decide the addiction part (whether to accept full addiction.) The only person who can stop my addiction is myself.

Q: Some addicts see themselves as victims.

A: Yes. Some addicts act the victim for a long time, "Woe is me. Poor me." They must progress beyond that stage.

Q: Is "The world owes me" behind the thinking of most addicts?

A: Many have that attitude. "I'm going to stay right where I am. I want the world to do something for me."

These addicts must reach the bottom. They experience loss of family, of job, or of source of income. There are only three endings: death, imprisonment or insanity. Corky was hospitalized twice. He was imprisoned twice. Left untreated, addiction always results in one of these three outcomes. Many of my patients have died. Others have been institutionalized. Some of them have gone to jail.

Q: Corky was institutionalized. Once his father had him admitted. Another time he entered on his own to beat a rap. Could he have turned to the institution during a weak moment? Does self-admission make sense?

A: When his father admitted him, was Corky willing?

Q: His stay in a Virginia institution was against his will.

A: The addict's life must become so unbearable that he wants to go. I don't believe that happened to Corky. He did not walk through those doors crying out, "I want to better my life." The motive cannot be, my mom or my wife wants me to go. I have patients who have been admitted five or six times. Each program lasts 28 days.

Q: What percentage of compulsive gamblers actually go to get out of gambling?

A: Realize one thing, addiction is always with you. You don't graduate to being clean and never gamble again. Temptation clouds your mind every day. The slightest stimulus can entice a return to gambling. The sun comes up and the world seems too hot. Therefore, I decide to start gambling again.

Q: He gambled because it became hot?

A: Yes. Today's a good day to gamble. Addictions morph. People can be addicted to one thing today and something else the next day. Addicts juggle between them. The rehabilitation process is vitally important. Those who succeed become able to look at their inner selves. Through treatment, they recapture their inner lost child.

Q: I have experienced inner child work. Is it that important?

A: That is the toughest process you will ever go through. Interior work is all about reclaiming your inner child. Finding his real self (inner child) enables the addict to at least slow his addiction.

Q: I embraced my inner child and promised him that I would never let him be harmed again. I heard his sobbing deep inside me. I finally faced emotional beating during my childhood. In adulthood, I let other people take advantage of my fears and past hurts. I remained extremely vulnerable.

A: Exactly. That vulnerability is always the outcome when you have been deprived. You reach adulthood having never found yourself. I remember my own childhood. I realize that I was competitive from the time I first came out of the shoot. I embraced competition. I competed to survive. When asked what I could have done differently, I say I would have been a golfer or a tennis player. My life was consumed by team sports. I needed to be obsessive to excel. I look back and wonder why. As a child, I couldn't answer that question. But I did wonder why. Why did I spend countless hours kicking a football? Today, I'm negative about all team sports.

Q: If your father had not driven you, would your life have been very different?

A: Most definitely. After many hours (and dollars) spent in counseling, I have concluded that my father did his best. I have met many other people with similar stories. My father was addicted to work. When he retired, he had three pensions. He was proud of that.

The most important commonality people with addictions have is that they never had any kind of spiritual life. I see a difference between religion and spirituality. That difference is hard to explain. I attended church as a child, but I had no relationship with God. During recovery, spirituality is the most difficult and final piece that returns to an addict's life.

Q: Progress in your addiction depends on an awakening of a sense of spirituality?

A: Most definitely. You have to. To become whole in recovery, the addict must develop a relationship with his higher power. Early in the process, addicts are taught to consider anything (even a plate) as his higher power. He has no concept. Once he begins talking to his higher power, he starts to realize that there is a God.

Any addiction, whether work-related, gambling, or to sporting events, shares a common defect. It lacks balance.

Q: Addicts behave like zombies?

A: Exactly. In an addict's mind, he feels alone. He sees himself as the only one in the world who suffers with this problem. During rehabilitation, he learns that he is not alone. It is not difficult for me to identify specific addictions. I am around addicts all the time. I try hard to empower them instead of doing it for them. The pain of addiction that I have experienced helps me now.

Q: I have heard that good counselors remain in therapy themselves. Is that true?

A: Ours is an ongoing process. We are never completely healed before the day we die. Everyday I work at balancing myself. Balancing affects four areas of life: spiritual, physical, mental, and social. Addicts are not able to socialize before first facing their addiction. If they are unable to know and like themselves, they cannot love someone else. The addict's world is full of abuse. I have encountered no recognizable difference in outcome between physical and verbal abuse. I was both beaten and yelled at. My outcome is that it hurts deeply inside.

Q: I notice tears in your eyes when you think of your father. I value your openness. When I started searching for Corky, I thought like a star-struck sports fan. My appreciation of Corky with his limitations has traversed so many layers. We have no way to completely understand another human being.

A: It is good to cry. It helps you heal.

Q: You welcome tears as healing?

A: Most definitely. I have shed enough and pounded enough pillows during my own counseling. I bitched and moaned and carried on. It was all worth it. Through addiction, I have met some wonderful people and lost other wonderful people along the way. That happens.

Q: How many have you lost?

A: I would guess I lost 50 percent of my friends. They died either for health reasons or through car accidents when they were high. Losing patients is an ongoing experience.

Q: How do you cope with such loss?

A: Sometimes deaths are family members. Addiction hurts families, even kills families. An addict in your home can even affect the animals. Think about it. If you understand addiction, you know why animals react the way they do.

Q: What animal behaviors are caused by the presence of an addict in its family?

A: Why does a dog suddenly bite when a family member raises his voice? Mental health and addiction affect everyone in the family. I spent time in rehab with all the members of a popular band, dealing with their drugs. Their names must remain anonymous.

Q: You have been in rehab?

A: I'm not afraid to say that I spent time in rehab.

Q: Why?

A: Dysfunctional relationships. I was an achievaholic. After my first marriage, I fell apart. I didn't understand what had happened. My counselor got down on his hands and knees to beg me to go to this place. He pleaded with me to find out why I was the way I behaved. I took him up on it. Thank God I did. It started the process of recovery including my continuing quest for balance. Otherwise, I could have crawled through life not knowing what the hell was going on.

Q: It takes courage to face yourself?

A: Courage, wisdom, strength, and surrendering prayer. That's what coping with addiction is.

Q: He had nowhere else to turn. When he took my money for his last gambling spree, Corky's money ran out. Defeated, he traveled to Kentucky, after borrowing bus money from his sister. He looked pathetic, wearing clothes and shoes that did not fit. This time the monks at Gethsemani accepted him. Fr. Dan Rocco urged Corky to try again. He was ready to accept God's invitation.

My question is this: after his life of addiction, could Corky become joyous like Scrooge on Christmas morning? Can anyone suddenly become loving and free of all additions?

A: No one can ever be free of addiction just like that. I don't think there is a magic wand. Total recovery can't be accomplished even by my higher power. Addiction requires a consistent change of attitude and behavior. No one can accomplish that in less than two years. Corky spent 18 months at Gethsemani in his mid '60s. He could never change that life style in such a short time. I don't want to say that God does not have the power to accomplish miracles. He does. But a permanent change requires practice. Only Corky, with the help of his higher power, could change over time. Does that make sense to you?

Q: It does. He appeared happy and free of addictions.

A: I believe that addiction remains with us until the day we die. Our challenge is to not let the addiction control us. We fight a 24-hour battle fueled by a desire to get better. Nothing permanent happens in an instant. I wish it could. God knows how much I wish it would. Addicts suffer so much pain. I can't adequately compare my inward pain to the physical pain I encountered in sports. The inward pain hurts so much more intensely.

Q: Will you ever get rid of it?

A: Will I overcome the pain? No. The pain lessens as I change my attitude and behavior. At times I thought the pain would never lessen. During those times, I worked my program. Thank God. I still feel the pain. It keeps me in reality.

Q: The pain draws you through life?

A: There is pain in everyone's life. We all experience mental, physical, spiritual, and emotional pain. Anyone not admitting to pain is in denial.

If a person can't acknowledge the pain inside, he will cope by switching to another addiction or compulsion. Corky must have experienced other addictions popping up later. New addictions might not have been immediate. Alcoholics Anonymous teaches that when you take alcohol away, the addict becomes a dry drunk. AA members spend years working on issues. I'm not pointing a finger. Recovery is not just abstaining; it requires constant work on the cause.

Q: What questions would you ask the Abbot?
A: I don't agree that he became addiction-free.
Q: Tell me what to ask.
A: Try this. What did you do to free him from addiction? What did Corky experience during his time at the monastery that made him so-called addiction-free? If you claim he became addiction-free, you should consider taking out a patent. I need to know, "How did you do it?"

XXXI

JUST ONE MORE GOOD DAY

During my third encounter with Fr. Dan Rocco, his contribution to *In Search of Corky* became a trilogy. Once again, Fr. Dan seemed serenely prepared for my arrival. Unexpectedly, we uncovered the most significant experience of Corky's life.

Q: This past weekend I enjoyed a new movie, "The Notebook." James Garner plays the older version of a lover who attempts to reclaim his wife from dementia. A young doctor assures him that coming back is impossible. James Garner disagrees saying, "With God, nothing is impossible." The movie depicts the death of their lifelong love relationship. Remembering my own fractured marriage, magnified by the rarity of lifelong commitments, moved me to tears. The story introduced nobility to aging.

A: Death is a rather weird phenomenon. I have befriended many people while they were dying. I talked with sick people who were experiencing illness that was not going to go away. They plead, "I just want one good day." They seem desperate to recapture something that will never be. The popular interpretation is that they are not being realistic.

I see the terminal person's request differently. He is yearning for that which is being offered to him. He wants to be free from what is binding him so he can be more complete during his movements through death. He seeks peace at last. Through memories is how he understands his passage. He interprets it as "One more good day." Reliving that day, he will be able to play golf or throw a ball again. That yearning will one day be fulfilled. He can only imagine the end through the limitations of the past experience.

Q: So the terminal person experiences his request as remembrance of a past event, but he is really looking forward?

A: He hears the call from beyond to let go of that which binds him. The more I witness people as they are dying, the clearer I identify this call. The response requires a fundamental choice. I choose whether to live in the past and regret who I am now. Or I choose to see the possibilities hidden within what I am now.

Q: The challenge of the cocoon to the butterfly?

A: Exactly. Our choice embodies the question of trust. The darkness and pain of terminal suffering cloud temptation. Each of us agonizes over our last temptation. For Christ, in the movie "The Last Temptation of the Christ," the devil sat on his shoulder telling him that he had already accomplished redemption. The devil urged Him to get off the cross. Only the pain of the nails enabled Jesus to realize that this was His last temptation. He must pass all the way through.

Q: Death is the deepest dread in all of our lives.

A: Exactly. It controls all of our lives. That is why the early Christians were able to go to their deaths for their faith. They came to accept and trust that there is more.

Q: How can I acquire that trust?

A: Through experience, I believe. You experience God's love for you. As you accept God, a bond forms. Nothing can take that bond away.

Q: Am I asking too much of you? Project what Corky experienced during his last hour.

A: It has to do with surrender. We can always draw back from surrender. In the Garden of Gethsemani, Jesus pleaded to have the cup taken away from Him. Up to the very end, He could have rejected the suffering. That is why, when people are dying, I whisper in their ear, "Keep your eye on Jesus." I am saddened that in a very Catholic home, a cross is not put in front of the dying person. The family would do well to play sacred music. A passage is taking place. We witness a Passover, but we don't help the person. We fail because we view death as finality rather than journey.

Q: A Passover is taking place?

A: Right. We go from the slavery of this world to a freedom. It is similar to the Passover of the Israelites. We, too, pass over into our promised land. We struggle with the temptation not to trust.

Getting back to your question about Corky, a lot depends on the surroundings you place yourself in when you die. The environment is very important. Corky went to Gethsemani. That speaks volumes. He traveled to the monastery for a number of reasons. He was running away. It was a layover. He had reached the end of his rope through his addiction. Or was he still searching? Gethsemani became the place where he felt at peace in order to make Passover.

Q: *He sensed that his death was approaching?*

A: Exactly.

Q: *He told me that the doctors gave him no more than six months to live. They predicted that he would just drop over while watching TV.*

A: That is what I mean. Where could he just drop over? He made a conscious choice to go to a place where there are no TVs. He was not denying imminent death. He was preparing for that event. He did not plan a purely functional death. He pondered, "Where am I going to put myself? How am I going to die?"

Q: *Are those the questions that all people ask?*

A: I think so. Not everyone deals with each question consciously. But we work it out as best we can. We examine our history and our aspirations.

Q: *You encountered Corky after he had been accepted at Gethsemani. Did you sense that he knew he was dying?*

A: No, I didn't. I was shocked when I learned of his death. That leads me to a more important question. How did he die? More important than his death, was what took place.

Q: *Corky didn't show up for work one afternoon. He collapsed in his room. Pills were all over the floor. It was a quick death.*

A: I suspect that he was in the process of dying the whole 18 months he was there. When did he die?

Q: *It was 2:30 in the afternoon on April 28, 1995.*

A: Check that out. What was happening when he died? Remember, the Transfiguration has been very prominent in our meetings. We met twice on that day. August 6th is important between us. Was anything happening when Corky died? Find out the context of Corky's death. You might not find anything. Study the person and the place. You need to understand the forces that a person brings upon a holy place.

Have you ever seen the classical movie "Monsignor Quixote"?

Q: *No.*

A: It is a great movie.

Q: Another assignment. "Barabbas" enlightened my view of Corky. At first, I didn't understand.

A: "Monsignor Quixote" stars Alec Guinness. The Monsignor is a descendent of the famous Don Quixote. He finds himself in conflict with his bishop, so he embarks on a journey in Spain. His companion is the Communist Mayor (Sancho) of his town. As a result of the Monsignor's bizarre behavior, his bishop orders him to stop celebrating the Eucharist. With Sancho, he seeks sanctuary in a monastery. In the middle of the night, the Monsignor arises to go say Mass. The monastery's abbot remembers that the bishop forbade Monsignor from saying Mass. Also at the monastery is an American professor who is devoted to finding artifacts from the famous Saint Ignatius of Spain. The Abbot, the professor, and Sancho follow the Monsignor through the halls. Monsignor enters the church to celebrate the Eucharist. He has no wine or bread.

What follows is a very beautiful scene. The Monsignor approaches his compatriot Sancho and says, "Body of Christ. Companero, you have to accept this." There is nothing in his hands. Sancho opens his mouth in acceptance. The Monsignor dies.

Companero means "sharer of bread." Because they have broken bread together, they are friends. The professor protests, "But nothing was there. It wasn't a Mass." The Abbot understands. "Which is easier, to change wine to water or air to the Risen Lord?"

The point is that at the end of Monsignor's odyssey, a culmination takes place. We never know whether he was in his right mind. That was the professor's perspective. The Mass was just part of Monsignor's movement towards death.

Q: To his death?

A: To his death and life eternal. That whole transition is really strong. I believe there are parallels in this story to Corky at the end of his life.

Q: You have pulled me in. Two weeks ago, The Bucks County players produced 'The Man of La Mancha.' That play was the first professional show I ever saw (30 years ago.) In 1975, I went on a Marriage Encounter. Featured were the songs describing the transformation of Dulcinea. I gained a whole different understanding of Don Quixote. Seeing the show again was like returning to where I started, but grasping it through different eyes. The message was still wonderful, but different.

A: You are not writing pure nonfiction. You are searching the movement of life. You seek to understand death and resurrection. You must understand how these elements come together.

Q: I was looking for the rhythm of life, death, and resurrection before you guided me. You pointed out that this book has become more about me. You lead me in a way similar to Henrie Nowen's description of his being pulled by a rope through life.

A: Pulling can also be described as birthing. The process determines how we move. Birthing is Passover. When you pass from the womb into the light, you leave the water. The entire process is birthing. How can we know, when we are in the womb, what life is like outside the womb? We don't. Through the love of our mother and our father, we acquire a sense of trust for the natural birthing of life. The birth in process, the pain, the suffering, and the oneness with the mother culminate in a sudden cry of life. It is the same with death.

Q: Have we ever heard the cry of death?

A: We have. Jesus rose from the dead.

Q: That is the cry? If we believe in Him, we join in His resurrection?

A: Yes. As Paul writes, "If the resurrection is not true, then none of our faith is true."

Q: When I visit, you seem to be waiting for me. Your insights lead me.

A: You are dealing with a theme that is universal. You are writing the story of a person who both attracts and repulses people. If Corky was simply a no-good rat, you would not be writing. There was something about him that convinced you that he was a nice guy. This created the tension in his personality. You uncovered dynamic tension. His struggle launched your own search for the truth.

Q: The pupil sits at the foot of his master. Do your answers inspire you?

A: They are part of me. Have you ever walked in the mountains or the forest? You have never been there before, but somehow you know the way. You know which is the better way to go. Something guides you towards your destination. Your senses choose the best way. Intuitively, you select the best place to cross a creek. This guidance comes from being at "one with."

Hopefully, we become connected to the Holy. That is why, when I was ordained a priest, I accepted connection through Holy Orders (an order of Holiness). Priesthood is ordered. It is not scattered or chaotic. I was offered orderliness. That doesn't mean that I cannot fall off the path. We all thrive on the orderliness of the journey. A lot of people go astray. They acquire addictions. They commit sins. Yet deep inside they intuitively know that there is something else. They sense what they "should be" headed towards.

That yearning for order is what I think was happening with Corky. It may, in turn, be happening with you. Obviously, you trust your call or you wouldn't be here. You are trying to steer your search towards a conclusion. The one person who should benefit from your search is you. Only you can decide if finding Corky is complete. Does this feel right?

Q: Everything you have said rings true. How the search will end remains mysterious.

A: You must finish the search. Then sit back and ask yourself the question, "What is the pattern of my own life?" You will draw upon the pattern of Corky's life.

Q: Because I am growing older, I have considered my pattern. One word that haunts me is failure. That word seems measured by achievement. Every goal I have attempted in life has, alas, failed. I have imitated the idealistic Don Quixote in the computer companies I have started. My marriage failed. I don't have a great relationship with my kids. But I never gave up hope that relationships may still work out. My personality is to remain optimistic. Why have I fallen short of my own expectations?

A: What expectations do we have of ourselves? Where do they come from?

Q: In my case, from my father. I spent the early part of my life (until the last few years) trying to please my father.

A: OK. Let me ask this question. Were you trying to please your father or were you trying to please The Father?

Q: Both. I named one of my companies "Alpha Omega Medical Systems." I didn't understand the reason at the time.

A: A lot of times we make our fathers God. We create an impossible situation. We cannot possibly please them. In reality, they might not ask so much from us. Mostly, we superimpose our notion that we must work out our own way to salvation. That is even more impossible. We cannot earn our own way to salvation.

Q: Corky's book represents my break from trying to please my father. I have changed professions. In the writing, I have trusted more. Has it stretched me towards maturity?

A: You must finish this transformation.

Q: What if someone reads it?
A: That fear is always present, if we place expectations before we finish the task. Fear of failure becomes our impediment to the accomplishment. Finish it. In completeness, you will experience the grace.
Q: Until now I could not envision the finished product.
A: At least you are now able to acknowledge potential accomplishment.
Q: I have a tendency to discount accomplishments.
A: Exactly. Why? Because you measure them against something else. Comparison is unfair to both you and what your have created.
Q: Can you think of anything else about Corky?
A: You question how to end the story. I suggest you let Corky finish it for you. Follow Cork's footsteps to Gethsemani. The conclusion will come to you. Attend services so the answers can come to you through prayer. All comes to us through prayer.
Q: Thoughts and inspirations come from nowhere. Even the decision to return to your office seems inspired. What made you hesitate about our third meeting?
A: I was balking because our encounter appeared to be just another meeting. It was only a mark on my schedule. Now that we have talked, my understanding has changed.
Q: You received something from our meetings?
A: Yes. If you can say that what you have created is beautiful, you have accomplished something worthwhile.
Q: The book is already beautiful. The writing is unyieldingly truthful.
A: We have discussed the four basic truths presented in the beginning of the Bible. One truth says, "Everything is *good*." A more accurate translation of that word is "*beautiful*." So God said, "This is beautiful." Beauty is an integral part of His world.

When you experience harmony, you connect intellectually, intuitively, and sensually to the experience of beauty. Keep this in mind when you visit Gethsemani. It is a place I have never visited.
Q: You must go.
A: I hope to. I almost went before Corky died.

My European professors used a gesture to describe something that is more. When they can't find the word, they say, "The best." Simultaneously, they rub their first two fingers against their thumb in a circular motion.
Q: In our country that same gesture signifies money.

A: There you go. When I studied in Europe, pure thinkers espoused great ideas. But it took the Americans to put the ideas into practice. To be practical, we reduce ideas to a skeleton. We take off all the flesh. When this happens, the idea loses its beauty. Contributions like Psychoanalysis and Economic Theories have been stripped down. Americans remove anything that is unnecessary. We lose "Something More." That is what mystery is.

Q: *Our world is devoid of mystery?*

A: We forfeit awe for the ebb and flow of being connected. You must cultivate that sense of awe. Then you will be on the right track.

Q: *Your interpretation of life strikes me as whimsically Irish. Your Italian heritage has become more apparent.*

A: It is becoming more aware beyond what is seen. When we profess our faith, we declare, "We believe in the visible and the invisible, the seen and the unseen." As someone is dying, I always call on the saints. I invite their connectedness. The saints tug at us. They prepare our journey. They serve as an integral unseen escort.

Q: *When I wrote The Preface, I questioned whether we are physical beings experiencing spiritual intervention or the reverse. My answer then was "both."*

A: Do not let the evidence betray the truth. Had Corky left Gethsemani before dying or rejecting his experience, you would have no story. His choice to stay may not have been conscious. Corky's gift to touch and manipulate people comes with a good and a bad side. His struggle towards his destiny included an unseen level. He groped with choice framed by coinciding events.

Q: *I heard him say, "My life has meaning." What is that meaning? Is he leading us from beyond his grave? Could he be trying to justify his existence?*

A: You cannot justify your life. You can only live it. When you try to justify, you progress into trying to earn. I hope that his words referred to the greater questions rather than simply justifying his life. His statement went beyond his human strugglers. We all devalue ourselves when we do evil things. Here is a great truth: "Remember, everyone is really trying as hard as he / she can."

Q: *You believe that?*

A: Sometimes.

Q: *Sometimes you believe the statement or sometimes people try?*

A: Sometimes they try. That is a judgment on my part. But trying is crucial. When their life on earth ends, most people have just tried to survive. They have been painfully aware of their weaknesses and their strengths.

Q: Key to my search is whether Corky ever stopped trying. Somewhere hidden in his strengths and weaknesses is his beauty.

XXXII

STRETCHING IN KENTUCKY

Jim Murray and I revisited Gethsemani. The Abbey was originally established on December 21, 1848, by Trappists from Melleray in France. Simple three-story buildings nestle in the rolling hills of Bardstown. The monks (between 50 and 60 at present) live in the enclosure area. Each day begins with VIGILS at 3:15 AM. It ends with COMPLINE at 7:30 PM. Seven intervals of formal prayer are shared along with Community Mass. Between services, regular work is scheduled. The meals are strict vegetarian. Each monk sews and washes his own robes (habit.) After evening services, a monk can expect a maximum of seven hours sleep.

Corky loved living at Gethsemani. He participated in the services and shared meals with the monks. Deep inside, he grew quiet. He experienced endless time of silent reflection. Corky never presumed to wear the monk's habit. He dressed plainly. He embraced the contentment of knowing that one day he would die here.

Upon our arrival, Jim departed for a conference with Fr. Alan Gilmore. I interviewed Bro. Rene Richie. He is currently the night gatekeeper. He befriended and worked with Corky during much of the time he lived at Gethsemani. Bro. Rene, a gentle man, volunteered to assist my search in any way possible.

Q: Bro. Rene, you knew Thomas Merton. What was his contribution to the monastery?

A: Because he was a free spirit, he helped the monastery a lot. Merton developed an advanced theology. As monks we lived rigidly, very behind the times. If you have been given the grace to live narrowly, you can do it. Our lives weren't bad. We spoke in middle age terminology. Thomas Merton tried to introduce the thinking of the 20th century.

Q: How do you remember Corky?

A: Mostly as a good man, a friend.

Q: Did you spend time conversing?

A: Occasionally I bumped into him. I invited him to meet my family when they visited the monastery. They were very impressed by him.

Q: Did Corky ever mention being incarcerated?

A: Yes. He assured me he signed himself in. In Reno, he won a pillowcase full of money ($44,000.) To keep it safe over the weekend, he hired a detective to stand guard outside his room. He never left his room. On Monday morning, only two hours remained before he left for the airport. He started gambling and lost all the money. He realized that he couldn't trust himself anymore. He felt hurt and tired. Corky told me, "Compulsive gamblers, when they lose their shirt, they don't show remorse."

Q: Your story sounds like a combination of two stories. Did you believe him?

A: I'm trusting. Others would have had doubts.

Q: Corky expanded his story of incarceration to include befriending a female doctor.

A: Yes, he did. I asked him how he got out. His answer was that he tricked his doctor.

Q: Was that institution near Reno?

A: No. I don't think it was. It was in another state.

Q: In another story, Corky smuggled a Canadian man in the trunk of his car.

A: I can verify that his border run really did happen. He smuggled the man through Detroit and over to Windsor. Along the way he stopped to stay at my brother's house.

Q: He spent a night with your brother before smuggling the man into Canada?

A: Corky promised to get him over the border to Windsor. The man had been a guest at the retreat house.

Q: In the story, I heard Corky carried a racetrack scorecard to engage the guard about which horse was running when. His distraction caused the guard to forget to examine his trunk.

A: That sounds logical and true.

Q: Many people have claimed that Corky wanted to help.

A: He always wanted to help people. He encouraged the nuns who live near here in Loretto. He raised funds for their battered women's program.

Q: He was always searching for a cause?

A: Yes.

Q: The tension of his life mobilized those who thought him wonderful and those who believed the opposite. Are you convinced that he overcame his addictions?

A: I certainly am.

Q: Was he free of gambling?

A: That is a good question. I never specifically asked him if he was free of his gambling addiction. I don't know if he could ever be totally free of addiction.

Q: You would know if he was in a position to gamble and refused.

A: I never saw that.

Q: Corky's spiritual director described God calling him to Gethsemani. Does that make sense to you?

A: Yes. When Jim Murray brought him here for the first time, Corky experienced God in the balcony of our chapel. He realized that God was here. He wanted all that he could get from Gethsemani. He felt comfortable and he wanted to stay.

Q: He lived at the monastery for 18 months. Did he ever desire to leave?

A: He never talked about that. He certainly did not show signs of that kind of desire.

Q: Corky was perfectly happy here?

A: That, I believe. He understood himself well enough to realize that he had it made here. He felt safe, secure, loved, and respected. When you are addicted, you know that you need help. He found help here. It was unsafe to leave.

Q: Could you describe the help he received? Are you referring to God?

A: His help came from knowing God was here and that he was permitted to stay. Abbot Timothy really wanted to help him. I held the job of night guest master up at the family guesthouse. Fr. Timothy asked me to leave that job so Corky could join us. I was very happy to do anything I could for Corky.

Q: Wonderful. I did not know of your sacrifice. Were you in the monastery on the day that Corky died?

A: Oh, yes.

Q: Who went to his room?

A: Bro. Roger and Bro. Thomas (who has since died.)

Q: I try to imagine his last night.

A: I have told you how generous Corky was. Corky's heart was in very bad condition. He had been hospitalized, which caused him to take nitroglycerine. Corky had loaned his car to someone, which caused him to walk from the monastery to the family guesthouse.

Q: The walk overtaxed his heart?

A: I'm thinking that. It was a meritorious way to die.

Q: Corky's spiritual director instructed me to search for something unique about the way he died. Each of us somehow prepares for death.

A: It was just his generosity. He had a bad heart, which meant he was not supposed to walk. He had been warned to be very careful. Corky willingly gave his car away forcing him to walk. I considered that act heroic.

Q: Did he expect to get the car back?

A: Oh, yes. It was only a loan.

Q: The guest-house is not far, no more than a quarter mile.

A: He did have to climb the hill.

Q: What was your opinion of Corky?

A: I liked him very much. He liked people.

Q: While here, did he become joyous?

A: He was always joyous. I never saw him sad.

Q: Corky lived most of his life as a very sad person.

A: Listen. If he had not been continually joyful, he would not have been invited to stay here.

Q: Joyous, even before he was admitted?

A: We were not able or willing to accept a troublemaker. Fr. Timothy showed a lot of trust by admitting Corky.

Q: I tried to lure Fr. Timothy into making negative comments. Conflict was consistent with Corky's life. Fr. Timothy would not.

A: Corky lived in our guesthouse. He never got in anyone's way. The job gave him responsibility.

Q: At the time of his death he worked as the night watchman. Did he actually patrol the halls of the guesthouse in the middle of the night?
A: Occasionally. He let people in and escorted them to their rooms. He was friendly to all the families. Corky was ready to help everyone.

* * *

Bro. Rene left me in his room. He returned with Bro. Ambrose (elder statesmen of the monastery.) Bro. Ambrose was cooperative and open.

Q: Corky's brother and sister both live in New Jersey. Where are you from?
A: I'm from Texas. The very fact that Corky came to a place like this shows that there was something very good about him. Some of our monks are not easy to get along with. My cousin arrived here unable to read or write English. Corky worked hard helping him get his driver's license.

Q: What is your cousin's name?
A: Carlos. Corky took the time to teach him the entire driver's manual. Corky did such a good job that Carlos passed on his first try with flying colors. No one could have helped Carlos unless he was a very good person.

Q: Was Corky totally free of depression while you knew him?
A: Yes. Even in the hospital he was helpful and cooperative with the nurses. He never spoke about himself or his career.

Q: Was he joyful all the time?
A: Yes. He joked and talked about topics that interested the monks.

Q: His seemed a special category in the monastery. Did anyone else share that status?
A: There have been a few special people over the years. During my early years, we communicated only through sign language.

Q: How long have you been here?
A: I have been here 64 years.

Q: Have you been happy the whole time?
A: Yes. It is hard to explain. I changed when I came here. I became content and comfortable. In the early days, we did not speak. Neither did we have machinery. No car, no tractors or anything like that. The monastery was completely self-sufficient. No vehicles left and no one came in. In our secluded life, we had little sense of time.

Q: The Second World War had not started?

A: I came in 1941. When Pearl Harbor happened, we knew nothing about it. One day in 1943 we were coming from chapel. The Abbot asked for prayers because we were at war. We knew nothing because we read no newspapers or listened to radio.

Q: *No people came here on retreat?*
A: The monks didn't speak with retreatants. Only those who were assigned guest master or retreat master made any contact. Retreatants didn't speak to us. Now teachers and outside theologians give us talks.

Q: *Did a large number of religious people pass through here?*
A: Not many have stayed for any length of time. Many of the youngsters became disillusioned because we emphasized service. They had trouble making sense out of our way of life.

Q: *I want to ask a difficult question. Do you believe Corky is in heaven?*
A: Yes, if only because he came here. No one visits who doesn't experience real contact with God.

Q: *Each person is called here?*
A: Yes. You have to be called. No person can persevere in this life without God's constant help. Life here is a calling in itself.

Q: *How could Corky have convinced you that he had no calling?*
A: Only through a calling can we enter into communion with God. The calling makes our life. The head of our order in Rome visits all of the monasteries. When he visited me, he asked, "Do you know that you are one of the oldest monks in our order? You knew the life when you entered. You know what the life is now. Is it as easy to become a monk now as it was then?"

I pondered a while. Then I responded, "Yes, father. Everything in the monastery has changed except its essence. That will never change."

Q: *Corky achieved total surrender?*
A: If he stayed and got along with everyone in the community, yes. We could never be selfish. We learned to get along with the brothers to stay here. Corky loved this place. He believed that he had reached heaven.

Another man lived here who could not take the silence. He was unable to make the total gift of himself. Obviously, Corky was successful in making that gift.

Right now we are going through an adjustment. We are trying to adapt to modern society. When I came here, I was on a different planet. We never bought anything at the store. We made our own clothes and grew our food. We rode in horse-drawn wagons. As times changed, we got rid of all our cows and our horses. In the '50s we embraced the modern world.

Q: Had Corky lived, would he have remained in the monastery?

A: Yes. He was a good man and he sincerely wanted to live a good life.

Q: I detect your have Hispanic roots.

A: I am originally from Mexico.

Q: Corky had Mexican roots. He lived in an area called the Landrillas.

A: I do remember him telling me about that.

Q: I have a picture of him interacting with the children. Seeing Corky with the Mexican children has led me to ask if Corky might have become a saint.

A: Yes. Corky was not a saint according to the canonization process. He was a saint in God's eyes. That is what really counts. He became a very good man because he kept trying. He learned what life is truly about. Sadly, he lived in the limelight. On his way here, he stopped often to think of God and give Him his due. Sports figures experience a difficult time focusing on what is important.

Q: Very encouraging. Did Corky come here trying to escape any problems?

A: It was apparent that something was not quite right. I thought his problem was gambling.

Q: Did he show any tendency to return to gambling?

A: His life had moved on. He lived only in the present. Have you visited our monastery before?

Q: This is my fourth visit to Gethsemani. At first, Bro. Alban encouraged me to continue the book. On my two most recent trips, I traveled with Jim Murray. He was Corky's friend and gave Corky's eulogy.

A: I remember that. His was a very meaningful talk.

Q: I asked for a copy of the eulogy but Jim never wrote it down.

A: It was straight from his heart.

Q: Thank you for your insights about Corky. I don't feel comfortable wishing you 64 more years of monastic life. What can you tell me about Thomas Merton while he lived here?

A: We arrived in the same year. At that time, we were separated. I served as a laborer while he became a monk. Although we lived in this same building, we only communicated through sign language.

Q: When did sign language end?

A: After Vatican II, in 1962.

Q: Did you get pretty good at it?
A: No, we really didn't need it. We didn't sign for conversation. We communicated, "I'm going to work. I'm going to bed. I'm going to pick a certain vegetable." Our lives were tied through a spiritual bond. Conversation was never necessary. Through our common spirituality, we felt close. We experienced each other at a deeper level.

A hard-working man named Mr. Head came here as a painter. Every time I saw him he was painting a hall or a window. He commented to me that here was the only place where he could put his wallet on a table and forget about it. Two years later, he could return. It would still be there.

Q: What year was he here?
A: 1943. There was an atmosphere surrounding Gethsemani. Once a nun visited us from Mexico. She stayed at the guesthouse. She loved it and felt such solitude. I smiled and signed that the solitude is deafening.

Q: What did you mean by deafening?
A: God is so present that He shouts, "I am here." People think that we find solitude in the stillness. That is true. But real solitude comes when we make direct contact with God.

Q: Can you advise me on how to make that connection?
A: Well, it depends on whether you are ready. If you are ready for His presence, you will hear God. In 64 years here, I haven't found anyone who has not experienced the grace of speaking to God. In this place you live with God. You hear Him, and you can almost touch Him.

Monasteries were once everywhere in the world. Particularly, they could be found in Europe. Most of them are now hulls. What has happened? Have people stopped looking for God? I don't think we stopped searching. I think we have failed in contemplation of God. Science has replaced spirituality. Sadly, we lack the time and the ability to rest with God.

Q: Corky claimed he could look into my eyes and read my soul. Does that sound like the Corky you knew?
A: Yes, very much so. He took a liking to my cousin at the time he came here to become a monk. Corky could see into him. Your story sounds very much like Corky. There are some people, chosen people, with whom you become one. Corky became one with a few chosen people.

Q: Were you one with Corky?
A: No. I had interaction with him about my cousin, but not much else. I can sense people who are good. Only they are capable of deep connection.

XXXIII

CROSSING THE FINISH LINE

In the evening, Jim Murray and I met for a vegetarian dinner in the Talking Dining Room. We sat at the table where, years before, we had discussed Corky with Fr. Timothy. When Fr. Damien joined us, he immediately put us at ease. He is a tall man of Irish and Polish descent. I couldn't help pondering the burden of responsibility he carried. He seemed weary.

Q: Yours is my final interview. Many believe that Corky could never change. I interviewed an addiction counselor who believed that instant cure of addiction was not possible. How much did Corky change?

A: Am I the last one?

Q: I have always believed that the story would end here with you.
(To Jim) At Gethsemane did he still have addictions?

Jim Murray: No. I saw changes. He came here to prepare for the end. That last year, I visited him for Easter with one of my sons. We ate breakfast together.

He became serious, "These guys have really taken good care of me. It's my heart. It is so damaged. I will probably be drinking a glass of iced tea, and I'll just keel over. It won't be while I'm out tilling the fields."

That is exactly the way it happened. He and I had traveled millions of miles. We were two sinners. I witnessed his journey back to his faith. He had been very angry. Here, he found the peace that he never imagined he would attain. Like all of us, he questioned his journey. His dark side lurked. The "bad boy" was part of his image.

I do know that he liked you (Fr. Damien) a lot.

Fr. Damien: We are talking about an addictive personality. All the Alcoholics Anonymous guys who come here trade their addictions for cigarettes or coffee. As a result, they can't sleep so they stay up all night.

Corky was wonderful. I am amazed that he has been dead 10 years. We still talk about the guy. There is nobody else we talk about like that.

Q: How did Corky first come here?

A: Jim Murray: I brought him here. It happened that we arrived on Holy Thursday. We attended a service in the middle of the night. Everything went black with the snuffing out of a last candle. Even an atheist could find God on campus. This is holy ground. I call it the Nuclear Power Center of prayer. Corky found something here that became very attractive to him. At last he found community and solidarity. He experienced solitude without losing himself. Prior to that night, he didn't know monastic life existed.

Coming into the church ignited Corky's determination to become a Trappist. He loved Fr. Alan and Bro. Alban. Corky thought much more deeply than people gave him credit for. He was a true searcher. His restlessness drove him to become homeless.

Fr. Damien: I know. It's amazing how he became one of us. He told so many stories. No one I have ever met remains so vivid in my mind. In spite of his pain, he always made fun of himself. Once he told me he had set the pro record for the most shots missed in a game.

Jim Murray: He wished he had taken another shot and missed.

Fr. Damien: He told another story about giving a talk to grammar school kids in New Jersey. He was enjoying a great time. The next day one of the kids came back to return his autograph. The kid complained, "My father considered you just a bench warmer."

He told that story often.

Q: How did you get to know him?

Fr. Damien: At one time, I served as boss in the kitchen. I went on a trip with Corky and a guy named Bob. The three of us stood about the same height. Bob lived by a rule that he would never pay more than the principal on any car loan. His car had been repossessed. Repo guys are usually just out of prison. They are not people to mess with. The three of us arrived at a sinister garage in Lexington. Bob was a colorful character—a white supremacist and all that. We walked in like Wyatt Earp.

Bob announced, "We want that stuff out of my van."

After collecting his personals, Bob barked, "Where are the guns?" The two of us were stunned to hear there were guns.

The reply, "We gave them to the police."

"I want my guns. Never mind the police stuff. I want my guns."

The repo guy retreated to the back. He returned with several machine guns.

I found myself holding one and blurted out, "Hey, is this thing loaded?"

Corky had been in prison. He knew how to handle the situation. He could talk to repo guys.

Q: The Abbot Gang rides again. Were you dressed as a monk?

Fr. Damien: Oh, no. We got all Bob's guns back. I just admired the guy. Have you heard all these stories?

Jim Murray: No. You are my first machine gun-toting Trappist. How did he talk you into that adventure?

Fr. Damien: The three of us were friends. It was important to Bob. So I took one of our cars and drove.

Q: Sounds like the John Dillinger mob.

Fr. Damien: Well it reminds me of his prison story.

Q: Which one?

Fr. Damien: The story goes that he was caught writing bad checks. While standing before the judge, he assumed that the judge would sentence him to easy time in a white-collar jail. But the judge hung one on him. Corky was sentenced to one of the worst prisons in California. Corky was the only white guy there. He was terrified. They put him in a cell with a psycho. His cellmate came after him armed with a pencil. Corky had reached the bottom.

He responded, "Do whatever you want. I could care less. If you want to kill me, kill me. I'm going to bed."

The cellmate was stunned. He had met someone who wasn't afraid of him. They became friends. No one in the prison bothered Corky. The psycho was his buddy.

Corky was released early because he had calmed his cellmate down. After Corky left, his cellmate was sent to a psychotic facility.

Jim Murray: Were you the one who found him dead?

Fr. Damien: No. I had previously anointed him in the hospital.

Q: Do you remember anything significant about his death?

Fr. Damien: He died up on the hill in his room. They found him on the floor. He died alone.

Q: On the day I arrived at Gethsemani, I met Bro. Alban. I was very tired and blurted out, "If God made a saint in our time, he could be Corky."

Fr. Damien: To make a saint, He might choose a layman. It would be amazing to have a non-religious. More unusual would be someone coming out of a bipolar disorder. In all the time he spent here, I never guessed that the guy was depressed. He really had a good cover.

Q: He was joyful the entire time he was here?

Fr. Damien: That is why we remember him so much. His joy stood out. He lifted everyone. Something about him sparkled. He was great at the front desk. One problem occurred after he began wearing short shorts. We agonized over how to tell him to stop wearing shorts in our Abbey. They looked like old time basketball shorts. When I told him, he understood.

Q: We have been told that he had more visitors at his grave than Thomas Merton. Are you laughing?

Fr. Damien: I'm remembering his funeral. Just today one monk mentioned that it was the biggest funeral we ever had. For a guy who was just a long-term guest, it was huge. We held it in the chapel upstairs. We acquired a great preacher. I asked this guy Jim at the last minute because he had taken weeks to prepare.

Jim Murray: Fr. Timothy, the abbot at the time, asked me while I was receiving communion.

He whispered, "Do you want to say a few words."

I'm Irish. Of course I'll do it. Do you remember the lady who was building a playground at that time? Later, she called me for fundraising help.

Fr. Damien: He was always a great greeter at the front door.

Q: He made everyone feel as though they were important?

Fr. Damien: Yes. He was everybody's friend.

Q: You never worried that he might take advantage of you. Did you ever consider him a wolf in sheep's clothing?

Fr. Damien: Oh, no. We accepted him where he was. It's funny. When you know someone really well, there isn't much you can say about them. Recently my aunt asked me to preach at her funeral. It was so much easier to talk about someone you don't quite know.

Q: You really believe that you knew Corky? Other people have complained about his face guarding (not being present to them.) Did he remove his mask with you?

Fr. Damien: He was a constant person. We held good conversations but I have trouble remembering them. I know he was a guy who wanted to be spiritual.

Q: Were you his spiritual director?

Fr. Damien: I don't know if he had one. I don't know if you can place that title on me. We talked. I presume that Corky also talked with Timothy.

Q: I tried to get Fr. Timothy to say something negative about Corky.

Fr. Damien: What do you mean by that?

Q: I suspected that Corky was close to wearing out his welcome.

Fr. Damien: That is not true.

Q: I'm not picking a fight.

Fr. Damien: I know. I really liked the guy. There have been few long-term guests with whom I developed that kind of relationship. That is why we agonized over the way he dressed. We just never observed anything negative. He wasn't contrived. All we had to do was tell him about his attire.

Q: If Corky had lived, would he still be here?

Fr. Damien: He had a relationship with one girl. Probably, that would have developed. He had no plans to become an oblate. So he probably would have moved on. He was happy here. Anyone from outside must be called to be at peace in a place like this. Our visitors have a wonderful time for a week. If they stay a month, our routine starts to gnaw at them.

Q: Thirty-day retreats separate the men from the boys?

Fr. Damien: Corky was able to keep his sense of humor. He always talked positively. Coming from his background, he changed.

Jim Murray: Most addictions have their AA groups. Corky's crisis drove him here more than once. After he arrived here, he experienced peace. He reached a comfort level, which enabled him to remove his mask. He became Corky in short shorts. He helped guys who didn't laugh, laugh. Retreatants spun stories about the guy they unexpectedly met at the Trappist Monastery. He was at peace in this place where you monks made him feel safe. He was in place, not out of place. Corky referred to you as his spiritual guy. Whatever conversation you don't remember was so profound that he considered it spiritual direction. He told me so.

Corky was tough on me. He disappeared off radar many times. He rarely told the truth. What I am hearing makes me feel good. Most of us live our lives keeping score. When we pray the "Our Father," we forgive those who trespass against us. Then we insert our own "buts." It is easier to pray for those who don't get in our way. Corky lifted everyone up. Even when monks were miserable to him, he stayed joyful. He saw Jesus in people. As a society, we are so negative. We stop here to fill our tank up. People come wounded. Corky arrived wounded. He experienced the extraordinary. I compare his journey to the story of the Prodigal Son. Corky played all three parts. In his past, he was the son who squandered everything. Here, he played the faithful son. He served as the trusted night watchman patrolling the halls with a flashlight while the monks slept. In his joy, he emulated the father after his son's return. It was not easy being the joyful friend to all the monks here.

Q: Was he really liked by all the monks?

Fr. Damien: Yes. A lot of our guys never want to get close. That is part of our rule. It was extremely rare that Corky became close to some of our guys. His stories still circulate. One day he was in Baltimore when he learned of a card game in Seattle. The next night he arrived in Seattle. He didn't feel it was right to sleep in a hotel. He spent 50 cents and slept in an all-night movie. He saved his money for the card game.

Q: You said the monks still talk about him.

Fr. Damien: I talk. I pray for him every night. He is on my list of people.

Q: I admit to asking him for guidance.

Fr. Damien: It's time. Surely, he couldn't be in Purgatory after 10 years.

Q: Is 10 years the cutoff?

Jim Murray: My goal is to be the last person in Purgatory.

Fr. Damien: I have a friend whose nine-year-old daughter died. My friend visited a medium.

When she walked through the door, the medium asked, "It's about your child, isn't it."

"How did you know?"

The medium responded, "I saw a little chair by your door. Did your grandmother die recently?"

She answered, "Yes."

"I see your grandmother behind you. She's holding your daughter. She has been taking care of your daughter since she died."

My friend asked, "You mean my grandmother is in heaven?"

The medium said, "Yes."

My friend disagreed, "Well, that can't be true. She was guilty of so many bad things."

The medium's response, "Time in heaven and Purgatory differs from our time down here."

10 years is enough.

Jim Murray: Would you say that Corky served as a bridge to many retreatants?

Fr. Damien: Yes. He was an easy guy to talk to. Most of the monks were not easy. Most are introverts. They preferred the solitude of enclosure. Corky disagreed: "Bring 'em on."

Q: *He didn't talk much about himself?*

Fr. Damien: I don't know about that. I just loved his stories. I liked everything about the guy. His best story was about the college game for all the marbles against West Virginia.

Jim Murray: Hot Rod Hundley was toying with the ball?

Fr. Damien: The game included two guys who became top picks in the country. Corky couldn't stand being taunted, so he punched the West Virginia guy.

Q: *I interviewed Hot Rod Hundley. He assured me the story is not true.*

Fr. Damien: (laughing) Is that so? I listened to that story so many times. It has become an urban legend.

Jim Murray: Part of his story describes the athletic director of West Virginia coming into the shower fully clothed to hug Corky. That story is true. Whether both guys confirm the punch is secondary. I met the athletic director before he died. He did go into the shower to hug Corky because he apologized for his behavior.

Fr. Damien: What a great story!

Q: *Not true, however.*

Fr. Damien: The significant part of the story was the athletic director's appreciation of another team's player. In college, I would not have been capable of apologizing in front of all those people. Both were good players. Both were chosen by the pros.

Q: *Corky told the punch story on local radio with James Brown as the host. I heard the tape. For many years, Corky believed it.*

Fr. Damien: He was a great man.

Jim Murray: You can't remember most of the things Corky said. Was that because you were so at ease? Paul has worked hard searching for the essence of Corky. Corky changed when he came here. During that process, he embarked on one final tour to apologize to people he hurt. Reconciliation is a step in the AA program. A friend of mine recently traveled to Australia to apologize. Even when she couldn't accept the apology, he accomplished part of his working program. I know Corky tried.

Q: Here is irony. I spoke with Fr. Rocco in New Jersey. Corky did visit him and others. He neither called nor visited me. That bothers me. He ripped me off, but never called me. I'm not good enough?

Jim Murray: He never called me, either.

Q: I'm comforted to hear that.

Jim Murray: God doesn't keep score. We each have our own agenda. Corky had his.

Fr. Damien: What was the guy thinking? We had a monk to whom I had not spoken in three years. When he first entered my office to describe his problem, I had responded "You're okay. I know you."

Because I said I knew him, he took offense. He had been working on knowing himself for his entire life. Now this Abbot thinks he knows me. We never know what will offend people.

What I take as an affront might not bother another guy. If you wait for an apology, it might never come. He may not know that he had anything to apologize for.

Jim Murray: Higher than judging is the spiritual way. At times, not judging is very hard. There wouldn't be wars or guys blowing themselves up if we all accepted the spiritual way. Peace is rare, even in this monastery. We live a frenetic pace, even in a Trappist monastery.

Fr. Damien: In here, the hardest thing to cope with is the different personalities. Diversity is also most difficult in life. The monastery differs only because I haven't chosen these guys. Outside, you can decide whom you want to be with and whom to ignore.

Q: My brother, Donald, is a priest in Virginia. In the past year, he described feeling overwhelmed. He doubted whether he could handle the load of a large parish. He has since found peace. His struggles led me to admire the priests in our parishes. Great numbers of parishioners rely on them. You seem to be describing something similar.

Fr. Damien: You have missed something. I have never felt so close to God. All other worries are beside the point. God really is in charge. That trust makes up for everything else. I have been amazed after I accepted this job. God showered me with His graces.

Q: I must ask. When the monks talk about Corky, what do they say?
Fr. Damien: I'm the one who talks most about Corky.

Jim Murray: We share something. I talk about Corky more than anyone else in my life. His crazy stories have accomplished something. Paul, you record our thoughts. From the day the monks arrive here, they are led by the Holy Spirit. One monk searching for himself, was offended when Abbot Damien met him for the first time and stated, "I know you." That went full circle. He disappeared for three years. That is Jesus to me. We will never know why the guy didn't talk for three years.

Paul, you have searched for years. Now you are here. This is funny. I can almost see Corky sitting here beside us. He seems to be prodding, "Tell them another story." He is also where we all want to go. If after you die, someone describes you as joyful, you have lived a Christian life. They might not approve of his personality. He took their money. He might not have apologized. But he has made Damien's list. That might be better than Schindler's list. Damien's is a wonderful list.

Can you imagine Corky patrolling these corridors while the monks slept? Here was symbolism. He waved his flashlight while the monks rested their bones. What are the odds against Corky, prisoner, nut house, and gambler admitting his past proudly?

"I slept in all-night movies and deserted tracks." He must have told me that a thousand times.

"I was homeless before anyone knew what that word meant."

He wasn't bragging. I saw only pathos. When he guarded these guys, he rejoiced at how they trusted him. He held the keys. They slept soundly because our joyful free spirit roamed the hallways in short shorts.

Think of the many women staying at the guesthouse. Corky's joyous spirit touched them. He loved the house and he loved those women.

Fr. Damien: The most important realization I have taken from our conversation is how deeply Corky's life touched both of you. I did not expect that.

The three of us had tears in our eye. The four of us cried together.

XXXIV

BLIND, BUT NOW I SEE

It was our time to leave the Trappists. A morning mist hovered over the cavernous Abby courtyard. Jim Murray stood next to me as we contemplated our 7 a.m. departure. The quiet seemed to speak.

"Let's say good-bye to the Corkster," Jim murmured.

Together we walked 30 paces to the last gravestone on the left. Jim knelt. We prayed silently. Next to Corky's stone nestled a tuft of flowers. It had long since lost its vibrance. Attached to the straw-like stalks was tied a blue ribbon. My thoughts drifted back to my first encounter with Fr. Dan Rocco. "The Tuft of Flowers" spared by the field worker had energized my search for Corky. Frost's poem spoke of one man preserving beauty to influence the follower. "Follow me," it whispered. Corky's mystical beacon had guided me to this place and the truth he found. The lifeless flowers told me that my journey had reached completion. Here he belongs. Corky, your soul has found meaning. All humanity strains, searching for the joy of acceptance. I believe that now your life is at peace.

Jim and I silently returned to our car. We were startled by a heavy "thunk." The main door of the monastery closed behind Bro. Rene. He wanted to add one last thought.

Calmly he said, "I just wanted to add something before you leave."

I thought back to how unapproachable the monks appeared during my first visit. Bro. Rene's manner had been open and childlike.

He confided, "Corky assured me how you can spot a compulsive gambler. After he loses everything, he can only think of where to get more money."

Jim responded, "Your wisdom is for me."

I thanked Bro. Rene for his gracious send off. Then, I mentioned the dead flowers we observed on Corky's grave.

With a twinkle he replied, "I know who put them there. My sister-in-law really loved Corky. She puts flowers on his grave to this day."

After nine years, Corky attracts the love of admirers. I pondered how far the search had progressed. I could feel his presence. His changed countenance spread like a vapor, hovering everywhere. I couldn't touch him. Instead, his spirit rested on me. I experienced a warm sense of connection. Another being shared all my inner thoughts. Mysteriously, he had walked with me until I learned to walk with him. Corky trusted me. "I want it written. I will help you." The meaning of his life lay hidden at the time he first spoke. What would I have written if I had traveled to interview Corky? I would probably have accepted his stories, never verifying his exaggerations. Can we ever fully understand another person? We can only approach another spiritually. I'm not sure why I have avoided judging Corky. The terrible offenses he committed remain very real to me. Those he helped and hurt continue to root for him. I'm truly happy that this flawed tortured man found his way home. I'm convinced he intends to lead others home. More important, I'm sure he can lead others home.

On earth, we experience no true happiness without gratitude. And, there is no true gratitude without humility. Corky found all three. His ascension began through humility. He sank to penniless, homeless, and directionless before seeking out Fr. Dan Rocco. Then, he became humble enough to accept the invitation to Gethsemani. At the abbey he recognized his home. Gratitude overflowed. Corky's tortured soul fell into waiting arms. His being blossomed with heavenly joy. Earthly happiness thrives only when embraced by heavenly joy.

Corky remained dangerous to himself and others. He slowed down to let The Quiet lead. He never forgot his past. He faced his past, lived in the present, and anticipated his future home. He understood his vision because he no longer felt alone.

On March 3, 1994, Corky penned a note from his heart to Bob Hardy and Peg. Bob's youngest son Tim and wife Tracy had welcomed their first son, Samuel. The note provides a glimpse of Corky's thinking.

> Dear Bob & Peg
> Thanks for shipping the remnants of my gear to me. I appreciate it greatly ... Also the note from Tim, Tracy and Samuel. I hope he's a super-star!
> Things are well with me .... for the moment at least... I've been in residence here since mid-October and while my many warnages protect my becoming a community member (that a bug with my insanities) I intend to remain here for as long as is permissable. My ability to manage myself in the world out there seems to be diminishing each year by leaps and bounds. I'm tired of continuing to injure people that I like and love ..... and being "sorry" just isn't enough any more.
> I am coming east soon to try to clean up sadnesses I left — I will see you then.   Love, Corky

"Being 'sorry' just isn't enough anymore." True sorrow. He clung to his conscience. Corky was still trying. Fr. Rocco assured me.

His life's message; "Don't ever give up. There is always hope."
Corky joined his plea across 15 centuries to the following cry:

> Late have I loved you,
> Beauty so ancient and so new,
> late have I loved you!
> Lo, you were within, but I outside,
> seeking there for you,
> and upon the shapely things you have made
> I rushed headlong,
> I, misshapen.
> You were with me, but I was not with you.

> They held me back far from you
> those things which would have no being
> were they not in you.
> You called, shouted, broke through my deafness;
> you flared, blazed, banished my blindness;
> you lavished your fragrance,
> I gasped, and now I pant for you;
> I tasted you, and I hunger and thirst;
> you touched me, and I burned for your peace.

Augustine

"He beat the tag." reminded Jim Murray.
He used a baseball phrase. The successful runner slides safely home under the fielder's tag. At the risk of being out, he grabs the prize. Corky did that.

* * *

Corky and I share signature traits. We are dreamers, lovers of competition, and absorbed in a quest. At our cores, we struggled with a crippling defect. We heard and followed spiritual voices. Perhaps, the following stories will explain our confusion.

I was 16 in the fall of 1952. I was playing left tackle for Malvern Prep when our season opened against Penn Charter in suburban Philadelphia. With limited substitutes, we played every down. Malvern got crushed, 28-0. Discouraged, I limped off the field. A strong arm wrapped around my shoulders. I didn't look up. An encouraging confident voice lifted my spirit. "You played a great game. Be proud. Your life won't always be like this." We walked together, seemingly alone.

In front of my locker I turned to stare into the face of Al Wistert, captain and left tackle of the Philadelphia Eagles. Al was coaching Penn Charter, but he walked me off the field. Forever, I will be grateful. That 16-year-old boy is still a loyal Eagles fan.

The seasons passed quickly until October, 2005. Jim Murray and I arrived at Rev. Herb Lusk's annual "People for People" dinner in North Philadelphia. His wonderful organization makes a difference for low-income families.

At the door in the next car squeezed Andy Reid, current Head Coach of the Eagles.

We shook hands and I looked Andy in the eye to offer, "It is a true joy for me to meet you."

A strong voice responded, "I know it is."

I turned and blurted, "Did you just say 'I know it is'?"

Andy returned eye contact. With a smile, he calmly responded, "I would never say anything like that. I said, 'It was also a pleasure meeting you.' But I'll use that line."

He spoke in a sincere, soft voice. The two voices I had heard were entirely different.

Imagine the confusion of interior messages. Internal voices linked Corky to me. They squeezed us down while shouting that we weren't good enough. Together, we have desperately tried to prove ourselves.

Corky's bravado masked his hope that he could induce people to like him. Inside, he heard that he was worthless. We thirsted for acceptance. The severe voice I attributed to Andy Reid was in my head. Similarly, cries from Corky's caves controlled his low self-esteem. After he accepted acceptance, his negative voices slowly grew silent. The root of the word *confidence* is *with faith*. When Corky surrendered his heart to God, faith in himself flourished.

My dear friend, Sis McKay, posed her explanation as to why Jim Murray and I were not included on Corky's farewell tour. Corky had grown sure that we loved him. His tour attempted to secure the love of others. I agree.

One final question remains. Did he make good on "In finding me, you will find yourself?" I believe that all lives unfold. Therefore, none of us totally finds ourselves. Certainly lives can be forever interdependent. He could have promised inserting the words "accept yourself." At that time I would not have understood his meaning. Corky and I embraced acceptance. That makes all the difference. That act makes it true for all of us. We become ready for Heaven only after releasing all our attachments on earth. Our faith has led us home.

XXXV

CORKY'S LEGACY

I searched nine years for Corky, seldom aware that I was learning. I focused solely on the prize. Why did he want his story written? Could I find him and mysteriously find myself? My challenge was to accept Corky, without judging him. Impressions he left clearly identified the thoughts and addictions that imprisoned him. Only the Truth led Corky to redemption. All human beings benefit from atonement. But only a chosen few accept redemption. Corky embraced his new-found reason to live.

Profound wisdom resides in the story of *The Holy Grail*. Parcival's mother sends him into the world in search of Truth. She burdens him with two principles which must never be broken. Her over-protective rules create his biggest obstacles. Parcival could never have imagined worse traits. The motherly advice:

1. Don't ask questions
2. Honor fair damsels

In modern terminology, Parcival was ordered to question nothing and place women on pedestals. Corky walked beside me on the beach. He sensed that we both shared these principles. In search of maturity, we must ask questions before smashing unhealthy pedestals. I struggled with an additional pedestal. I honored pseudo-fathers. My earthly father dominated my adolescent years. He died when I was 24. I was left incapable of decision-making. My answer—attach myself to another dominant male.

While searching for Corky, I asked many questions. He hovered just ahead, which enabled him to lead. I wrote stories about the truth that I was learning. Life questions gained answers during my search. My pursuit is finished, but the search for myself continues. Let me finish with insights I have gained.

Silence Negativity

From moment to moment, chance events shape our understanding of reality and dominate our moods. We choose between positive and negative.

Dale Carnegie advocates the sublime benefit of optimism. Simply avoid the Three "Cs." Never Criticize. Don't Condemn. Minimize Complaints. The core of all relationship problems festers from destructive negative traits. When criticism, condemnation, or complaints creep into human interaction, the seeds of negativity have been sown. The venture is doomed to fail.

Jesus was the greatest psychiatrist. He never intended to limit or control lives. "Love one another" permeated his teaching. Rarely did he criticize anyone. He focused on his disciples' good, while encouraging the down-trodden. His ministry lifted despairing souls. While he healed them, he instructed them to free themselves of criticism. Jesus saved his criticism for the hypocritical Pharisees, who basked in judging others. "No one," he preached, "has the right to criticize." When we devalue another person, we accuse them of not measuring up to our standard. How prideful. Critical people are most annoyed when they encounter their own faults in others. Observe your culpability the next time you criticize someone else.

Our most antisocial behavior is condemnation, full-blown judgment. "Remove the plank from your own eye before attacking the splinter in someone else's." Most adults struggle with memories of past relationships. No one can escape being betrayed, belittled, or wrongfully accused. Failed relationships magnify valid reasons to condemn (judge) former partners. Yet Jesus pleaded not to judge. He wanted us free of negativity even if that meant forgiving a guilty spouse. Only after releasing judgment can we be ready for a new relationship. Allowed to fester, judgments gain control. New relationships never survive control. Along with money, control is at the root of all evil.

Complaining people eventually isolate themselves. They can only be tolerated by other complainers. Positive people don't really listen to them. They endure complainers by tuning them out.

Does Dale Carnegie's optimism bring happiness? Are we happier and more successful when we avoid criticism, condemnation, and complaining? I think so. Our positive attitude enables us to admire the beauty of others. Forgiveness replaces negativity, introducing the joy of being open to others. Negative complainers might think you naïve and childlike. They live their conflicted view of life. Avoid judging them. There lies our challenge.

The Lost Art—Valuing Maturity

Not many developers in the competitive software industry keep a client for seventeen years. During a cross-country site visit to Seattle, my client welcomed me home to visit her family. This unexpected opportunity included a day spent with her hundred-and-one-year-old father. The experience was profound.

Joe's mind was clear. He seemed anxious to share wisdom he had gathered over a century. He began by showing me assorted framed pictures of cherished family members. Joe's loving gallery preserved their eternal stares as he relived their stories. He described their contributions while he emphasized their unique qualities. To each faded image, he specified the number of years they had lived. He slowed as he came to the innocent children. These angels had offended no one before dying young. Each of Joe's days began with reading his newspaper. Reverently he removed Dr. Billy Graham's article. He saved each in a special box.

When our day ended, Joe accompanied us to dinner in downtown Seattle. He observed everything and everyone. When it was time to part, he carefully selected four articles which he presented to me. I was deeply touched by the experience of Joe. After I returned to New Jersey, I thanked him through the following letter:

> Dear Joe,
>
> It was truly a joy meeting and experiencing dinner with you. Unlike the majority in our youth-oriented culture, I value and revere the wisdom of your age. Observant living strikes me as the only valid path to wisdom. I have agonized over how to convince my children, "Listen to me; I haven't been brain dead all these years."

Each of your family pictures preserves their individual wonderful stories. I thank God that I have met you. May it become His will that we again meet here and beyond the veil.

Our world suffers from blindness and confusion. I admire Billy Graham because he serves as a battlefield doctor. He ministers to his patient's soul. At times, I fear that good has lost—that evil is prevailing. But, in our hearts we trust that in the end, our lives will be vindicated. God has always reigned.

I hope you are well. You have become a treasure for us all.

Paul

What value do you put on older members of your family? What do you want thought about you as you approach your last birthday? Social workers observe that our personalities don't really change as we age. Our personality only expands on what we have been. Scary thought. If I grow up, I want to become more like Joe.

Find and Follow Your Passion

How am I different from single men who seem to just exist? Hopefully, it is the uniqueness of an enlightened vision. Purpose is only possible in lasting relationships. Friendships are no longer measured in numbers. I seek belonging. I accept responsibility and hope for success found only in a meaningful relationship.

Passion in life flows when we understand who we are. An Indian legend describes a tiger cub that separates from his family and is adopted by a family of goats. For years he munches grass, looking and sounding like a goat. Passion appears one day when the King of the Tigers bounds into the goat's clearing. With fearful eyes, the goat family flees. But the baby tiger gasps, unable to run. The pathetic little tiger stares, fascinated by the King. The Tiger King understands. He lifts the little tiger by the back of his neck and carries him to a pond. The cub stares at his reflection. Stunned, the baby tiger cannot understand the connection. In desperation, the King Tiger shakes the youngster. No reaction. Inspired, the King throws a piece of raw meat in front of the cub. Timidly, the baby sniffs. He tastes the meat. The cub gurgles a squeaky little roar and becomes a tiger.

Thirty years ago, I encountered this story. My search for raw meat never ends. Sometimes, I just sniff. I have made a specialty of "road kill." But, individual passion, our inner drive, alone makes life meaningful.

Lukewarm or unfulfilled yearnings cloud the purpose of life. Limitless possibilities appear when we discover who we were meant to be. We thrive through uncovering our passion. Don't settle for the life of a goat. Examine carefully your reflection. A grazing world awaits your inspiration.

Look Inside for Answers

"God gives us everything we need to live our lives, but nothing that we already possess." Ruth Stapleton's (President Jimmy Carter's sister) quote has guided me these many years. It advocates two seemingly conflicting truths. First, God grants us everything we need when we ask him. Our prayers are heard. Because He loves us more than we can imagine, we expect God to respond to our prayers. He delights in our requests. The Good Father gives us answers with things good. The second part of Ruth's statement appears to limit the first. God does not grant our request when we possess the ability to obtain it ourselves. He withholds His gifts consistent with our free will. We were created with the ability to solve the problem. Why insist that God solve it? We choose *not* to act. God will not act against our free will. It appears that God refuses or fails to help us. In truth, we fail to risk trusting our own capabilities. Whenever we ask, if there has been no response, the solution lies somewhere within us. Examine your passion, where your gifts are hidden.

Many years ago, I accepted Jesus as my Lord. In those early days, all my prayers seemed to be answered. One summer day, I stood on the Avalon, NJ pier. It had been a morning of fruitless fishing. I prayed a request to catch a big fish and cast one final time. A huge fish hit. I dragged him towards the pilings. One excited fisherman announced that it was a weakfish (so-named for its weak mouth). I lifted the fish, but a giant wave smashed into the pier.

"Lost," the men groaned.

The wave receded. The fish was still on my line. Its weak mouth held my hook. We lowered the nets. The fish flopped on the pier. I felt like a child on Christmas morning. When I asked for gifts, God gave them to me.

Reality gradually changed. The child was growing. More and more answers became, "No." Had God's seed fallen on rocky ground? Like a child, I questioned whether God still loved me. I was convinced that, "He could give me what I wanted." Why wouldn't He? Then I entered into darkness. My marriage ended. Then my business failed. I lost my house, prompting my best friend to sue me for what was left. Friends I counted on disappeared. My family stopped calling. Collectively, the sources of my self-esteem dried up. I discovered the prayer of Jonah.

I understood "The jaws of the nether world slammed shut behind me forever."

My dignity became less important. I wondered if anyone remembered that I existed. I was capable of only one prayer, "Yes, I'll go through this."

I pleaded to go home, but God didn't take me. All reasons to live disappeared. Would the pain ever end? As Jesus hung on the cross, in Jerusalem business went on as usual. Most people weren't aware that he was suffering. He lost everything, especially his dignity. Through his pain, he saw signs of life. His deepest suffering was isolation. Our faith is most tested when God seems not to care.

My resurrection experience was more mysterious than my death. I had fantasized that one day I would awake, basking on a desert island. I would be sipping cool pineapple juice (all I had to do was enjoy). Instead, my resurrection proved the lack of zippers on cocoons. Without struggle, I would have remained locked in the past forever. I could have completely avoided resurrection. My fight out of the jaws of hell was exhausting. I'm grateful for my struggle. I could have been imprisoned by my past. I no longer fixate on my misfortunes.

Trusting the gifts God gave me involved risk. I tried new things. I joined an improvisational acting group. I started a new business and took up tennis. Most important, I risked loving again. Walls erected to hide my pain melted. Each risk contributed to new growth. My vision of life slowly expanded. Newly discovered talents fortified the new person. The more I risked, talents and insights became visible. They had hidden dormant inside me all along. They surfaced through my death experience. But God never handed them to me. Remember Ruth Stapleton's quote: "He gives us nothing that we already possess." When your prayers don't seem to be answered, look inside yourself. God will always help us recognize our talents. We cannot use them if we never recognize them.

Silence the Lullaby

"For I have miles to go before I sleep." My favorite line from the poems of Robert Frost points towards our earned reward promised for the final steps of our lives. Current beauty must never distract us from our promise to accomplish all that we can. The purpose of our lives, including its trials, sorrows, and hills absorb our energy. In hope, we yearn to sleep in peace with God. "Well done, thou good and faithful servant."

Examine your vision. Are you really awake? Anthony DeMello advocates that "waking up" is critical to life's happiness. Awake, we embrace reality. Asleep, we accept life's lullaby without thinking. So much of our understanding accepts the voices around us. Don't accept what we hear as truthful. Identify goals and values that others have accepted. Listen to the following flawed statements:

"You really look cool in that red Chevy."

"If you really cared about me, you'd know what to say."

"The Powerball Jackpot is up to ninety-five million—you have to play."

Does anyone notice that you look cool (or if you thaw)? Shallow observers are caught up in being "cool" themselves. And, could my loving you ever be linked to reading your mind? Finally, your legitimate chance of winning the lottery is ridiculously poor. Fill a football stadium with white ping-pong balls. Drop in one red ball. Shake the stadium. Could your ball really be picked? When the jackpot increases, there are more balls. The chance of selecting your ball decreases.

We fall asleep when we accept other people's values at the expense of examining our own. Our youth-oriented culture embraces exclusively young ideas. Platitudes thrive everywhere. Immature reasoning is born of limited experience. Words like "cool" and "awesome" have become lazy substitutes for real meaning, inclusionary buzzwords keeping the speaker in control.

When we accept popular falsehoods, we become driven like zombies. On this mindless trek, we encounter suffering. Our response is to lash back and take control over others. Our sleeping culture directs us to seek revenge. But retribution and resentment always lead to blind emptiness. Happiness thrives from serving, not hurting, others. Awake, we remember, "I have come to serve others." We have discovered how to live. When I fall asleep and want to "be served," my life becomes closed and unhappy. Ignore the empty noise of our world. Happy are those awake now who sleep when God's lullaby sounds.

Don't Fear What You Are—A Child

Life's most profound experiences are usually not understood on the day they occur. Meaning evolves over years. I traveled to Fatima, Portugal in

1990. I went on a pilgrimage when I was befriended by Fr. Hugh McSherry who lived in Fatima as chaplain for The Blue Army. He entertained me for a full day, describing the events of Our Lady's apparitions. He emphasized their relationship to the history of the First and Second World Wars. When our time waned, he announced, "I have spent this day with you because you are destined to *Spread the message of Fatima.*

I never saw Father McSherry again. I assumed that showing the Fatima story in the United States was my destiny. I bought a videotape about Fatima. Not one person showed an interest in my trip or viewing the tape. Years passed. The tape was given to a friend.

I forgot about spreading the message. Three years passed. I received a call from my friend Joe. He invited me to speak about my Fatima trip on a men's retreat. I couldn't refuse. But I did not foresee the obstacles ahead. The retreat had rules. All talks must be written and critiqued in advance. Therefore, I was expected to write each detail of my trip and describe the meaning of Fatima. To my surprise, I couldn't write the first word. I tried everything. I just couldn't.

I realized that I didn't understand exactly what the message of Fatima was. Joe rescued me. "Just give the talk." No writing was a rare exception to the rules. I became terrified at the prospect of giving a talk without knowing what I would say.

Weeks later, I humbly accepted standing in front of forty men without a script. Joe was introducing me; I closed my eyes. I pleaded with God to put His words in my mind. Whatever He put in my mind, I promised to repeat. My only role was to stay out of the way. Once I relinquished control, I listened to the message along with the men in front of me.

A sense of peace filled me. I began by explaining the logistics of my visit. I clung to the podium at first. But soon, I found myself standing among the men. They were facing me in their chairs. I directed them to close their eyes and relax with hands on their knees. After we shared some deep breathing, I invited them slowly to think back to their childhood. They were five years old. Then I spoke the following words:

"Examine your face. Look into your eyes. They are the only part of you that has remained unchanged over all these years. See the truth, the sweetness and the open heart that was you then. That child is the real you. Your journey has put layers of experience upon you. But, that child is you. Love that little boy. Let him lead you now. Let him walk you back to God. In this same way Our Blessed Mother wants to lead you back to Jesus. Her loving heart is guiding you to Jesus so he can hold you, heal you, and lead you home to Him. This is Mary's message of Fatima."

In the quiet, I sat back down next to Joe. Under my breath, I whispered, "That was a real surprise to me. I guess it was pretty bad." Joe just said, "Look at the men." They were still in meditation. All were sobbing quietly.

Many years have passed since I heard Father McSherry's words—"Spread the message of Fatima." He is now with Mary. Together, I hope they smile at my second attempt at spreading the Fatima message.

He called a little child over, stood in their midst and said, "I assure you, unless you change and become like little children, you will not enter the Kingdom of God. Whoever makes himself lowly, becoming this child, is of greatest importance in that heavenly reign." (Matthew 18:2,3).

Look Beyond The World You See

Jimmy Hoffa disappeared on July 29, 1975. My understanding of all truth changed that day forever. On a Sunday morning, my wife and I sat talking on my bed.

We were participating in a Marriage Encounter. Suddenly I was lifted up and floating in the beautiful blue sky. Head tilted back. I could only look up. My body remained sitting on the bed. From every direction I was surrounded by a beautiful chorus of voices, blending perfectly in a melody I didn't know. I sensed that I was privileged to hear hymns in praise of God. I could see nothing. But, around me swirled the warm beauty of God's heavenly chorus. My heart expanded in a joy that I hadn't known existed. I wished that I could join or remain with the choir forever. I had been raised Catholic. I did not read the Bible. Days later, I found the passage, "Eye has not seen, nor ear heard the joy that God has in store for those who love Him." It's true. Heavenly joy cannot be imagined by limited mortals. Believe me. A spiritual world exists in a place we cannot see. Heaven is our true home. Look up instead of down. No worldly allure can hold us here. I was removed from the singing because I had to go. Had I stayed among the angels another instant, I would have burst with joy.

Two weeks later, I calmly described the choir to a priest who taught me in high school. He listened attentively.

His response stunned me, "At least you know that God exists."

This man I respected wasn't sure that God existed. He added, "I believe that we all experience direct intervention and inklings of God's Glory. It is easiest to deny them. We label them dreams or fantasies. During the Old Testament, God communicated His will through dreams and visions. The prophets believed. Maybe acceptance made them prophets. Today, encounters with God are discounted as illusion or coincidence."

Ignoring spiritual intervention makes little sense. God cares more about us than we can imagine. As you read, examine your own experiences. Open your spiritual eyes. One singular experience beckons to you because you have never revealed it to anyone. Ponder God's promises. I assure you, it is real. You need to share your spiritual encounter with someone you trust. In breaking your silence, you declare the experience true. Take this risk. It will change your life. Truth bursts forth from the final verse of my favorite hymn:

> "When Christ shall come mid shouts of acclamation,
> And take me home. What joy will fill my heart.
> Then I will bow in humble adoration and here proclaim,
> My God, how great Thou art."

With halting voice, I sang this verse at my mother's funeral. In a glorious eulogy, Father Don (my brother) beautifully pictured mother sailing to the distant shore, "'Mid shouts of acclamation." Her real home beckoned from where we someday also will be. Mother lives. Let those who open their eyes see the truth.

On Our Own It Is Too Late

Three decades have passed since I was blessed by God's choir. The years have brought changes through the shifting content of my prayer requests. My youthful pleadings centered on accomplishments and comforts. My focus was goal-orientated, rooted in personal achievement and family status. Abruptly, my goals changed with the end of my marriage. My requests changed. Fear and the hope of survival launched me into my second journey. Prayer requests changed with God's grace.

Later that wonderful Sunday, I heard an interior voice, "Ask anything and I will give it to you." Without hesitation I requested to stop drinking. Desire for drink left instantly. But my life changed in many ways. I began reading the Bible. Although I was grateful to stop drinking, deep inside I regretted my request. Wouldn't it have been better to ask for Solomon's gift—an understanding heart (wisdom)? For 24 years, I prayed constantly for Solomon's gift. I didn't understand that Solomon eventually offended God. He broke God's covenant. After gaining enormous worldly success, he was punished. His son was deprived of Solomon's kingdom.

Solomon offended God in three ways. First, he mounted his own standing army instead of relying on God for protection. Secondly, he took 700 wives and 300 concubines. Still worse, he extracted a 666 gold talents tax from his people.

Solomon received wisdom, but he never enjoyed the heart of God. Six hundred and sixty-six is only mentioned one other place in the Bible. In Revelations, that number refers to the beast. Today we live in the most evil of times. Where does this number point? Most people think of a person when referring to the Anti-Christ. But, the Anti-Christ might be an attitude.

Worship of money, an evil force deeply oppressing Christian values, has seduced our world. We are bombard by television, movies, concerts, and political rhetoric. Wealth has replaced values as the criteria for self-worth. Luxurious living is hailed as the American dream. Love of money seeped into our hearts without detection. By Biblical standards, a more wealth-oriented world has never existed.

Can we change the values of our world? Most people live entranced by their lifestyle. Can we wake them up? In truth, nothing can change the world's view. Solomon couldn't. We must pray, do our best. and hope.

As the world darkened, my prayer has changed. I now plead with God for David's gift. I long for the Heart of God. May He draw me nearer to our wonderful Father. At our weakest, He is strongest. Approach God as a little child. Through innocent faith we will find the fruits of our hope. Only after we become totally dependent on Him, He will act. He will make justice dawn for us like the sun. Bright as the noonday will be our vindication. The calf and the lion will lie together when a little child leads them. We were created for God's world. You'll see.

Corky's March of Gethsemani

From birth, Corky was drawn toward his final resting place. He introduced me to the Trappists and their house of peace. His life pointed to another Gethsemani where a church is built over the rock where Jesus wept. Inside the church sits a tabernacle, an unusual carving on its front. That art is not a crown of thorns or a chalice. It is a pelican. Why this bird?

Pelicans are the noblest of birds. They mate for life. Love of family compels one partner to guard the nest of babies, while its spouse searches for food. During this time, they dedicate their lives to providing for their children. If tragedy befalls the 'searcher' and the mate does not return, the remaining bird never leaves the young. As food becomes scarce, the pelican literally tears off pieces its own flesh to feed the babies. In one final act, the bird rips out its own heart. While dying, the heart is fed to its young.

Our selfish illusionary world doesn't understand Jesus and the pelican. "Unless a man lays down his life for his friend, he cannot enter the Kingdom of Heaven." What did Jesus says to us on the last night of His life? He pleaded with us to serve others (sacrifice selfish interests) pointing us to meaning and happiness (The Kingdom of God). We must focus on others. Isn't selfishness an exquisite definition of sin?

With halting steps, Corky battled and overcame selfishness, the impossible change. God's love consumed him. It was an honor to chronicle Corky's Calvary. His life acquired great meaning.

All wounded healers must be tried by fire. How does the process of refining gold work? The chemist sits over his kiln watching the intense fire purify mineral rock. He must catch the exact moment (as God does) when the rock is transformed to pure gold. If he waits too long, part of the gold melts and is lost. If he removes it too soon, the gold is not pure. The moment he awaits happens when he sees his reflection in the gold. God saw His reflection

Corky became gold. His joy magnifies his Lord.

"While I will never speak to you in your head, I will always speak to you in your heart."

"Racetrack escapes included the Professor, Rocky, Corky, and Jim." The Four Amigos at Saratoga Race Track

"I must avoid all confessional things, but I'll give you my impressions." Fr. Daniel Rocco

"We went outside to talk about Corky." Paul Arizin

"If he said 'good morning' I would put on my pajamas and go to bed." Bert Bell.

"I'm the one who talks most about Corky." Jim Murray and Fr. Damien.

"She puts flowers on his grave to this day." Jim Murray and Bro. Rene in the morning mist.